Adventures in Raspberry Pi®

Carrie Anne Philbin

WILEY

This edition first published 2014
Reprinted January 2014, September 2014

Registered office

John Wiley & Sons Ltd, The Atrium, Southern Gate, Chichester, West Sussex, PO19 8SQ, United Kingdom

For details of our global editorial offices, for customer services and for information about how to apply for permission to reuse the copyright material in this book please see our website at www.wiley.com.

A catalogue record for this book is available from the British Library.

ISBN 978-1-118-75125-1 (paperback); ISBN 978-1-118-75123-7 (ePub); ISBN 978-1-118-75122-0 (ePDF)

Set in 10/12.5 Chaparral Pro Light by Indianapolis Composition Services

Printed in the United Kingdom at Bell & Bain

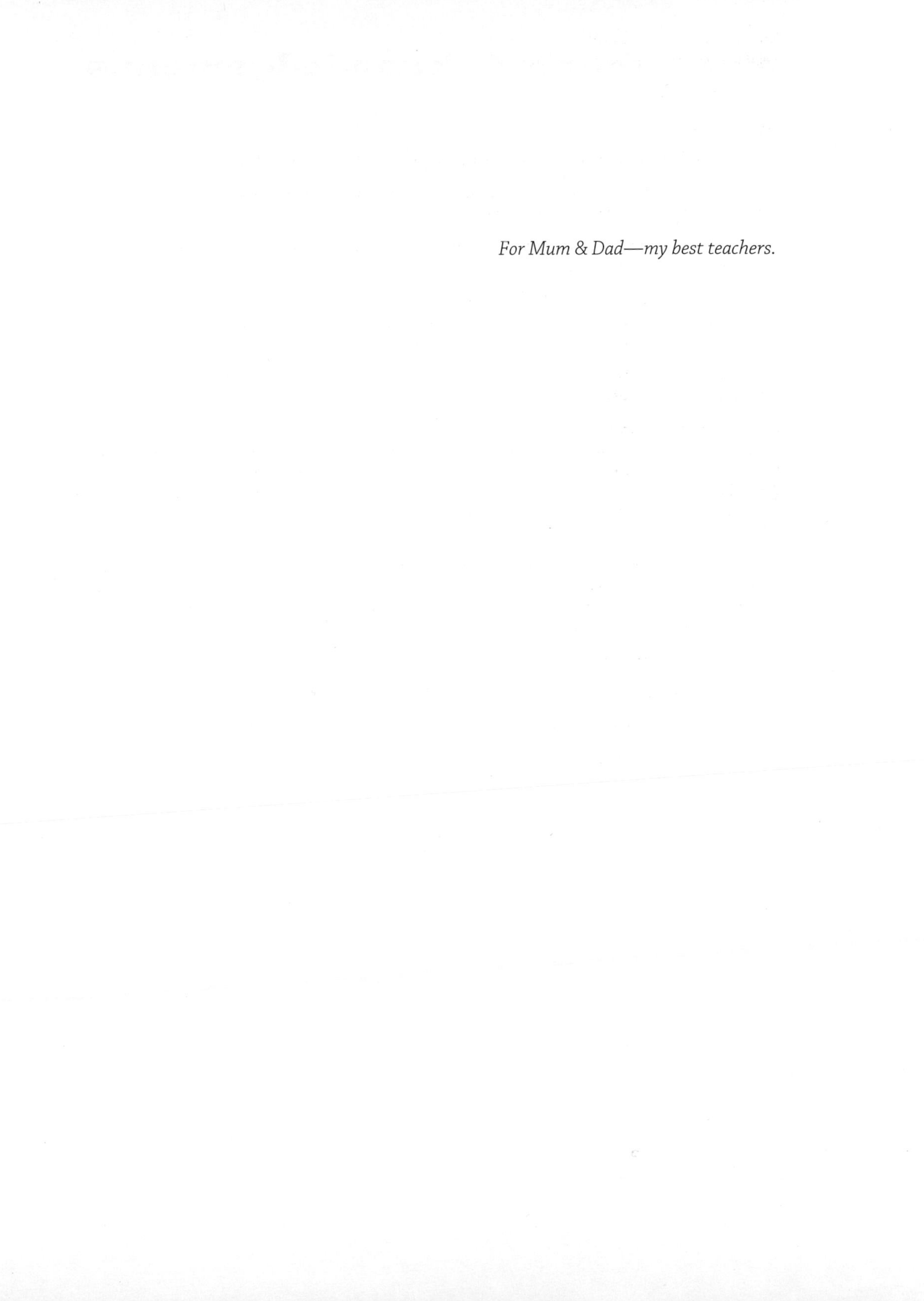

For Mum & Dad—my best teachers.

Publisher's Acknowledgements

Some of the people who helped bring this book to market include the following:

Editorial and Production

VP Consumer and Technology Publishing Director: Michelle Leete
Associate Director–Book Content Management: Martin Tribe
Associate Publisher: Chris Webb
Executive Commissioning Editor: Craig Smith
Development Editor: Sara Shlaer
Copy Editor: Grace Fairley
Technical Editor: David Whale
Editorial Manager: Jodi Jensen
Senior Project Editor: Sara Shlaer
Editorial Assistant: Anne Sullivan

Marketing

Associate Marketing Director: Louise Breinholt
Marketing Manager: Lorna Mein
Marketing Executive: Polly Thomas

Composition Services

Compositors: Jennifer Mayberry, Sarah Wright
Proofreader: Wordsmith Editorial
Indexer: Potomac Indexing, LLC

About the Author

CARRIE ANNE PHILBIN is a high school-level Computing and Google Certified Teacher and a member of the DfE Computing expert panel reviewing the new Computing School Curriculum in the UK. She is also the founder and presenter of the award winning *Gurl Geek Diaries* (`www.geekgurldiaries.co.uk`) and vice chair of the *#include* Computing At Schools initiative (`http://casinclude.org.uk`) to get more girls and minority groups into computing. Currently, Carrie Anne is working with the Raspberry Pi Foundation to improve the teaching of Computing in schools.

Acknowledgments

I would like to express my deep gratitude to the Raspberry Pi Foundation for allowing me to set my creativity free on their marvellous invention. In particular I'd like to thank Alex Bradbury and Dr Sam Aaron for their enthusiastic encouragement and patient guidance. Their willingness to give their time so generously is very much appreciated. I would also like to thank David Whale and the Raspberry Pi Community for their useful critiques of this work. Thanks to Jennifer Mayberry for her design work and Sarah Wright for much of the art.

Special thanks should also be given to the staff of Pimoroni for providing necessary equipment in order to complete elements of this book, as well as members of CAS #include and the Rainham Library Book Club, for keeping my progress on schedule with their kind words of encouragement.

My special thanks are also extended to my good friends: Emma, Sian, Helen, Viv, Lizi and Kylie who are a constant source of inspiration in my life.

Finally, I wish to thank my parents, brother and sister-in-law for their patience, support and encouragement throughout.

Contents

Adventure 3

Creating Stories and Games with Scratch . . .45

Adventure 4

Programming Shapes with Turtle Graphics . . .77

Introduction

ARE YOU AN intrepid adventurer? Do you like to try new things and learn new skills? Would you like to be a pioneer in creating technology? Do you own a Raspberry Pi, or are you considering getting one? If the answer is a resounding "Yes!" then this is the book for you.

What Is the Raspberry Pi and What Can You Do With It?

The Raspberry Pi is a computer. A very small computer. In fact, it is roughly the size of a credit card. Don't be fooled by its size; as we know, good things come in small packages. However, the Raspberry Pi does not come in a package at all. It does not come in a case (although you can build one, as discussed in Adventure 1) and its circuit board and chips are fully visible, as you can see in Figure 1. You can plug a Raspberry Pi into a digital TV or monitor and use a USB keyboard and mouse with it, making it very easy to use, and because of its size you can easily transport it anywhere.

The Raspberry Pi gives you the opportunity to build and control a device that does what you want it to do. For example, you can deploy your very own robot arm, controlled by a program that you have written. You can design and create your own role-playing game, or produce beautiful computer art or music, all by using code.

FIGURE 1 The Model B revision of the Raspberry Pi, about the size of a credit card

Just because the Raspberry Pi is small doesn't mean you can't do big things with it. Here are just a few examples of some incredible Pi projects:

- Launching teddy bears into space using high altitude ballooning (`www.raspberrypi.org/archives/4715`)
- The ultimate bird feeder—it's solar-powered, takes photographs and tweets images of birds! (`www.raspberrypi.org/archives/4832`)
- Crazy customised Halloween costumes like Doc Brown from *Back to the Future* (`www.raspberrypi.org/archives/4856`)
- A robotic sailboat (`www.raspberrypi.org/archives/4109`)
- Pi-controlled sculptures like the 15-foot tall Mens Amplio with a brain that lights up (`www.raspberrypi.org/archives/4667`)

In the final chapter of this book, you'll use your Pi to build a jukebox that plays your favorite tunes and displays track information on an LCD screen. And with the skills you learn throughout the book, you'll be ready to dream up your own exciting projects—and create them.

Who Should Read This Book?

Adventures in Raspberry Pi is for any young person who has an interest in making things happen using computing. You might perhaps be unsure of how to get started or want to further your current skills. Whatever your reasons, this book will be your guide for a journey with your Raspberry Pi, the most important item in your backpack. Your trek will take you from setting up your Pi, through learning the basics of programming, to discovering how to create your own project. By the end of your adventures you will have acquired the skills you need to become a pioneer of technology!

What You Will Learn

This book will help you discover some of the amazing things you can do with your new Raspberry Pi, and introduce you to many of the developer tools and projects available to you. With this book, you will learn how to set up and use your Raspberry Pi easily so that you can experience its potential for yourself. You'll learn the skills you need to design and create your own computing projects.

You'll find out that you can give instructions to your Raspberry Pi in a variety of ways, using different programming languages and tools. The adventures in the book allow you to experience programming using Scratch, Turtle Graphics, Python, Sonic Pi and Minecraft Pi.

You will also learn some computing (and electronics) concepts that you can apply to other devices and programming situations. Many fundamental computing concepts are similar for all programming languages, so once you understand the basics of programming in one language you can apply that knowledge to others very easily.

What You Will Need for the Projects

First and foremost, of course, you need a Raspberry Pi. If you don't already own one, you can buy a Raspberry Pi from a distributor in your country by visiting the official Raspberry Pi website (`www.raspberrypi.org`) and following the links listed under the "BUY A PI" banner. You will also need a monitor or other screen, a mouse and a keyboard to connect to your Raspberry Pi.

Each chapter—adventure—in the book notes any special items you need to build the project covered in that adventure. Along with your Pi, some projects require Internet access to enable you to download software or other materials. You'll need headphones or speakers to listen to the music you make in Adventure 7. For the projects in Adventures 8 and 9, you will need some specific cables, wires, LEDs, resistors, and other hardware. You can purchase these items from your local electronics store, or from various online retailers.

As final ingredients, you'll need some curiosity and a willingness to try new skills!

How This Book Is Organised

Every chapter of the book is a separate adventure, teaching you to use new skills and concepts while you create a project. The book is organised so that as you progress, the concepts and projects get more complex, building on what you learned in earlier adventures. Each chapter begins with an introduction to the language or tool for that adventure, provides instructions for downloading, installing, and setting up whatever you need, and usually gives you a short task to help you become familiar with the tool. After you've got the basics, I lead you step by step through the instructions for the main project.

In Adventures 1 and 2, you learn how to get started with your equipment and use common text commands, perhaps for the first time. These two chapters are necessary for the beginner Pi explorer, as further adventures will depend on the skills covered here.

The two most common ways to program a Raspberry Pi are to use the Scratch or Python languages that come preinstalled on the Pi's main operating system, Raspbian. Adventures 3, 4 and 5 get you started with the basics of these languages. In Adventure 3, you use Scratch, a simple drag-and-drop programming language, to design and create your own computer game, while getting an introduction to the programming concepts of loops and variables. Adventure 4 is a bridge between Scratch and the more conventional programming language, Python. In this adventure, you use Turtle Graphics to create shapes and spirals with both programming languages. In Adventure 5, you learn how to create an adventure game program that asks for user input, uses lists, imports functions and prints text to the screen, all using text commands written in the programming language Python.

Adventures 6 and 7 take programming on the Raspberry Pi further by looking at two developer tools that you can download and use with the Raspberry Pi: Minecraft Pi and Sonic Pi. Minecraft Pi enables you to interact with and adapt the popular computer game Minecraft, using Python code to build your own transporter. With Sonic Pi, you can create electronic music by writing programs.

Another exciting aspect of using the Raspberry Pi is that it gives you the option to add on to the main board by using GPIO pins. Adventure 8 looks at the GPIO pins in more detail, introducing you to electronics and computer programming while you build a program that uses a marshmallow to make a light blink (yes, you read that right).

Adventure 9 draws on the computing concepts and skills learned through completing the preceding adventures in this book to create one big project—a jukebox. In this chapter, you learn how to plan, design and create a project from start to finish.

Finally, the Appendix suggests where you might go next to learn more about the different aspects of computer science and Raspberry Pi—including how to locate or set up your own club to share project ideas with others.

The Companion Website

Throughout this book you'll find references to the *Adventures in Raspberry Pi* companion website, `www.wiley.com/go/adventuresinrp`. (It's a good idea to bookmark that site so you can return to it as and when you need to.) The website includes video tutorials to help you out if you get stuck, and code files for some of the more extensive projects.

Conventions

Throughout the book, there are some special boxes to guide and support you. They use the following key:

These boxes explain complex computing concepts or terms.

These boxes are hints to make life easier.

These boxes include important warnings to keep you and your Raspberry Pi safe when completing a step or project.

These boxes feature quick quizzes for you to test your understanding or make you think more about the topic.

These boxes provide explanations or additional information about the topic at hand.

These boxes point you to videos on the companion website that will walk you through the tasks at hand.

You will also find two sets of sidebars in the book. *Challenge* sidebars ask you how you might expand on the projects in the book to make changes or add new features. *Digging into the Code* sidebars explain some of the special syntax or programming language, to give you a better understanding of the computer languages.

When following steps or instructions using code, especially in adventures using Python, you should type in the code as set out by the instructions. Sometimes you need to type a very long line of code, longer than will fit on a single line in this book. If you see a ⮐ symbol at the end of a line of code, it means that line and the following line are part of a single code line, so you should type them as one line, not on separate lines. For example the following code should be typed on one line, not two:

```
print("Welcome to Adventures in Raspberry Pi by ⮐
Carrie Anne Philbin")
```

Most chapters include a Quick Reference Table at the end to sum up the main commands or concepts from the chapter. You can refer to these guides when you need a refresher on the commands.

Whenever you complete a chapter, you unlock an achievement and collect a new badge. You can collect badges to represent these achievements from the *Adventures in Raspberry Pi* companion website (`www.wiley.com/go/adventuresinrp`).

Reaching Out

In the Appendix you will find ways to take your Raspberry Pi knowledge further, with references to websites, organisations, videos and other resources. Many of those resources include forums where you can ask questions or get in touch with other Raspberry Pi users.

You can also contact me by sending me a message through my website, `www.geekgurldiaries.co.uk`.

Time to start your adventures!

Adventure 1

You Have a Raspberry Pi. Now What?

IN THE PAGES of this book you'll discover how to do great things with your Raspberry Pi. You'll create art and music, programs, games, even create your own jukebox! But first, you need to get your system working.

If you are new to Raspberry Pi, the initial tasks of getting it set up and running might seem a little daunting but it is not that complicated to do. By setting up the Raspberry Pi yourself you will learn more about how it and other computers work. You will encounter technical jargon and procedures that you may not have come across before. In this chapter, I show you how to set up your Raspberry Pi so it is ready for you to use for the first time. I explain what **hardware** and **software** you need, and tell you how to put it all together into a working system. You'll also learn how to create a backup copy of your system in case you need to replace it at some stage in the future.

Hardware refers to the physical elements of the computer that you can see and touch. This includes everything inside the computer case, known as components.

Software is the term given to the programs that run on the computer system. Programs are what make the hardware work, for example by making a calculation or organising your files. There are two main types of software: systems software, which runs and manages your computer; and application software, which performs a specific task or function.

What Hardware Do You Need?

Of course, the first thing you need is a Raspberry Pi. If you have used games consoles or computing devices before, you'll notice something different about Raspberry Pi—it doesn't come with a power supply, a charger or any connecting cables. It doesn't have a storage device to keep your programs on either, or even a case!

So, to get started, you will first need to get the following hardware together (see Figure 1-1):

- A Raspberry Pi
- A micro **USB** power adapter
- A USB keyboard and mouse
- A desktop computer or laptop with an SD card reader/writer—this is to enable you to prepare an SD card with the software you need to run your Raspberry Pi
- A 4 GB **SD card**, like the kind you find in a digital camera
- An **HDMI** cable—you will be using this with an HDMI TV or monitor
- A monitor or TV

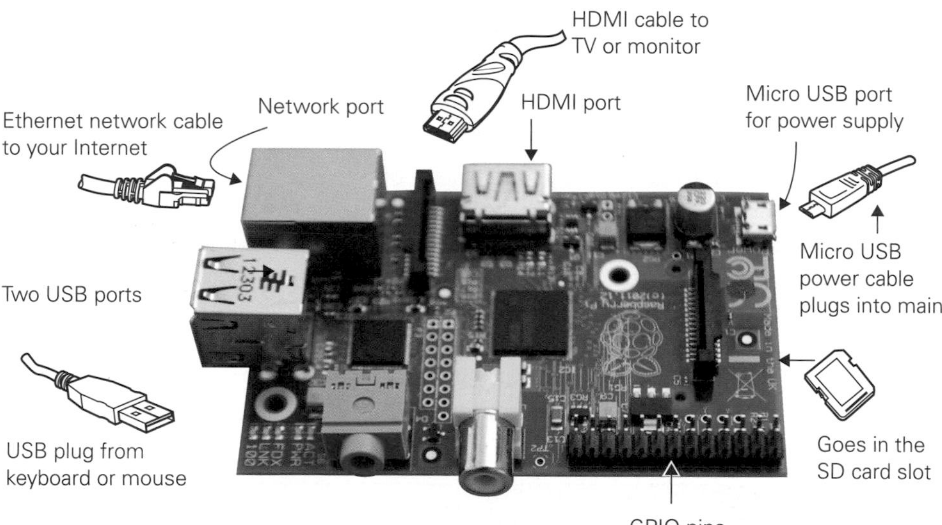

FIGURE 1-1 The essential hardware you'll need before you can use your Raspberry Pi.

HDMI stands for *High-Definition Multimedia Interface*. HDMI devices are used to transfer video and audio data from a source device—such as your Raspberry Pi—to a compatible HDMI device like a digital TV or monitor.

USB stands for *Universal Serial Bus*. You have probably used a USB port on a computer to plug in a webcam or a portable memory device like a memory stick.

An **SD card**, or *Secure Digital memory card,* stores data or information. SD cards are most often used in digital cameras, to store images that can then be transferred to a computer using an SD card reader.

What Other Equipment Is Helpful?

The following additional accessories are not vital but you might want to consider acquiring some of them to improve your Raspberry Pi experience.

- **A case**—To protect your Raspberry Pi from damage and make it easier for you to carry, think about buying a case like the PiBow shown in Figure 1-2, designed and manufactured by Pimoroni (`http://shop.pimoroni.com/products/pibow`). The great thing about this case is that it's colourful and fun, and the ports are also labelled to remind you where each cable should be inserted.

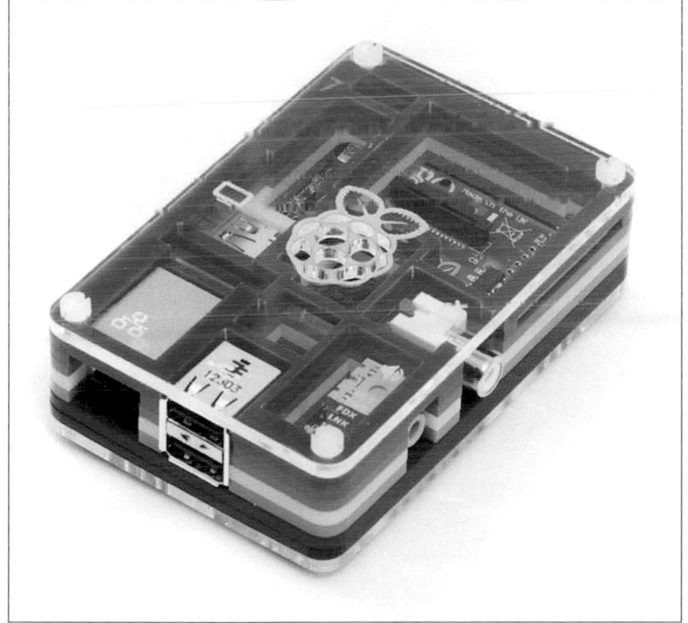

FIGURE 1-2 The PiBow case can help protect your Raspberry Pi.
Reproduced by permission of Pimoroni

If you don't want to spend cash on a case, why not create your own by using the Raspberry Pi Punnet? This template can be printed onto card, and then cut out and folded into a box. You can really let yourself get creative here and customise your case using pens, paints, stickers or coloured card to create a masterpiece. You can download the template from this site: `http://squareitround.co.uk/Resources/Punnet_net_Mk1.pdf`.

Want a sturdier case? Build one with Lego blocks! You can find instructions to build the Lego Raspberry Pi case shown in Figure 1-3 on the official Lego website at `http://www.thedailybrick.co.uk/instructions/Building%20Instructions%20[Raspberry%20Pi%202].html`.

FIGURE 1-3 Build a Lego case for your Raspberry Pi.
Reproduced by permission of The Daily Brick

- **A few spare SD cards**—It's worth having a few extra 4 GB **SD cards** just in case the one you're using becomes corrupted or stops working for any reason. They are also useful for backing up your files and projects—I explain how to do this at the end of the chapter.
- **An SD card reader/writer**—You'll need an **SD card reader/writer** to enable you to put the Raspberry Pi operating system software onto an SD card. You download the operating system software onto your computer, plug the card reader into a USB port on your computer and use it to copy the OS onto an SD

card that you can then load onto your Raspberry Pi. Many desktop computers and laptops are already fitted with an SD card reader and writer but if your computer or laptop doesn't have one, you will have to get an external USB card reader.

- **A Pi Cam**—The Pi Cam is a Raspberry Pi camera board accessory for the Pi (`http://cpc.farnell.com/jsp/search/productdetail.jsp?sku=SC13023`). It connects to the Pi with a flex cable and can be used to take digital images of whatever the camera is pointed at.
- **A Wi-Pi**—The Wi-Pi (available from `www.farnell.com`) is a small wireless dongle designed to be connected to a USB port on the Raspberry Pi so that you can add your Raspberry Pi to a wireless network, perhaps to share an Internet connection or files with other computers on the network.
- A PiHub—As the Raspberry Pi has only two USB ports, you may find you run out of ports to plug in all your devices like a keyboard, mouse and WiFi dongle. The PiHub (`http://shop.pimoroni.com/products/pihub`) is a USB hub designed to work with the Raspberry Pi so that you can have access to more USB ports.

Setting Up the Raspberry Pi

Getting your Raspberry Pi up and running takes just three main steps. First, you need to download the operating system software and copy it onto an SD card. Next, you hook up the hardware—the mouse, keyboard and other components. Finally, you install the software onto your Pi and configure a few settings. The next few sections walk you through this process for a smooth launch. Don't worry: Doing the actual steps is much easier than reading these instructions!

For a video that walks you through the steps of setting up your Raspberry Pi, visit the companion website at `www.wiley.com/go/adventuresinrp`. Click the Videos tab and select the SettingUpRaspberryPi file.

Downloading and Copying the Raspbian Operating System

All personal computing devices need an **operating system** (OS) to make them run. You've probably used a computer or laptop before, and the likelihood is that your computer's operating system was Microsoft Windows for a PC, or Mac OS X for a Mac computer or Macbook. The Raspberry Pi can run a number of operating systems, but the OS most people use is **Raspbian**, which is a distribution of the free **Linux** operating system. The projects in this book assume you are using Raspbian on your Raspberry Pi, and the instructions in this section tell you how to download and install it.

MORE ABOUT OPERATING SYSTEMS

An **operating system (OS)** is a type of software that allows people to create, store and manage files and applications that contain information on a computer. Examples of popular operating systems include Microsoft Windows, Mac OS X and Linux.

Linux is a free, open source operating system. This means that the programming code it is made with is free and open for anyone to look at and possibly improve on. There are many versions, or distributions, of the Linux operating system available. **Raspbian**, the OS you use on the Raspberry Pi, is a Linux distribution. You may have heard of some other well-known Linux distributions, such as Ubuntu, Debian, or Fedora.

Raspbian was created by a community of thousands of volunteers world-wide. You can connect to this community and learn more about Raspbian and Linux at `www.raspbian.org`.

Preparing an SD Card to Store Your Software

A desktop or laptop computer uses a permanent storage device called a **hard drive** to store information and applications. The Raspberry Pi doesn't have a hard drive, however, so your operating system, applications, and information all have to be stored on a removable SD card. This type of storage, known as **flash memory**, is the same as the kind you use with a digital camera to store all your photographs.

Before you plug in all the cables and so on, you first need to prepare (or *flash*) an SD card with the software the Raspberry Pi needs in order to run. This means that you format your SD card and copy the free Raspbian OS onto it. If you don't do this step, your Raspberry Pi won't recognise it as a storage device (like the hard drive of your computer) from which you can **boot** software. Don't worry if these terms are unfamiliar to you—all will become clear as you read through this section.

The first thing a computer does when you turn it on is to start up, or **boot**, the operating system.

You can buy SD cards with the Raspbian software preloaded onto them. This type of card allows you to get up and running straight away and you can skip the instructions on how to install the Raspbian software. However, I recommend you walk through the installation steps in this chapter, rather than using a preloaded card. It's useful to learn how to complete the formatting process yourself so that you understand how it's done and can start fresh if anything goes wrong.

Your SD card must be formatted, as described in the following steps, before any software is loaded onto it.

1. The best way to ensure that the card is formatted correctly for use is to download, install and use SD Formatter 4.0 (`www.sdcard.org/downloads/formatter_4`) from the SD Association to your desktop or laptop computer. (The built-in Windows formatting tool will only format the first partition and not the entire disk, so it is important that you use the SD formatter 4.0 tool instead.)
2. To download SD Formatter, follow the link in Step 1, and select either SD Formatter 4.0 for Windows Download or SD Formatter 4.0 for MAC Download. Read and agree to the terms and your download will begin. Once the download is complete, extract the file by clicking on Extract All and then run the setup application following the onscreen steps.
3. With the SD Formatter installed on your computer, run the application. Make sure that it has the right drive selected for your card; for example it might be labeled D: or F: (see Figure 1-4).You can find out which drive is your SD card by looking in My Computer on a Windows computer or using Finder on Mac OS X.

The program will wipe all data from the card so make sure you select the correct drive!

4. Click the Option button and select FULL (erase) from the drop-down menu. When you are ready, double-check that you have the correct drive selected, and click Format.

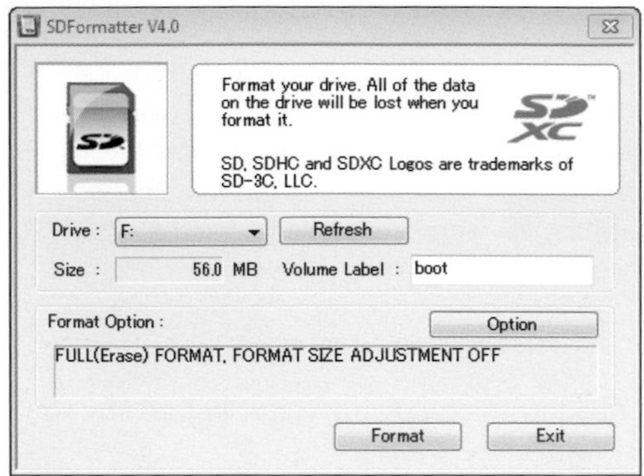

FIGURE 1-4 Formatting an SD Card using the SD Formatter application

Making It Easy with NOOBS

With your SD card formatted, you're ready to copy the Raspbian software onto it. The ***N**ew **O**ut **O**f **B**ox **S**oftware (NOOBS)* produced by the Raspberry Pi Foundation allows you to copy the files you need straight onto the SD card like you would do with photo or document files. It gives you the option of selecting which operating system you want to install, and even provides recovery should you accidentally delete all your software files.

All the projects in this book are designed to run using the Raspbian OS included in the NOOBS software. I recommend ensuring that you use the latest version of NOOBS before starting any projects in this book, otherwise you may have difficulty getting some of the projects to work.

First, you need to download NOOBS onto a desktop or laptop computer with an SD card reader. After you download the software, you will save it to an SD card for use with your Raspberry Pi. The following steps walk you through the process:

1. Navigate to the Raspberry Pi website at `www.raspberrypi.org` and click the Downloads tab at the top of the page. The New Out of Box Software that you are want to download is at the top of the page. Click the link to select the latest NOOBS .zip file.

   The download file is a compressed .zip file. Save the compressed file to your desktop or laptop computer, and then extract the files by right-clicking on the file and selecting the Extract All option (on a Microsoft Windows computer). You will then be given the option to extract the files to a directory or folder of your choice so that you will easily be able to find after the extraction is complete, as shown in Figure 1-5.

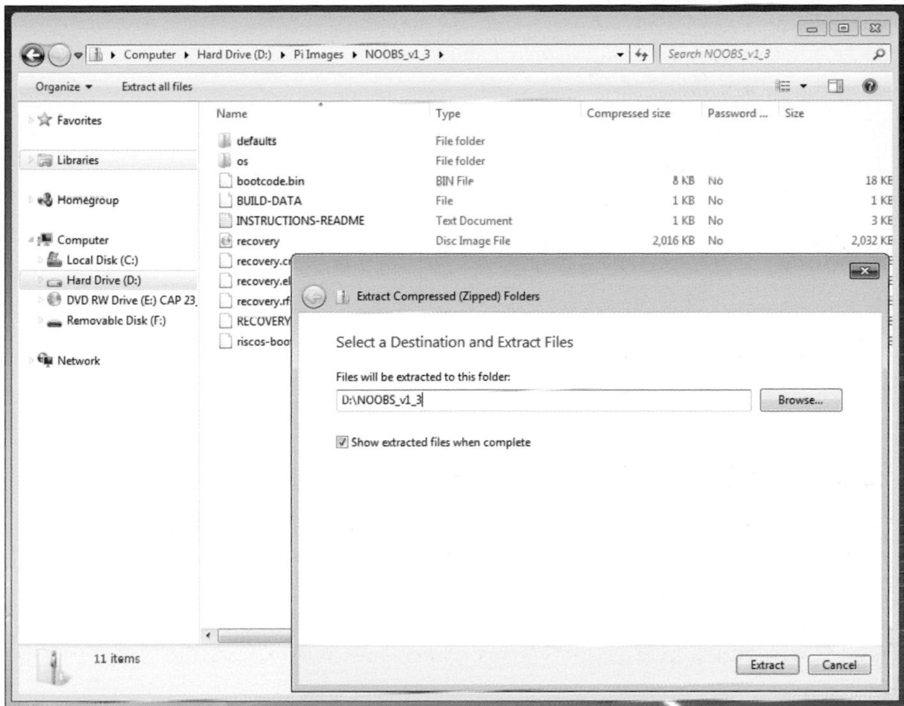

FIGURE 1-5 Extracting NOOBS to a directory on a windows computer

2. Place your formatted SD card into the card reader slot on your desktop computer or laptop. Now copy the extracted NOOBS files from the directory or folder on your computer and paste them onto your newly formatted SD card. You can do this either by dragging the files from one window to another, or by highlighting them all with your mouse, right-clicking, and copy/pasting the files onto the SD card.

You should always download the latest version of NOOBS as the software is being updated all the time. The latest version is usually listed at the top of the page with a version number.

Plugging in the Hardware

Now it's time to get your Raspberry Pi up and running. Find yourself a solid surface, like a desk or table, big enough to hold all your equipment. Make sure it's near some mains plug sockets. Ideally, you should also have access to a network device like a router because you will likely want to access the Internet on your Raspberry Pi at some point but this is not necessary at this point to set up your Pi.

As noted in Step 5 of the following instructions, do not plug in the power supply until you have completed the first four steps.

Set up your Raspberry Pi using the following steps:

1. Place the SD card with the NOOBS files you have loaded onto it into the SD card slot of your Raspberry Pi.
2. Plug a USB keyboard and mouse into the USB slots on the Pi.
3. Next, connect the HDMI cable from your TV or monitor to the HDMI port on the Pi and turn on your TV or monitor. Some TVs and monitors accept input from lots of different sources, so you may have to make sure that you set your TV or monitor to the HDMI setting. Some TVs and monitors will auto-detect the HDMI when you power up your Raspberry Pi.
4. If you think you'll be using the Internet on your Pi, connect a network cable to the Ethernet port.
5. Finally, to start the Raspberry Pi, plug in the micro USB power supply. It is important to do this step last, as the Pi does not have a power button so the boot process will begin as soon as you plug it in.

Okay, your Pi is running!

Installing and Configuring the Software

When you power up your Raspberry Pi with a NOOBS SD card for the first time you will need to complete the setup of the software.

The new system will load and begin to resize the SD cards partition. Partitions are used to separate parts of a storage devices from each other. Once NOOBS completes this task your card will have three partitions: one called the *boot* partition, which holds all the files needed to start and run your Pi; one called the *recovery* partition; and one to store any files that you create, or applications that you add later.

The NOOBS software gives you the choice of installing one of several different operating systems, including RaspBMC and Pidora as well as Raspbian. To use the projects in this book, you should install Raspbian. See Figure 1-6.

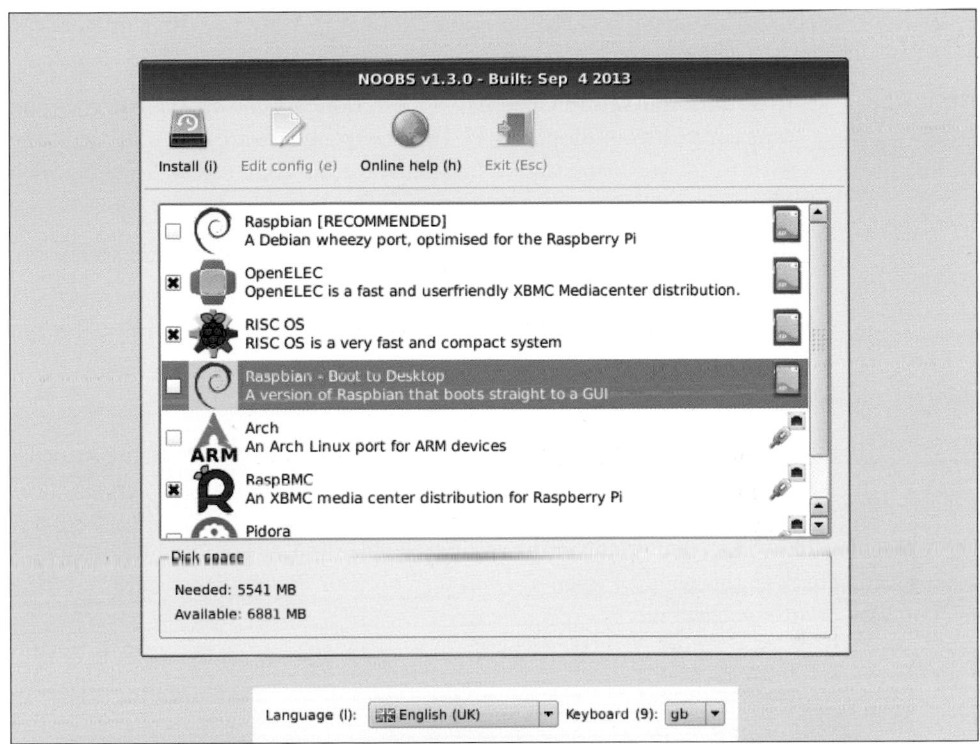

FIGURE 1-6 Selecting an operating system to install using NOOBS

In future releases of NOOBS you will be able to install more than one operating system at a time from the list provided. You might like to try another OS, such as Risc OS, at a later date. You can always use NOOBS on a different SD card, configured for another OS.

Follow these steps to install Raspbian:

1. Select the operating system that you wish to install—Raspbian—and click Install OS. At this point you can also change any language settings.
2. A warning will appear asking if you are sure you want to install the operating system as it will overwrite any file system already on the SD card. Click Yes.
3. After installation of the operating system, on the first full boot, a window like the one shown in Figure 1-7 will load, asking you to provide some configuration

settings. This screen is called the `raspi-config`. Here you can configure the following settings:

- **Internationalisation Options**—This option lets you set the language and time zone for your Raspberry Pi. For example if you are in the UK, you may wish to set your language to English and time zone to GMT—Greenwich Mean Time.
- **Enable Camera**—If you have a Pi Cam (a Raspberry Pi camera accessory), you should enable it here so that you will be able to use it.
- **Add to Rastrack**—Rastrack (`http://rastrack.co.uk/`) is a website that pins your Pi's location to a map of the world to let other people know you have a Pi and where you are located.
- A**bout raspi-config**—Use this option to learn more about the `raspi-config` application.

You do not need to change any of the settings at this time, as you have the option of coming back to this window whenever you turn on your Pi, by typing `sudo raspi-config` after you log in.

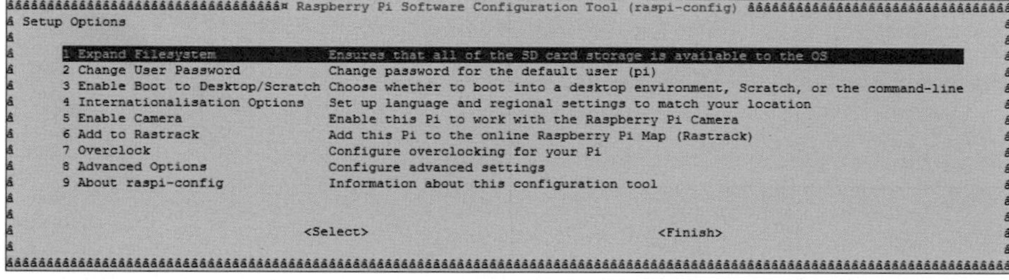

FIGURE 1-7 The `raspi-config` menu

USING NOOBS FOR RECOVERY

If anything goes wrong at any time after first running your Pi with NOOBS and installing an operating system—for example, if you manage to corrupt your file system, or if you would like to try one of the other operating systems packaged in with NOOBS—simply hold the Shift key when booting your Raspberry Pi and you will be taken to the recovery screen.

Logging in to Your Raspber

While your Raspberry Pi is booting up, you will see a lot of text moving ver the screen. This tells you that the operating system is loading. It looks a litt don't worry; you are not supposed to be able to read it. If something wrong, this text can be helpful to see where in the process the error occur

Once the start up (boot) of your Raspberry Pi has taken place, you will se ing prompts asking you to log in with your username and password:

```
raspberrypi login:
password:
```

The default user for the Raspberry Pi on Raspbian is called *pi*, and the default password is *raspberry*, so type **pi** for your login name at the first prompt and **raspberry** for your password in the second and press Enter.

Like many computing devices, you won't be able to see what you type into the password box for security reasons. Don't worry if you make a mistake, you will get another go.

After you log in and provide the password, the following text will appear:

```
pi@raspberry ~ $
```

The Raspberry Pi is asking you to give it a command. Type **startx**, as shown in Figure 1-8.

FIGURE 1-8 Logging into Raspberry Pi and starting the desktop environment

The window shown in Figure 1-9, called Xwindows, will load. Congratulations! You've reached the **graphical user interface** for the Raspbian operating system. Read on to explore the interface a bit.

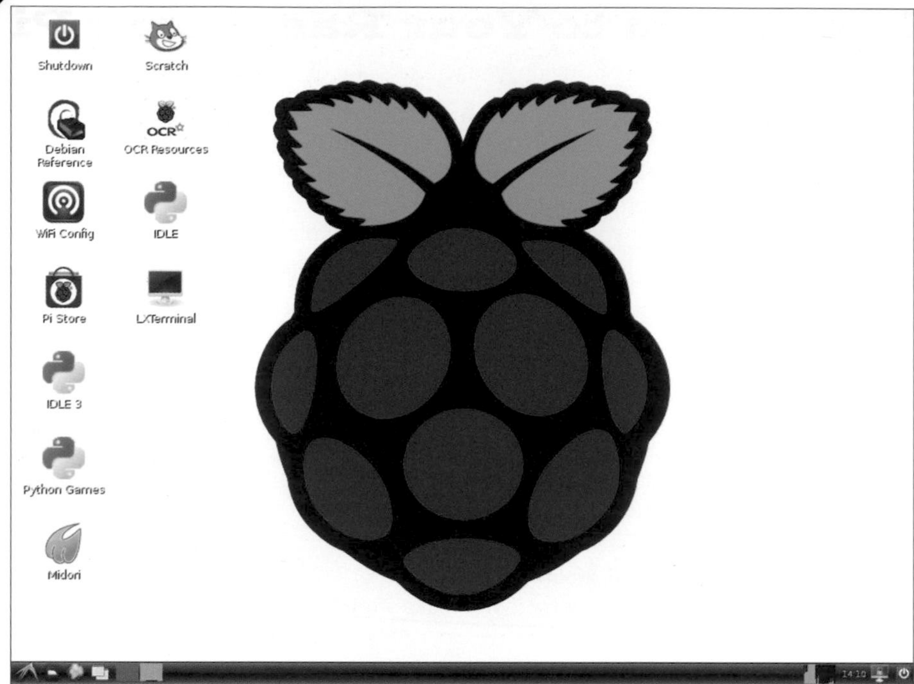

FIGURE 1-9 The Raspbian desktop

You may be used to using desktop computers or laptops that have windows, a mouse pointer, and a desktop. This is typical of a **graphical user interface,** or **GUI**.

Exploring the Desktop in Raspbian

As you just saw, typing startx after logging into the Raspberry Pi loads Xwindows, or the graphical user interface, of the Raspbian operating system.

You will see the default Raspbian desktop shown in Figure 1-9, with the Raspberry Pi logo, a taskbar across the bottom with the time on the far right, and the main menu (arrow) icon on the far left. The desktop also displays a number of icons for applications that you can launch by double-clicking with your mouse. Some of the most commonly used applications are Scratch (see Adventure 3), Python (see Adventure 5), and Midori (a web browser) that you can use to browse the World Wide Web if your Pi is connected to the Internet via an Ethernet cable or a wireless adapter like the Wi-Pi. There are even some games for you to try out using PyGame. Spend a few minutes checking out what applications are available by clicking on the main menu and then each of the submenus in turn. Figure 1-10 shows the applications available under the Accessories submenu.

To learn a little about how your Raspberry Pi is set up, try the following steps:

1. Click on the main menu icon in the left corner of the taskbar.
2. From the main menu, select Accessories➜File Manager to open the file browser (Pcmanfm). If you are logged in as the user *pi*, the browser will display the contents of your home directory (`/home/pi`). This directory will be fairly empty as you are yet to begin your programming adventures with Raspberry Pi. You will see a directory called `Desktop`. If you double-click that folder icon, you will see it contains all the shortcuts to the applications that you see on the desktop.

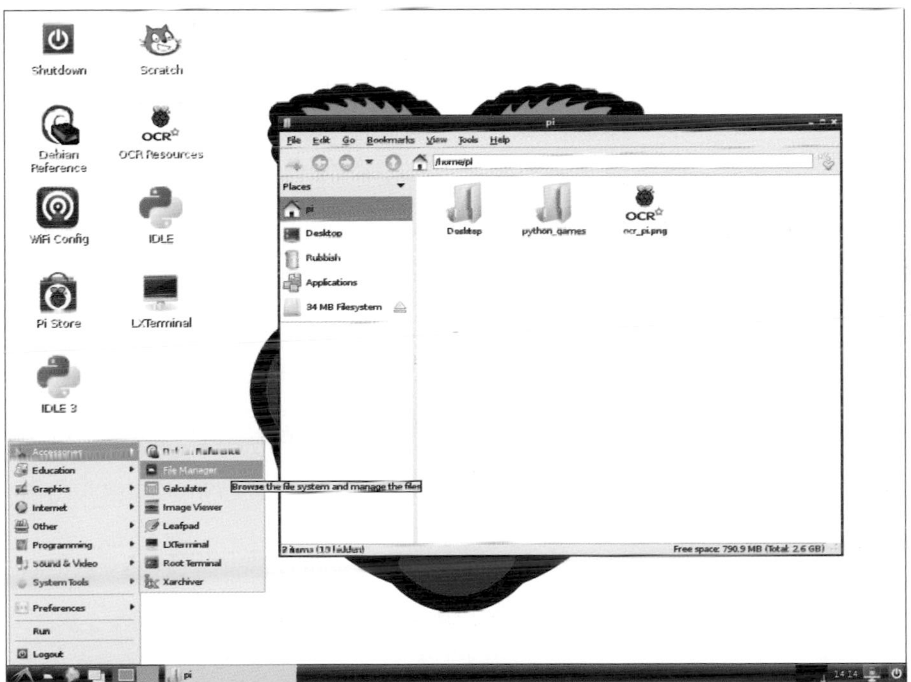

FIGURE 1-10 Using the main menu and file browser in Raspbian

Shutting Down Your Raspberry Pi

When you shut down your Raspberry Pi, it is very important that you don't simply remove the power supply but make sure you always instruct the OS to shut down safely. The latest version of NOOBS has a Shutdown desktop icon for shutting down your Raspberry Pi cleanly if you are using the GUI—just click the icon and your Raspberry Pi will do all the work.

However, if you are not using the GUI you will not see this icon, and will need to use a text command to shut down your Raspberry Pi. You can learn how to do this in Adventure 2, in the section "Using Shutdown and Restart Commands".

Backing up an SD Card Image

You have only used your Raspberry Pi once so far, but you have already made changes to the configuration of the operating system. As you move through the projects in this book, you may wish to make copies as you go along to make sure you don't lose any of your work if your SD card stops working for any reason. It is very easy to do this using a free Windows application called Win32 Disk Imager. Download this application from `http://sourceforge.net/projects/win32diskimager/` before continuing with the following steps.

1. First, if you have not yet shut down your Raspberry Pi, follow the instructions in the previous section to do so now, using the following command:

   ```
   sudo shutdown -h now
   ```

2. Take your SD card out of your Pi and place it into your computer's SD card reader.
3. Run the Win32 Disk Imager on your desktop computer by locating the folder into which you extracted it and double-clicking the application icon.
4. In the Image File box (see Figure 1-11), type a name of your choice for your backed up image—Adventures_In_Pi, for example.
5. Click the folder icon to browse to a location on your computer where you would like to save your backed up image.
6. Click Read to copy the image from the SD card to your computer.
7. Wait for the progress bar to become full before closing the software and removing your SD card.

In the future, when you become more skilled, it's likely you will have multiple cards with different project images on them. You can save all these to your computer separately. It's a good idea to back them up in this way, to keep all your files safe. It is also best to store one image on one SD card and use separate cards for each project you work on.

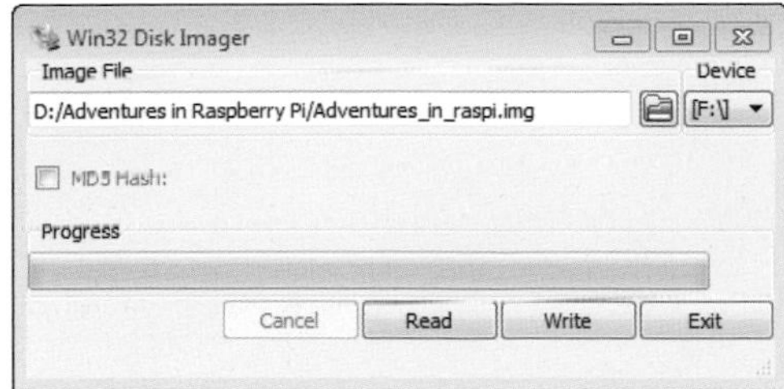

FIGURE 1-11 Using Win 32 Disk Imager to make a backup of an SD card.

Raspberry Pi Startup Command Quick Reference Table

Command	Description
`startx`	Launches the Raspbian desktop environment (GUI).
`sudo`	Gives the user *root* or *super user* permissions.
`sudo shutdown -h now`	Shuts down (halts) the power to the Raspberry Pi.
`sudo shutdown -r now`	Shuts down the power to the Raspberry Pi and then restarts it.

Achievement Unlocked: Your Raspberry Pi is up and running!

In the Next Adventure

In Adventure 2, you learn about the power of text commands. You will use commands to instruct your Raspberry Pi, and discover how to navigate the file system, launch programs and download more applications to use with your Pi.

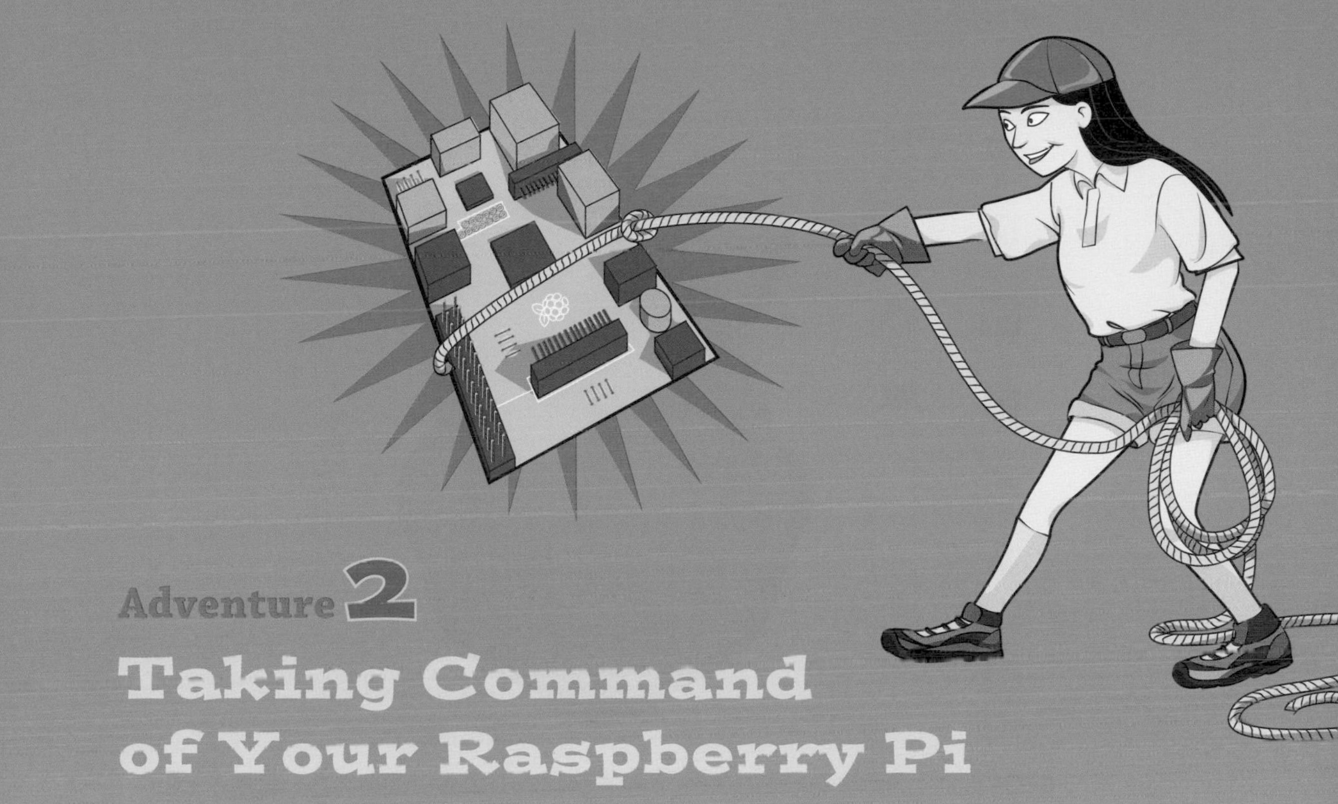

Adventure 2
Taking Command of Your Raspberry Pi

NOW THAT YOUR Raspberry Pi is up and running, how do you tell it what you want it to do? Well, there are a number of ways to communicate with computers, depending on what operating system (OS) it uses. Many of today's OSs—like Microsoft Windows and MAC OS X—use graphical user interfaces (GUIs). These have icons that you click with a mouse, making the computer very easy to use. Raspbian, the OS you are using on the Raspberry Pi, has a GUI (see Figure 2-1). You can access the GUI by typing **startx** straight after you log in, as you did in Adventure 1.

If you use the Raspbian GUI, you simply click the icons to access the software programs. As an alternative to the GUI, you can communicate with the Raspberry Pi using text-based instructions, known as **commands**, without the need for a GUI. This form of communication is called a **command-line interface**, and the window into which you type the commands is called a **terminal**. Although the GUI might be more user friendly and easier to understand than text commands, text commands can be faster when you become more experienced in using them. You can also do more things with text commands, such as writing scripts, which are small programs that combine a series of commands to carry out routine computing tasks. In later adventures you will write your own scripts to make something happen.

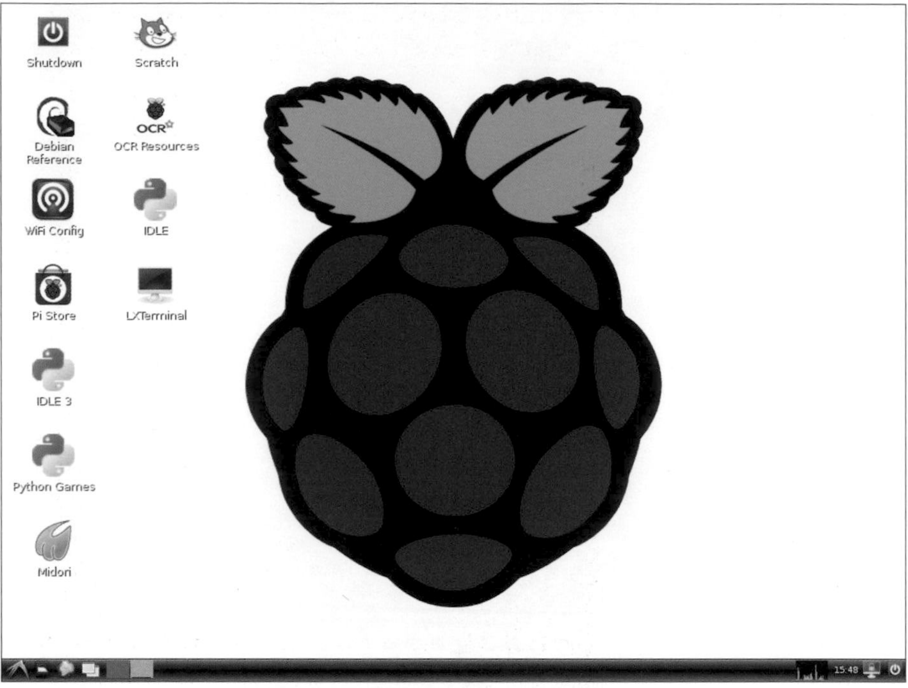

FIGURE 2-1 The Raspberry Pi GUI

A **command-line interface** (**CLI**) allows you to communicate with a computer using text commands.

A **terminal** is a screen window that gives you access to the command-line interface. The graphical LXTerminal is an example.

When you first log in to your Raspberry Pi with your username and password, you will see the $ prompt on the screen, which tells you that the computer is waiting for you to type a command. In Adventure 1 you typed the command **startx** at the $ prompt to start the desktop environment (GUI) but you don't have to use that command—you can type in any command that the computer knows about.

By pressing CTRL+ALT and one of the function keys between F1 and F6, you can switch among six different virtual terminals. You can log in to any of the terminals and type commands at the prompt. If you press CTRL+ALT+F1 after typing `startx`, you will see your original terminal. CTRL+ALT+F7 will take you back to the desktop environment.

For example, suppose you have written a book report on *Hamlet* and you want your Raspberry Pi to delete it. You might try typing the following command at the prompt:

```
Delete the file hamlet.doc
```

If you do this, the file won't be deleted, but you'll get this error message:

```
-bash: Delete: command not found
```

This is because you can't just type any command and expect the Raspberry Pi to understand it! It will only respond to a command when it is composed of a particular set of defined words that it already understands. These commands can be very specific and often need to be typed in a certain order to work. To delete your report, you must use a command that Raspberry Pi understands. In this case, you need to use the `rm` (remove) command:

```
rm hamlet.doc
```

If you learn these commands, you won't be limited to using a GUI and you'll be able to navigate file systems and program the computer by using simple text commands. This can sometimes be faster and more convenient than doing the same tasks in a GUI. Many of the projects and tutorials in this book use some text commands, so this chapter introduces you to some basic commands that will help you save some time.

Exploring the Terminal

In this section, you'll become familiar with some common Linux text commands by using the graphical LXTerminal within the desktop environment, as shown in Figure 2-2. You can open this terminal in one of three ways:

- Log in and type the command `startx` to enter the desktop environment, as you did in Adventure 1.
- Open the LXTerminal from the desktop by double-clicking the icon with your mouse.
- Select LXTerminal from Accessories in the main menu.

To see a video about using the LXTerminal and the other tasks in this adventure, visit the companion website at `www.wiley.com/go/adventuresinrp` and select CommandLine.

When LXTerminal is loaded, you will see a black screen with the line `pi@raspberrypi ~ $`, as shown in Figure 2-2.

FIGURE 2-2 The LXTerminal open in the Raspbian Desktop Environment

You may recognise the line `pi@raspberrypi ~ $` from when you logged in, before you launched the graphical user interface using the command `startx`. Let's break down the parts of this line.

- `pi` refers to your *username*. You have logged in as the user *pi*.
- `raspberrypi` is the **hostname** of your device; this name identifies it on a network. So you are the user *pi* on the device *raspberrypi*.
- After the hostname comes the current directory, which is represented by the ~ symbol (this symbol is called a *tilde)*. This is a short way of referring to your home directory, which is `/home/pi` when written in full.
- Finally, the Raspberry Pi asks you what you want it to do, by displaying the `$` symbol as a prompt to enter a text command (see Figure 2-3).

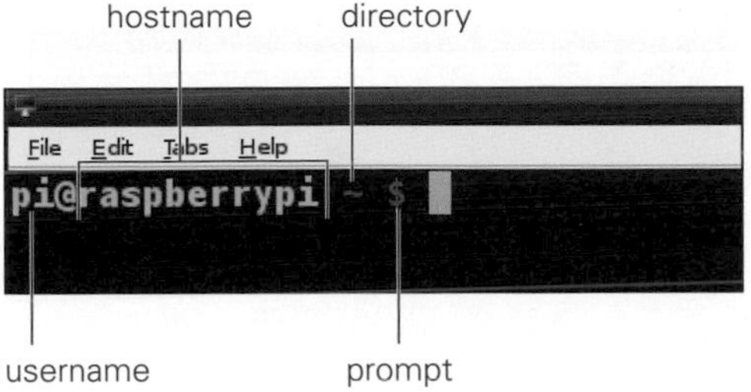

FIGURE 2-3 Breakdown of `pi@raspberrypi ~ $`

Now try to interact with the computer by typing a command: type **date** into the terminal and press Enter.

The Raspberry Pi tells you the date and time without needing to display a graphical clock, and the command provides you with a response quickly.

A **hostname** is a word that identifies a computing device on a network. The hostname of the Raspberry Pi is `raspberrypi`.

Commands for Navigating Through Your File System

One of the most important tasks of an OS is to organise files and folders (called *directories* in Linux). These files and directories are organised into a tree-like structure, in which directories can contain other directories and files. The File Manager, shown in Figure 2-4, is a tool that lets you see what that structure looks like graphically. You can access File Manager by clicking the icon next to the main menu icon on the taskbar at the bottom of the desktop environment.

You can use simple commands to navigate through the file system using the command line. As with any navigation, you need to know where you are—your starting point—before you can find your way forward. Type **pwd** at the terminal prompt and press Enter:

```
pi@raspberrypi ~ $ pwd
```

FIGURE 2-4 The File Manager view of my Raspberry Pi file system

The Raspberry Pi will respond by displaying this line on the screen:

```
/home/pi
```

The `pwd` command asks the Raspberry Pi to ***p**rint the **w**orking **d**irectory*, or show which directory you are currently working in. The `/home/pi` response that appears shows that you are currently located in the `pi` directory, which is inside the `home` directory.

As you can see in Figure 2-5, if you give the command `ls`, it tells your Raspberry Pi to **output** a *list* of the files and directories in the current directory. To see a list of files and directories that are in `/home/pi` (the `pi` directory in your Raspberry Pi's home directory), type **ls** at the `$` prompt and press Enter:

```
pi@raspberrypi ~ $ ls
```

Output refers to the data that your computer gives in response, after you have typed in a command.

```
pi@raspberrypi ~ $ pwd
/home/pi
pi@raspberrypi ~ $ ls
Desktop    indiecity  minecraft-pi-0.1.1.tar.gz  python_games
Documents  mcpi       ocr_pi.png                 Scratch
pi@raspberrypi ~ $
```

FIGURE 2-5 Using the `ls` command to show a list of the files and directories on my Raspberry Pi

Figure 2-5 shows that inside `/home/pi` are six directories listed in blue (such as Desktop and Scratch), as well as one file in pink (`ocr_pi.png`) and one in red (`minecraft-pi-0.1.1.tar.gz`). This list does not really tell us much about those files or directories. To learn more about the contents of the directory you are in, type **ls -l**. You are still using the `ls` command, but this time adding the `-l` (which stands for *long*) **parameter** or option. This tells your Raspberry Pi to show the list in a longer, more detailed format:

```
pi@raspberrypi ~ $ ls -l
```

Parameters modify the way that the standard command works (a bit like ticking a tick box in a GUI program). Most Linux commands have lots of parameters that modify the way that they work. Just to be clear: the `-l` parameter is a lowercase L, not the numeral 1.

As you can see in Figure 2-6, the Raspberry Pi will now give you more information about the files and directories that were listed in Figure 2-5. This information includes the size of the file, the date it was created, the owner of the file and what kind of permission you have to access it.

To move between directories or folders in the tree-like structure, you can use the `cd` (*change* ***d****irectory*) command. Try moving into the Desktop directory by typing **cd Desktop** at the prompt:

```
pi@raspberrypi ~ $ cd Desktop
```

To move between directories or folders in the tree-like structure, you can use the `cd` (*change* ***d****irectory*) command. Try moving into the Desktop directory by typing **cd Desktop** at the prompt:

```
pi@raspberrypi ~ $ cd Desktop
```

```
pi@raspberrypi: ~
File Edit Tabs Help
pi@raspberrypi ~ $ pwd
/home/pi
pi@raspberrypi ~ $ ls
Desktop    indiecity  minecraft-pi-0.1.1.tar.gz  python_games
Documents  mcpi       ocr_pi.png                 Scratch
pi@raspberrypi ~ $ ls -l
total 1460
drwxr-xr-x 2 pi pi    4096 Apr 22 08:28 Desktop
drwxr-xr-x 3 pi pi    4096 Apr 20 15:20 Documents
drwxr-xr-x 3 pi pi    4096 Apr 22 08:25 indiecity
drwxr-xr-x 4 pi pi    4096 Feb 11 10:52 mcpi
-rw-r--r-- 1 pi pi 1459472 Feb 11 11:05 minecraft-pi-0.1.1.tar.gz
-rw-r--r-- 1 pi pi    5781 Feb  3 05:07 ocr_pi.png
drwxrwxr-x 2 pi pi    4096 Apr 14 14:23 python_games
drwxr-xr-x 2 pi pi    4096 Apr 20 15:20 Scratch
pi@raspberrypi ~ $
```

FIGURE 2-6 Using the text command `ls -l` to list more information about files and directories

The next prompt from Raspberry Pi will read like this:

```
pi@raspberrypi ~/Desktop $
```

Notice how `~/Desktop` has appeared as part of the prompt. This reminds you that you are now in the Desktop directory, which in turn is inside your home directory.

You are now inside `/home/pi/Desktop`.

To go back to /`home/pi`, type the command **cd ..** (that's `cd` followed by a space and two full stops).

```
pi@raspberrypi ~ $ cd ..
```

The `cd ..` command will move you up the directory tree to the parent directory. For example, if you are in `/home/pi/Desktop` and type `cd ..` you are moved upwards through the file system to `/home/pi`. To check where you are in the file system at any time, type **pwd** to see your current directory, as shown in Figure 2-7.

```
pi@raspberrypi ~ $ cd Desktop
pi@raspberrypi ~/Desktop $ pwd
/home/pi/Desktop
pi@raspberrypi ~/Desktop $ cd ..
pi@raspberrypi ~ $ pwd
/home/pi
pi@raspberrypi ~ $
```

FIGURE 2-7 Navigating the file system in Raspberry Pi's LXTerminal

If you are ever lost in the file system and can't remember where you are, just type **pwd** to find out.

Understanding sudo

When you are logged into Raspberry Pi as the user *pi*, you have only limited access to the ability to perform tasks on the device. This restriction prevents you from accidentally deleting important files. Sometimes, however, you will need to do things that affect the whole system, such as installing a new program or adding a new user. The `sudo` command lets you temporarily act as the *super user* (or *root* user) and gives you permission to do whatever you want on the system. This includes deleting every file on your disk so you must be very careful when you are logged in as sudo!

You may need to use `sudo` for some applications. Can you think why?

Some applications require the ability to make changes to protected parts of the system or to interact with protected devices such as the GPIO pins, and so must run as an administrator. For instance, if you run the `apt-get` command to install or upgrade an application you must run it with `sudo` or else it will fail because it doesn't have permissions to update the necessary files.

Launching Programs from the Command Line

You can use text commands to launch programs from the command line, too, which is often quicker than navigating the main menu and clicking an icon. It is also handy to be able to do this if you do not have a mouse plugged in.

Try this. In LXTerminal, type the following command at the $ prompt:

```
leafpad
```

The leafpad application on the Raspberry Pi opens. (The leafpad application is a text editor in which you can enter text. It is included with your Raspberry Pi installation.)

Managing Files and Directories

You may sometimes want to create files, or copy, move or delete them. The following Linux commands are useful for managing your files:

- `cat`—displays the contents of the text file
- `cp`—makes another copy of a file
- `mv`—moves a file to a new location
- `rm`—deletes (removes) a file
- `mkdir`—makes a directory
- `rmdir`—deletes (removes) a directory
- `clear`—allows you to clear the terminal

Type the following commands into the LXTerminal window, in the order they're given here. See if you can explain what is happening at each step:

```
pwd

cd to desktop

ls

touch hello

leafpad hello

rm hello

cd ..
```

Installing and Updating Applications

The New Out Of Box Software, or *NOOBS*, that you learned about in Adventure 1 includes some applications that are installed along with the Raspbian operating system. You can see these application icons on the desktop and also in the main menu. In future adventures you will use Scratch and Python IDLE 3, which are already installed.

If you connected your Raspberry Pi to the Internet as described in Adventure 1, you can use text commands to download, install and update additional applications that you may wish to use.

Downloading and Installing Applications

It's easy to find new applications and install them on your Raspberry Pi. The Pi Store (`http://store.raspberrypi.com/projects`), for example is full of both free and for-pay apps that you can download and use much like the Apple App Store. Try typing the following command in a terminal and then pressing Enter:

```
sudo apt-get install scrot
```

Scrot (which is short for **scr**een sh**ot**) is an application that enables you to take pictures of the display on your Raspberry Pi screen. The `sudo apt-get` command tells Raspberry Pi to use the Internet connection to find and install the application on your Raspberry Pi. This command requires `sudo` because by installing a new application you are asking the Raspberry Pi to change system files.

You will see the terminal window fill with writing and, after a few seconds, the terminal will ask you to check that there is enough space on your SD card to install the application. At this point you can either press the Y key for yes, to continue with the installation, or the N key for no, which will cancel the installation. Figure 2-8 shows the screen display for the scrot installation process. About halfway down the screen, you see the question "Do you want to continue [Y/n]?" and see that I answered yes (y) to install the application.

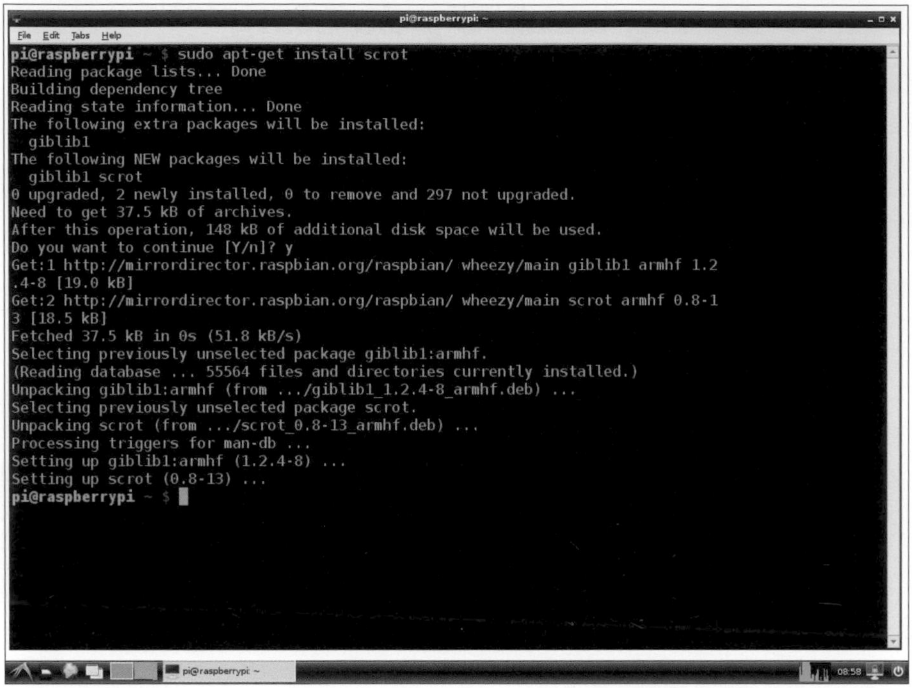

```
pi@raspberrypi ~ $ sudo apt-get install scrot
Reading package lists... Done
Building dependency tree
Reading state information... Done
The following extra packages will be installed:
  giblib1
The following NEW packages will be installed:
  giblib1 scrot
0 upgraded, 2 newly installed, 0 to remove and 297 not upgraded.
Need to get 37.5 kB of archives.
After this operation, 148 kB of additional disk space will be used.
Do you want to continue [Y/n]? y
Get:1 http://mirrordirector.raspbian.org/raspbian/ wheezy/main giblib1 armhf 1.2
.4-8 [19.0 kB]
Get:2 http://mirrordirector.raspbian.org/raspbian/ wheezy/main scrot armhf 0.8-1
3 [18.5 kB]
Fetched 37.5 kB in 0s (51.8 kB/s)
Selecting previously unselected package giblib1:armhf.
(Reading database ... 55564 files and directories currently installed.)
Unpacking giblib1:armhf (from .../giblib1_1.2.4-8_armhf.deb) ...
Selecting previously unselected package scrot.
Unpacking scrot (from .../scrot_0.8-13_armhf.deb) ...
Processing triggers for man-db ...
Setting up giblib1:armhf (1.2.4-8) ...
Setting up scrot (0.8-13) ...
pi@raspberrypi ~ $
```

FIGURE 2-8 Using the `apt-get install` command to download and install the scrot application

You will remember from earlier in this chapter that you can use a command to open an application. Once you have installed scrot, you can open it and see it work by typing **scrot** into a terminal window. Scrot will take a picture of your screen, called a *screen capture*, and store it in the home directory. Use the File Manager to find the image—it will be labelled with a filename that starts with the date and time the picture was taken and end in `.png`, which is a common image format. Once you have found the file, click it to view the image.

Learning More About an Application

Each Linux application or command has a "manual" file that gives a description of the application and lists the options or features that are available. To read the manual for any application, use the command `man` followed by the name of the application. For example, to see the manual for the nano text editor, simply type **man nano**. Figure 2-9 shows the manual for the scrot application.

The manual lists the options available with the application and shows you any extra functions that are available for you to use if you wish. For the scrot application, for example, you can choose to have a timer delay before it captures the screen. It is always a good idea to read an application's manual, and it can be very helpful if you forget the order in which you need to write the commands.

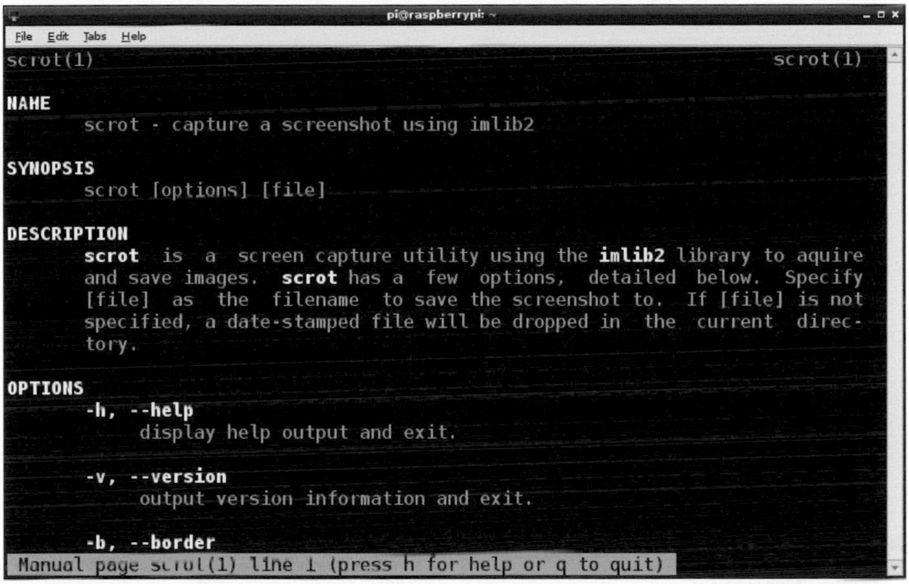

```
scrot(1)                                                        scrot(1)

NAME
       scrot - capture a screenshot using imlib2

SYNOPSIS
       scrot [options] [file]

DESCRIPTION
       scrot  is  a  screen capture utility using the imlib2 library to aquire
       and save images.  scrot has a  few  options,  detailed  below.  Specify
       [file]  as  the  filename  to save the screenshot to.  If [file] is not
       specified, a date-stamped file will be dropped in  the  current  direc-
       tory.

OPTIONS
       -h, --help
            display help output and exit.

       -v, --version
            output version information and exit.

       -b, --border
 Manual page scrot(1) line 1 (press h for help or q to quit)
```

FIGURE 2-9 Accessing an application's manual to learn more

Upgrading Your Apps

It is good practice to upgrade the applications that you have installed approximately once every two weeks, or before you download and install a new application. Upgrades for an application may provide new features, correct "bugs" that have been causing problems in the application and resolve security issues that may threaten your system.

To upgrade your applications, you should first type the following command to download information about any new versions of applications that are available:

```
sudo apt-get update
```

Next, type the following command to actually install the upgrades:

```
sudo apt-get upgrade
```

Editing Files

The `nano` command opens a text editor, which is an application that allows you to edit text files. This program is useful if you wish to make changes to lines of code or individual settings inside a file. The following instructions walk you through the stages of using nano to create and edit a text file (see Figure 2-10).

1. Create a text file on the desktop. To do this, first use the `cd` command to navigate to the Desktop directory, and then use the `nano` command, like this:

```
pi@raspberrypi ~ $ cd Desktop
pi@raspberrypi ~/Desktop $ nano hello
```

2. The nano program will open a text file called `hello`. You can type anything you like into this text file—as you can see in Figure 2-10, I typed in "Hello Raspberry Pi Adventurers!" Try typing your favourite quote from a film or the lyrics of a song.

3. To exit the text editor, press CTRL+X. The following message appears:

```
Save modified buffer (ANSWERING "No" WILL DESTROY CHANGES) ?
```

If you want to save the changes you have made to the file, press Y for yes. If you do not want to make any changes, press N for no.

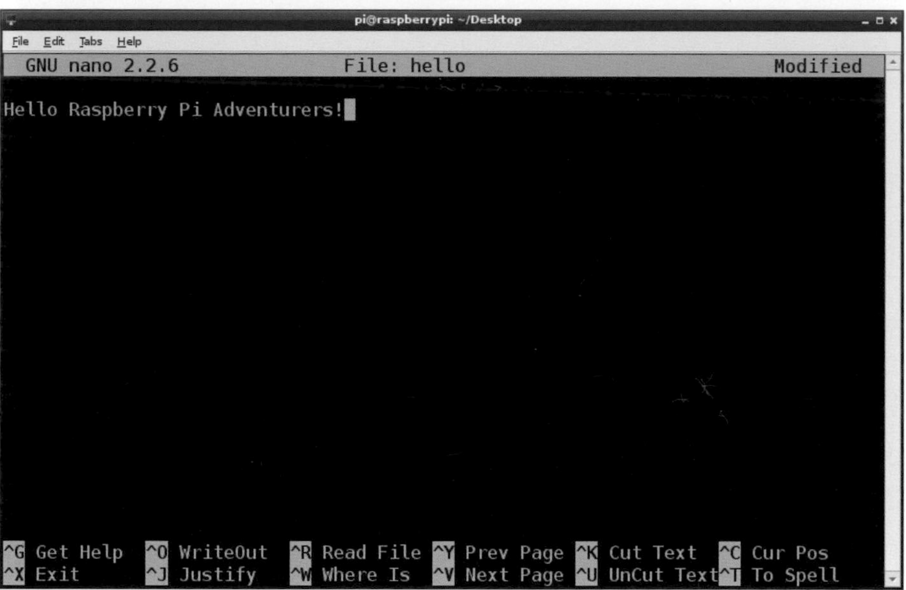

FIGURE 2-10 Using nano to edit a text file

To learn more about using nano to edit files, run the `man nano` command and read the manual.

Using Shutdown and Restart Commands

When you start a Raspberry Pi, the device follows a set of instructions to load the OS. Similarly, when you shut it down, it should follow a set of instructions to shut down the OS in such a way that the file system stored on the SD card stays complete and uncorrupted. It is therefore very important that you don't simply remove the power supply but make sure you always instruct the OS to shut down safely. From the GUI, you can simply use the Shutdown icon on the desktop to shut down the Raspberry Pi, as described in Adventure 1. Alternatively, from the LXTerminal, you do this by using the `shutdown` command.

First, make sure that you close any open applications. After all applications are closed, type the following command to start the shutdown process from the command line:

```
sudo shutdown -h now
```

The `-h` option in this command stands for *halt*. When the system is "halted", it is safe to remove the power.

Sometimes, you might simply want to restart the OS. The following command, with the `-r` (*restart*) option, will shut down and then restart the Raspberry Pi:

```
sudo shutdown -r now
```

Continuing Your Text Adventure

To learn more about commands and using terminals in Linux, click on the Debian Reference shortcut on the desktop of the Raspberry Pi and explore the information in that program. To recall or review the commands in this chapter, refer to the following Quick Reference Table.

Command Line Quick Reference Table

Command	Description
`cat`	Displays the contents (*catalog*) of the text file.
`cd`	Change directory. For example, the command `cd Desktop` moves you into the Desktop directory.
`cd ..`	Move you up the directory tree to the parent directory.

continued

Command Line Quick Reference Table (continued)

Command	Description
`cp`	Makes another copy of a file.
`clear`	Allows you to clear the terminal.
`date`	Displays the time and date.
`ls`	Displays a list of files and folders in the current directory.
`ls -l`	Provides a list that includes more detail about the files. The `-l` parameter is a lowercase L (for *long*), not the numeral 1.
`man`	Displays the *manual* or description file for the command.
`mv`	Moves a file to a new location.
`mkdir`	Makes a directory.
`nano`	Opens the nano text editor. To open a specific text file, add the file name; for example, `nano hello` opens the `hello` text file.
`pwd`	Prints the working directory (shows which directory you are currently working in).
`rm` *`xxx`*	Deletes (removes) the file named *xxx*.
`rmdir`	Deletes (removes) a directory.
`startx`	Launches the Raspbian desktop environment (GUI).
`sudo`	Gives the user *root* or *super user* permissions.
`sudo apt-get install` *`xxx`*	Tells the Raspberry Pi to use the Internet to find, download, and install the *xxx* application.
`sudo apt-get update`	Downloads information about any new versions available for applications on your Raspberry Pi.
`sudo apt-get upgrade`	Installs available upgrades for all applications on your Raspberry Pi.
`sudo shutdown -h now`	Shuts down (halts) the power to the Raspberry Pi.
`sudo shutdown -r now`	Shuts down the power to the Raspberry Pi and then restarts it.

Achievement Unlocked: Your Raspberry Pi responds to your commands!

In the Next Adventure

In Adventure 3, you will learn some basic programming skills. You'll create a crazy monkey animation and a role-playing adventure game using the graphical programming language and environment known as Scratch.

Adventure 3
Creating Stories and Games with Scratch

IF YOU CAN put together a jigsaw puzzle, you can create a computer program using Scratch! With just a few clicks, you can have a bat fly around a castle, make a ninja sneak past a guard or conjure up a flock of butterflies floating through a garden.

Scratch was developed by the Massachusetts Institute of Technology (MIT) Media Lab to help young students learn basic control and programming concepts (`http://scratch.mit.edu`). It is free to use and has become very popular throughout the world. There is even an International Scratch Day, which is held every year to celebrate and share the things people have created using the language.

Scratch is a graphical programming language. This means that, instead of writing text commands, you connect blocks of code together to make a script that makes something happen. You can use Scratch to create interactive stories and computer games in which you draw the scenery (called the **stage**) and the characters (called **sprites**). You can also create music and art with Scratch.

In this adventure, you'll begin by creating the Scratch equivalent of a typical Hello World! computer program and making Scratch Cat say "Hello". After that, you'll create a program with a monkey who moves around the screen and changes his facial expression. Finally, you'll create an entire role-playing game incorporating a variety of backgrounds and different ways to win points.

Sprites are the characters that can be programmed to do something in Scratch. The sprites wear costumes that can be customised.

The **stage** refers to the background for the sprites. You can add scripts to the stage to allow the sprites to interact with it—for example, you might draw a wall that stops your sprite from moving beyond a certain point.

Getting Started with Scratch

If you are using the latest version of the Raspberry Pi operating system Raspbian, Scratch will be pre-installed and you'll see the Scratch cat icon (see Figure 3-1) on your desktop. To open Scratch, double-click the icon or open the main menu on the bottom left of the screen, navigate to Programming and click on Scratch (see Figure 3-2).

FIGURE 3-1 The Scratch cat

You may have used Scratch in school but it might look a little different on your Raspberry Pi. This is because you are using Scratch version 1.4 on the Raspberry Pi, and there are other versions, including Scratch 2.0, which you may use in school or code clubs through a web browser.

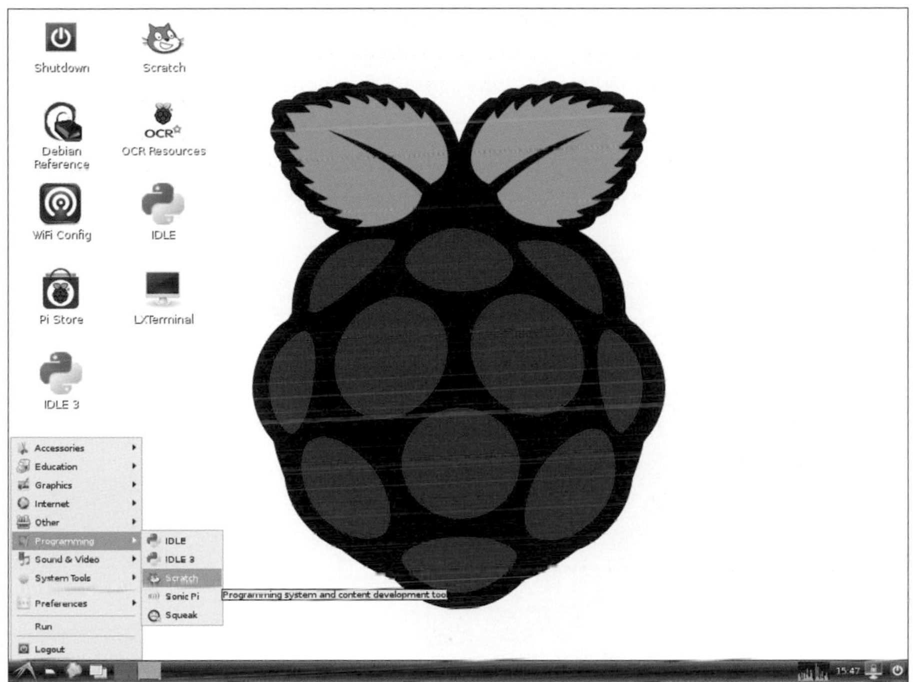

FIGURE 3-2 Opening Scratch from the Raspbian menu

The Scratch Interface

The interface for Scratch includes four main panes, identified in Figure 3-3:

- **Stage**—Your animations, stories and games are displayed in this pane so that you can see what happens as you add backgrounds, characters and scripts to your creations. The stage is set on a grid with an x axis and a y axis so that you can program events or actions to take place at a specific location on the stage; for example, you can have a star appear in the top right corner of the stage by giving the appropriate x and y coordinates.
- **Sprites palette**—This pane displays the sprites or characters that you create for your project. To see or edit scripts or costumes for a sprite, click on the sprite in the palette.
- **Blocks palette**—The Blocks palette is divided into two portions. The top portion has eight labels—Motion, Looks, Sound, Pen, Control, Sensing, Operators and Variables—each of which corresponds to a group of blocks that you can use to program your projects. Click on a label, and the blocks available for you to use appear in the lower portion of the pane. To form scripts, you select the blocks you want to use, drag them onto the Scripts tab (see the next bullet) and fit them together.

- **Scripts tab**—The centre pane of the interface has three tabs along the top: Scripts, Costumes or Backgrounds, and Sounds. When the Scripts tab is selected, you can drag the programming blocks into this pane and fit them together to build your scripts.

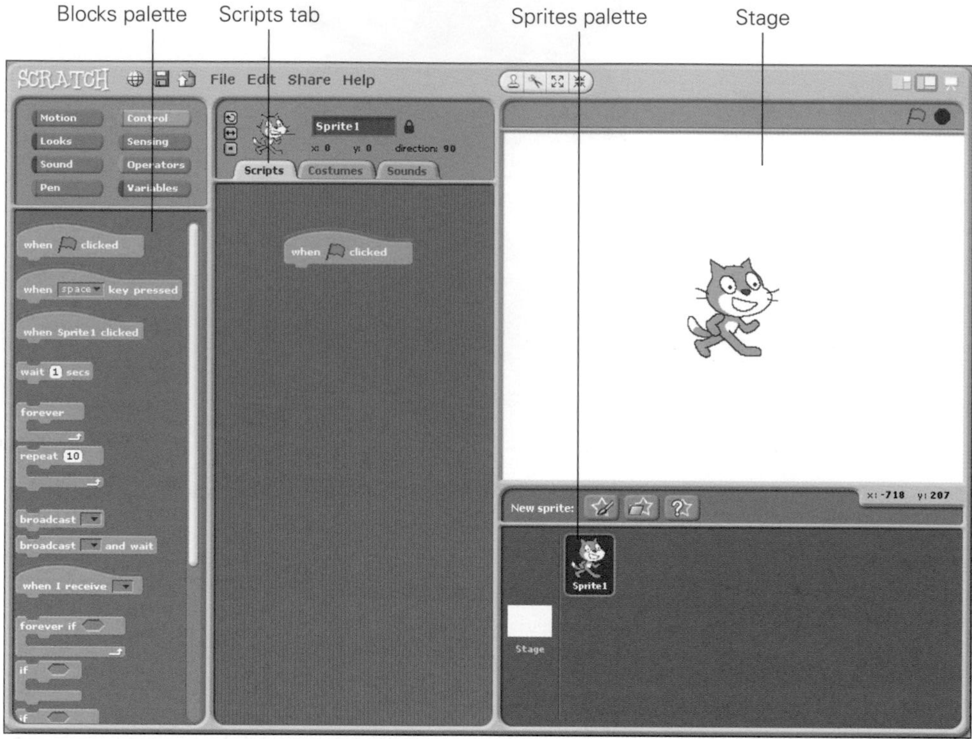

FIGURE 3-3 The Scratch interface

A Quick Hello from Scratch Cat

The best way to learn how to use Scratch is simply to use it! In this project, you will learn the basics of using Scratch by following some simple instructions.

1. To begin, make sure that that the cat sprite with the label Sprite1 is selected in the Sprites palette and the label reads Sprite1.
2. In the centre pane, click the Scripts tab. You will drag blocks onto this tab to create a "script" that tells your program what actions to perform.

Notice that the cat and the label Sprite1 appear at the top of the tab to indicate that the current script will be applied to that sprite. Always check that you have selected the correct item before working in the Scripts tab.

3. Next, click the Control label at the top of the Blocks palette to see all the control blocks available.

4. Drag the control block labelled `when [flag] clicked` onto the Scripts tab, as shown in Figure 3-4. This control block is the "start button" of your program. It means that when the green flag above the stage is clicked, the script you have created will run.

5. Next, click Motion at the top of the Blocks palette to see the available motion blocks. From the list of choices, drag the `move 10 steps` block to the Scripts tab and connect it with the control block that you placed in Step 4, as shown in Figure 3-4.

Some of the blocks have sections in the code that you can customise. For example, in the motion block `move 10 steps`, you can change the 10 to any number you like.

6. Now click Looks in the Blocks palette, drag `say Hello!` to the Scripts tab and connect it to the motion block you placed in Step 5.

7. Click Sound in the Blocks palette, drag `play sound meow` to the Scripts tab and connect it to the looks block you placed in Step 6.

8. Finally, save your file, and then press the green flag in the top right corner above the stage to see your script work.

FIGURE 3-4 The blocks for a quick Hello from Scratch cat

When completing a Scratch program containing scripts, it is good practice to save your work at regular points and test that it works. To do this, click File→Save As and then press the appropriate key to start your script. Scratch files can be saved into the Scratch Projects folder on your Raspberry Pi. As you move through the instructions in this chapter, I'll remind you to save your work at end of each section.

Congratulations, you have written your first program using Scratch! Of course, you can do much more with Scratch than just move a cat around the screen. Next, you'll take a look at the parts of Scratch that you can design yourself—the stage and costumes.

Setting the Stage

If you are creating an animated story or computer game using Scratch, you'll want to set the scene by changing the background from its plain white default. You can do this in two ways: by designing and drawing your own background or by selecting an image from the Scratch library.

To prepare to change the background image, click the Stage icon, which is situated next to the Sprites palette. Select the Backgrounds tab. You now have a choice between editing the current background or adding a new one.

- To edit the current background, click the Edit button in the Backgrounds tab in the centre of the screen and the Paint Editor window appears, as shown in Figure 3-5. Use the drawing tools to draw a setting for your animation or game. For example, you might want to draw a room or a maze.
- To add a new background, either click the Paint button to open the Paint Editor window and create a scene, or click the Import button to use a scene from the image library (see Figure 3-6).

  Scratch also has an option for you to use webcam images as backgrounds for your Scratch projects. Click the Camera button to access this option. Before you can use this function you will need to have either a webcam plugged into a USB port or the Raspberry Pi Cam plugged into the camera slot on the Pi board.

To see a video that walks you through the Scratch interface and shows you how to create backgrounds and characters, visit the companion website at `www.wiley.com/go/adventuresinrp`. Click the Videos tab and select the QuickHelloFromScratch file.

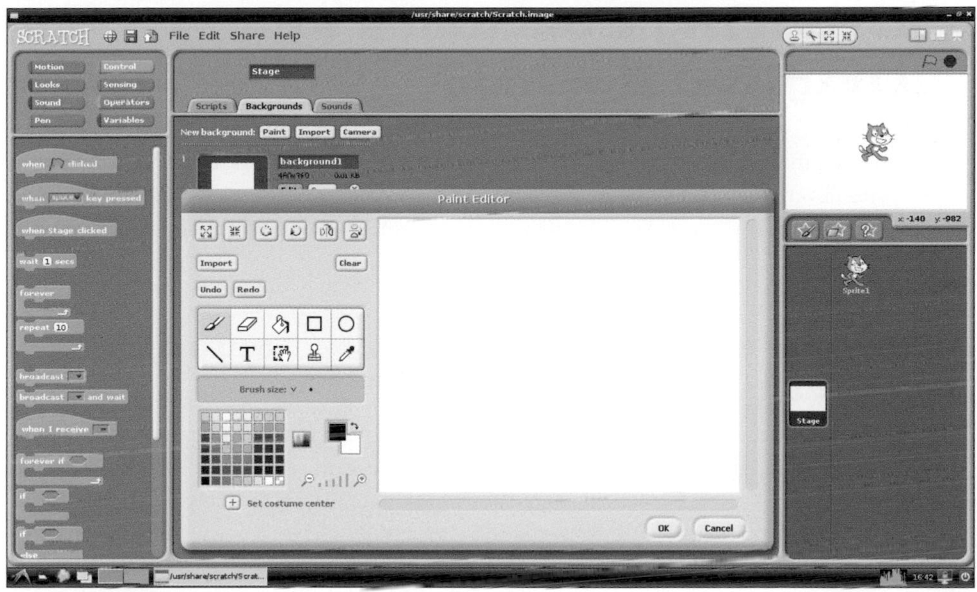

FIGURE 3-5 The Scratch Paint Editor window

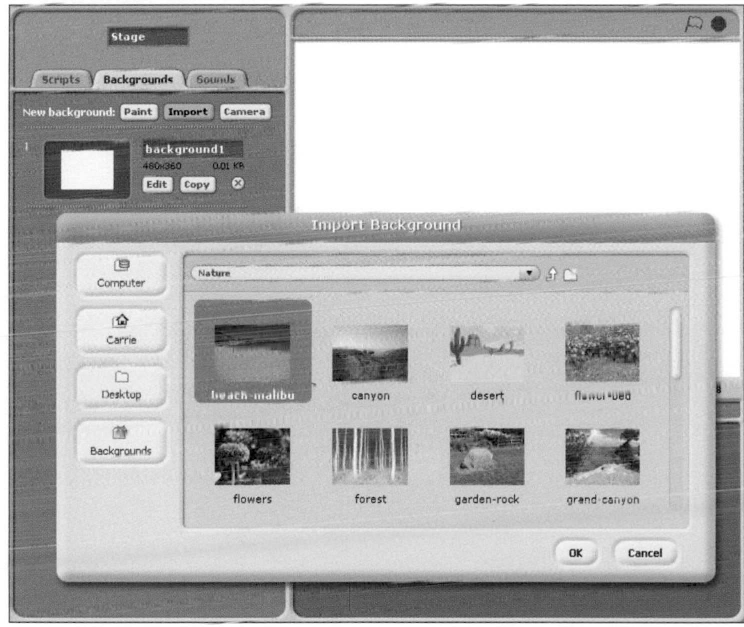

FIGURE 3-6 The Import Background window

Creating Costumes and Original Sprites

Of course, you won't always want to use Scratch Cat as your sprite—you may want other animals, people, astronauts, flowers or even a basketball! Scratch has its own sprite library, much like the background image library, which you can use to get more sprites for your project. You can also edit these sprites, or simply draw original sprites of your own.

Using the Scratch Sprite Image Library

To use a sprite design from the Scratch Sprite Library click the Choose New Sprite from File icon at the top of the Sprites palette (the icon with the folder and star), as shown in Figure 3-7. Browse through the Things, People and Animals folders until you find a sprite you want to use. Select it and click OK to add it to your Sprites palette.

FIGURE 3-7 Using the Sprite Image Library

Editing an Existing Sprite

Select a sprite from the Sprites palette. In the centre pane, click the Costumes tab to switch from Scripts to Costumes. To edit the sprite, click the Edit button next to the picture of your sprite under costume1 to open the Paint Editor window (see Figure 3-8). You can then use the drawing tools to add your own enhancements to the Scratch cat sprite—why not give it a cape or a moustache? You'll learn more about how to change costumes to create variations of sprites in the next section.

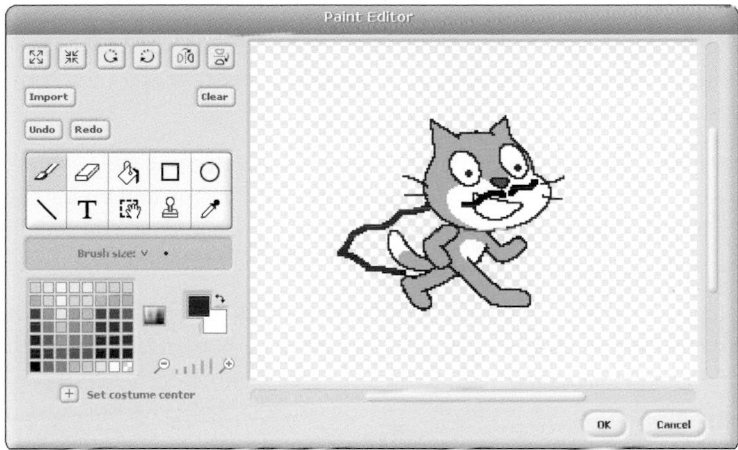

FIGURE 3-8 Editing an existing sprite using the Paint Editor—love the moustache!

Creating Your Own Original Sprites

To create original sprites of your own, click the Paint New Sprite icon above the Sprites palette (the icon with the paintbrush and star). The Paint Editor window is displayed, and you can use a freehand paintbrush or shapes to create your own characters.

Play around with Scratch a bit to get comfortable with the different aspects of the application. When you have a good feel for how it works, move on to the next section to create an animated monkey!

Animating a Crazy Monkey

It's only natural for adventurers to come across challenges, especially on an expedition through a wild jungle. A crazy monkey jumping all over the screen with a variety of facial expressions is definitely going to be a fun challenge!

For a video that walks you through the Crazy Monkey Animation project, visit the companion website at `www.wiley.com/go/adventuresinrp`. Click the Videos tab and select the CrazyMonkey file.

1. To begin, open a new file by selecting File➜New. Delete the Scratch Cat sprite by right-clicking on it and selecting Delete from the menu that is displayed.

   For this project, you need a jungle style background and a monkey sprite. You can draw your own using the Paint Editor in Scratch, or use the forest background and the monkey sprite from the image libraries as described in the previous section. Alternatively, if your Raspberry Pi is connected to the Internet, you can download the jungle background and monkey sprite used in this project from the Adventures in Raspberry Pi website at `www.wiley.com/go/adventuresinrp`.

2. With the monkey sprite selected, click the Costumes tab. Rename the costume to Monkey1 by clicking on the sprite name above the Edit button and typing the new name. Click the Copy button to make a duplicate of the monkey. You should now see two monkeys on the Costumes tab: Monkey1 and Monkey2.

3. The next step is to change Monkey2's expression. Click the Edit button for Monkey2 to open the Paint Editor. Use the paintbrush tool to erase the mouth on the monkey and replace it with a different one (see Figure 3-9). You can continue to duplicate the monkey as many times as you like, changing the expression on each one.

FIGURE 3-9 Duplicating a sprite and changing the costume. Notice the different expression on each monkey's face.

4. Continue to make copies of the costume and edit each new copy with a different face. You can even change the eyes or move the tail!

5. Now click the Scripts tab. You are going to create a set of blocks to switch among the costumes that you have created. In the Blocks palette, click Control and drag the `when 🏴 clicked` block onto the Scripts tab.

6. Next, click Looks in the Blocks palette and add `switch to costume Monkey1` (see Figure 3-10). You can use the drop-down arrow in this block to select the costume (expression) you want to start with.

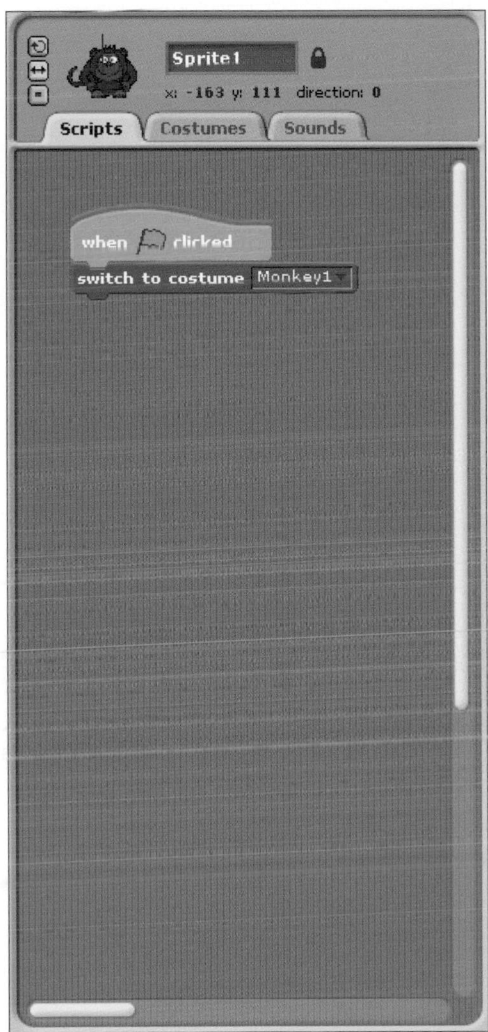

FIGURE 3-10 First steps in the Crazy Monkey script

7. In the Blocks palette, click Control to switch to the control blocks. Under the first block in the Scripts tab, add the control block `forever`. Inside the `forever` block add the control block `wait 1 secs` and the looks block `next costume`. Figure 3-11 shows the script at this point.

   The `forever` block is a **loop**. It runs the same sequence of blocks over and over again until you stop the program. In this case, you are making the monkey change his facial expressions, over and over again. In computing, this kind of repetition is called **iteration**.

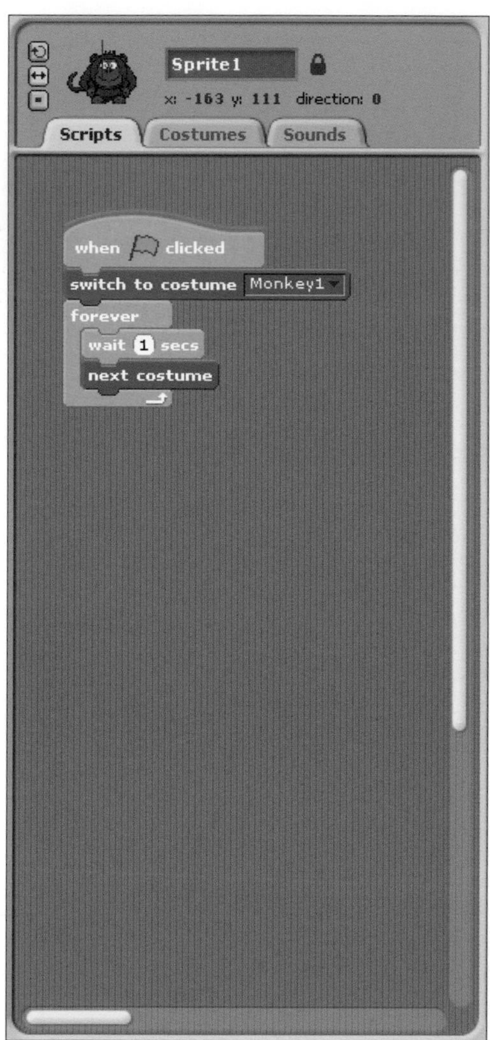

FIGURE 3-11 The Crazy Monkey script with a `forever` block

What do you think will happen when you click the green flag? Try it and find out if you are correct.

Next, add some more animation to your monkey by having him move as well as change facial expressions.

8. With the Scripts tab still selected, underneath your first block add another `when clicked` control block.
9. Next add the motion block `go to x:0 y:0`.

The stage area in Scratch uses the coordinates x and y to refer to where your sprite will appear on the stage. If you want your sprite to begin in the middle of the stage, use `x:0` and `y:0`. If you want your sprite to appear in the top left portion of the stage, use `x:-163` and `y:11`. Notice that when you select a sprite with your mouse you can see its coordinates at the top of the Script tab (see Figure 3-12). Move the sprite with your mouse and watch as the coordinates change to reflect the new position. There is also a handy graph background showing the x and y axes that you can import from the library to help you.

10. Again, you need to use a `forever` control block to repeat some instructions. Inside the `forever` block, add three blocks from the Motion Blocks palette: `move 10 steps`; `turn 15 degrees right`; and `if on edge, bounce`.
11. Note the three small buttons next to the monkey sprite at the top of the Scripts tab (see Figure 3-12 for reference). These control a sprite's rotation. Click the middle button, which directs the sprite to `only face left and right`. This will add more animation to the monkey sprite and allow him to move more than just his mouth.

Save your animation by clicking File➜Save As and naming it `jungle animation` inside the Scratch Projects folder.

Figure 3-12 shows the completed script. Notice that I have added a third block of commands to include a sound effect for the animation.

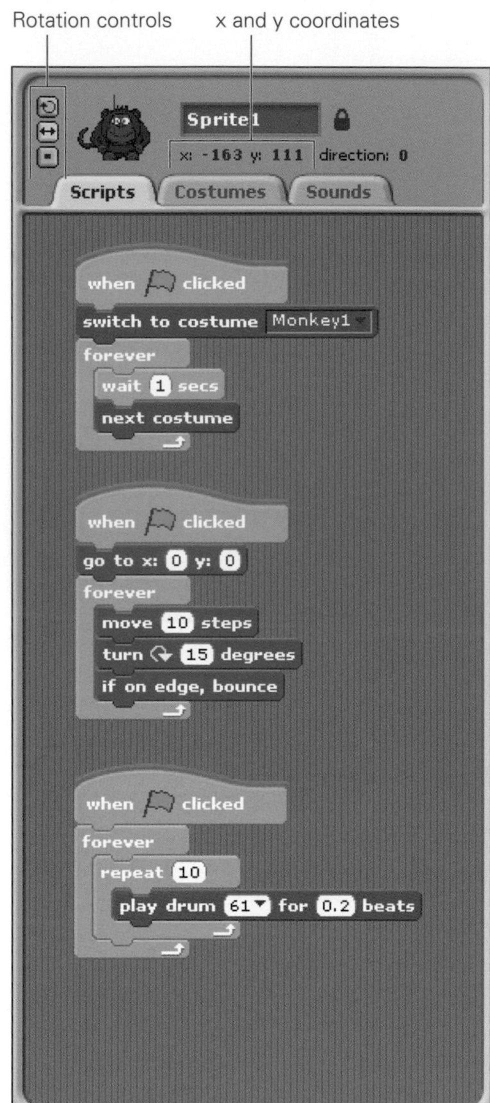

FIGURE 3-12 The completed Crazy Monkey animation script in Scratch

What do you think the monkey will do now? Will he still change costumes? Click the green flag to find out!

CHALLENGE

If a moving monkey with different faces is not exciting enough, you can add some sound effects. Why not have a go yourself? What block do you think you should begin with? See the lowest block of commands in Figure 3-12 if you need help.

Creating an Adventure Role-Playing Game

Now that you have conquered the crazy monkey in the jungle, it's time to move on to the next level by creating a first-person adventure role-playing game in Scratch.

In this project, you will learn some programming concepts that are common no matter what programming language you use (such as loops, `if` statements and variables) by creating a game in which a single player can move through locations or rooms to reach a magical key, trying to avoid deadly flowers along the way.

For a video of the Adventure Game project, visit the companion website at `www.wiley.com/go/adventuresinrp`. From the Videos tab, select the ScratchAdventureGame file.

Creating Your Sprite and Stage

To begin, you need to draw an Adventurer sprite from a top-down or bird's eye view; see the sprite in Figure 3-13 for an example. (Don't forget to delete the Scratch Cat sprite first by right-clicking on it with your mouse and selecting Delete from the menu that appears.)

Click the paintbrush icon next to New Sprite to open the Paint Editor window, and use the tools to create your sprite. Make sure that you draw your Adventurer sprite facing towards the right, as this will become important later on in this project. You will also need to create an outside cave and inside cave stage background, labelling the locations `Outside` and `Inside`, respectively. So that you do not lose any of your work in this project, you should save your work as you go along. Refer back to the "Setting the Stage" section earlier in this adventure for a reminder on how to create a background. Figure 3-13 shows my version of the completed game in progress.

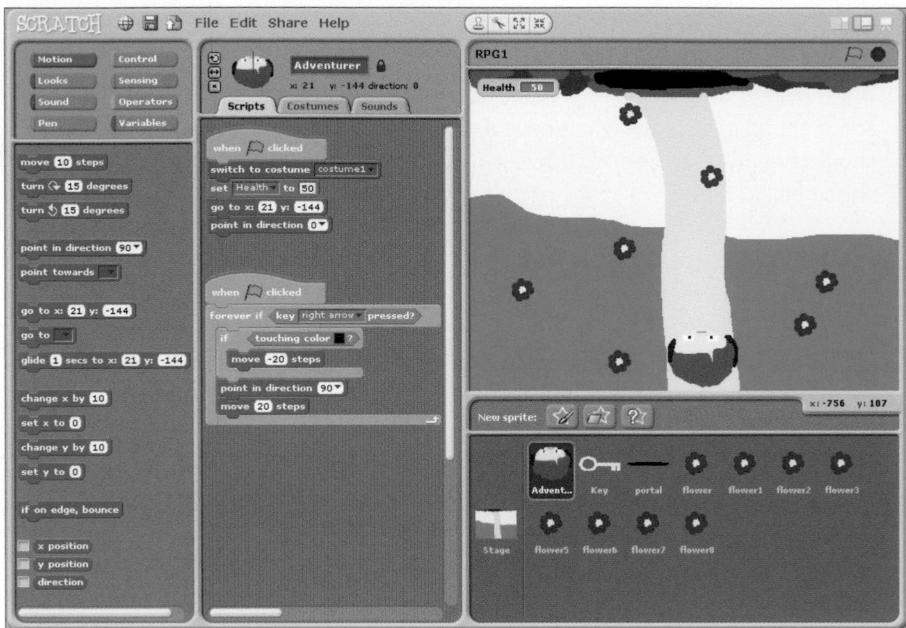

FIGURE 3-13 Scratch adventure role-playing game

Setting the Start Position of the Adventurer Sprite

When the game begins, the Adventurer character will always start at a certain point on the stage; after all, an adventure needs to start somewhere.

1. To set the start point, click the Adventurer Sprite and position it on the stage where you want to start the game.
2. On the Scripts tab, drag the control block `when` 🏁 `clicked` and the motion block `go to x: y:` (see Figure 3-14).
3. Set the x and y coordinates to where your Adventurer sprite is located on the stage. You can find its exact coordinates by looking near the top of the Scripts tab, between the sprite's name and just above the tab labels.
4. You can also add a Motion block to `point in direction _` if you want the Adventurer sprite to be looking up, right, left or down at the start of the game. The value you type into the block will determine the direction the sprite faces: Use the value 0 to make the sprite look up, -90 for the left, 90 for the right or 180 for down. Try changing the value to see how your sprite responds (see Figure 3-14).

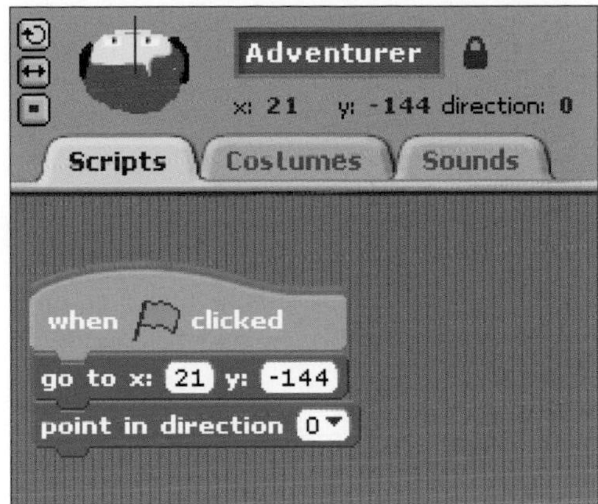

FIGURE 3-14 Setting the start position for your sprite

Creating Variables: Including Health Points for the Adventurer Sprite

In role-playing games, players (or rather, their characters) typically start with a certain number of 'health points' or 'lives'. As you play the game, these points may decrease as you encounter foes or increase when you collect certain objects or overcome obstacles. You can create **variables** in Scratch to allow for values that change, and use these variables inside different scripts. You can set the health points to a certain value—for example, 50—at the start of the game and create scripts that will add or take away points when triggered—for instance, finding a useful tool might add 10 health points. This feature will make the game more interesting.

A **variable** holds a value that can be changed. The health variable in your adventure role-playing game is an example of a value that can be changed and used inside different scripts.

1. To create a variable, click Variables in the Blocks palette and then click Make a Variable. The New Variable window opens and asks you to type a name for your variable.
2. Name your variable `Health` and ensure that *For all sprites* is checked before clicking OK. Figure 3-15 shows the window with the correct settings.

FIGURE 3-15 Creating a variable

3. You'll see some orange blocks added to your Variables palette, and a small counter box appears on the stage (see Figure 3-18).
4. Add the block `Set Health to 0` to the starting point script you have already created. You can then change the value of `Health` from 0 to 50. This means at the start of the game when the green flag is clicked, the Adventurer sprite will start with 50 health points. Figure 3-16 shows the script up to this point.
5. Remember to save the work you have done so far by clicking File➜Save. Then test that your scripts work by clicking the green flag icon.

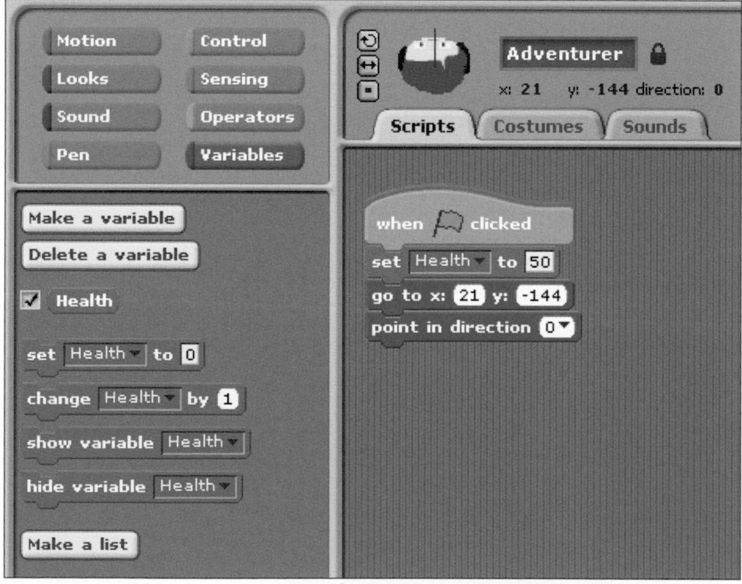

FIGURE 3-16 The Adventurer sprite start script so far

Controlling the Direction and Movement of the Adventurer Sprite

An important part of any computer game is being able to control the movement of a sprite using keys or buttons. In Scratch you are able to create more than one script for a sprite or for a stage, which can be run in parallel with each other. These multiple scripts running at the same time are called **threads** in computing. You need to create a number of scripts for the Adventurer sprite to be able to control the sprite's movement.

1. Underneath the first script you created to set the start position and health variable, add a new `when 🏴 clicked` control block.
2. Next add a `forever if` block. Notice that this block has a hexagon shape in it. This is designed so that you can add extra blocks, such as operators or sensing blocks, to add a condition. This means that the blocks contained within the `forever if` loop will only run if the condition is met. For this project, click Sensing in the Blocks palette and add a `key right arrow pressed` block by dragging it with your mouse and placing it inside the hexagon shape. This creates a **conditional** statement. Notice that you can change which key is referenced by using the drop-down menu on the block. This allows you to set different keys for different directions of movement, as you will do later in this project.

> In computing, a **conditional** statement is one in which an action will be taken only if a certain condition is true. For example, in the block you create in Step 2, the `forever` part of the `forever if` block will loop the sequence of instructions contained within its structure only if the right arrow key on the keyboard is pressed.

3. Now add the motion block `point in direction` inside the `forever if` loop and set it to 90, which will point the sprite to the right.
4. Underneath this block and still inside the `forever if` loop, add the motion block `move 0 steps` and change the value of steps to 20. See Figure 3-17 to see how the script should look at this point.
5. Test that this script works by clicking the green flag to start all the scripts, and then pressing the right arrow on the keyboard.
6. Create three more scripts like this one for the left, up, and down keys, changing the values to move the Adventurer sprite in the correct direction for each arrow key. Save and test your file.

FIGURE 3-17 Controlling the direction and movement of the Adventurer Sprite

Entering a Cave and Switching Backgrounds

The action in a role-playing game typically involves the characters moving among different scenes. In this game, the Adventurer sprite begins outside a cave and has to cross the stage to get to the cave entrance before going inside. At the start of this project you were asked to create two backgrounds for the stage: one outside the cave that you have been using so far, and one for the inside of the cave. But how do you get the Adventurer sprite to switch between these backgrounds? You need a script for each of the backgrounds, another script for the Adventurer sprite and another for the stage.

Adding a Script to Make the Adventurer Sprite Move Between Backgrounds

Scratch programs are built up out of a collection of small scripts. Sometimes you need a way to communicate among these scripts when certain things happen in your adventure game—for example, when you move the Adventurer sprite from one location or background to another. This next script will use a new sprite to act as a trigger, so that when the Adventurer sprite touches it, a message is **broadcast** to all the sprites and the stage at the same time, to alert them to the change.

1. First, you need to create a new sprite to act as the cave entrance. Simply click the Paint New Sprite button (the paintbrush icon) on the Sprites palette and use the circle tool to draw an ellipse that matches the entrance of your cave (see Figure 3-18). This ellipse will be your new sprite.
2. Name the sprite *portal* and position it at your cave entrance on the opposite side of the stage from where your Adventurer sprite starts. This new portal sprite will act as the trigger to move between the two backgrounds.
3. Select the Adventurer sprite from the sprite palette and add another new script to act as a thread on the Adventurer sprite Scripts tab. Add a `when` 🏴 `clicked` control block onto the Scripts tab of the Adventurer sprite, and add the `wait until _` block to it. This is another type of conditional block, but unlike with the `forever` loop, the sequence of instructions happens only once when the condition is true. In this case the condition will be true when the Adventurer sprite 'touches' the portal sprite.

4. Add the sensing block `touching _` into the hexagon space on the `wait until _` control block, and use the drop-down menu to select the portal sprite, so the block now reads `wait until touching portal`.

5. Next, add the control block `broadcast _` and select New from the drop-down menu. Name the new broadcast message `Level`.

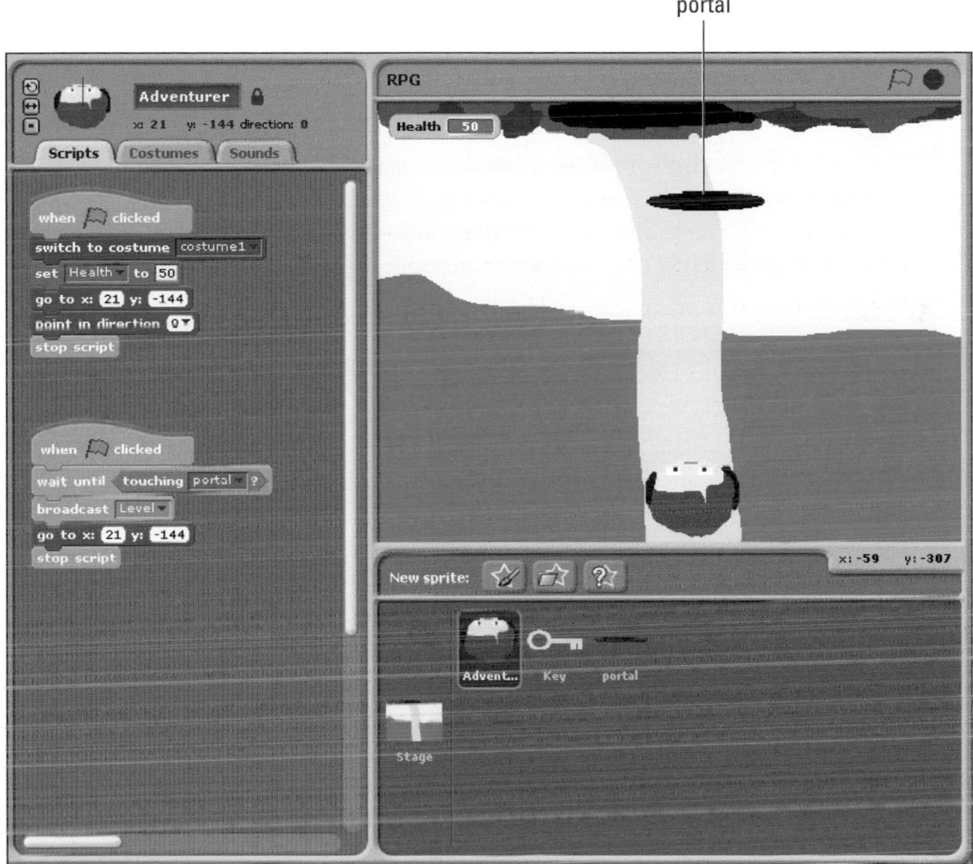

FIGURE 3-18 Cave entrance portal sprite and script. Notice the counter block in the top left corner of the stage.

A **broadcast** message is used to coordinate the actions of different sprites and the stage. It keeps all the scripts running for each sprite and keeps the stage synchronized. In this case, when the Adventurer sprite touches the portal, a message called *Level* is broadcast. This message triggers a script for the stage to switch to the `Inside` cave background that you created.

Adding a Script to Switch the Stage

So far, you have created a portal sprite that broadcasts a message when touched by the Adventurer sprite, but that does not solve the problem of switching the backgrounds of the stage. You need to add a script to the stage so that it responds to the message that was broadcast when the portal sprite was touched.

1. Click the Stage icon in the Sprites palette. Add the control block `when 🏴 clicked`, followed by a `switch to background _` looks block, and select `Outside` from the drop-down menu. Make sure that you have labelled your stage backgrounds as `Inside` and `Outside` to correspond with your location designs.
2. Next add another control block, but this time use `when I receive` and select the broadcast message `Level` from the drop-down menu. Add the `switch to background _` looks block and this time choose `Inside` from the drop-down menu. Figure 3-19 shows this script. Save your work so far and test to see if it works.

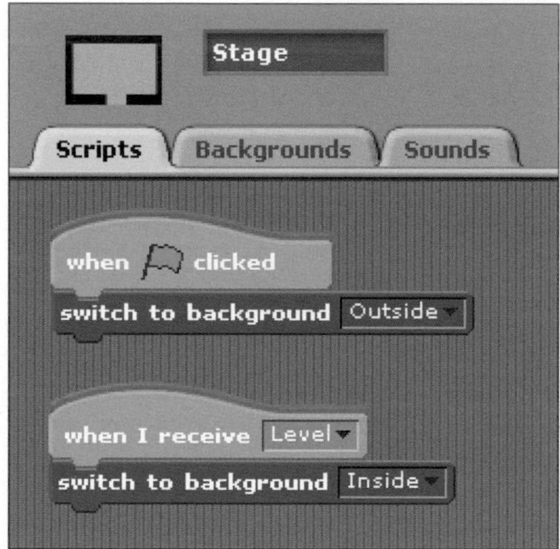

FIGURE 3-19 Using broadcast on the stage to switch between backgrounds

3. Whenever you are creating more complicated scripts for multiple sprites and on the stage, it is a good idea to test that they work. Click the green flag and use the arrow keys on your keyboard to navigate the Adventurer sprite to the portal and see what happens.
4. You may find that your Adventurer sprite is not positioned at the entrance of your `Inside` cave background. Simply drag the Adventurer sprite to where you would like it to start from on this stage background, make a note of the x and y

coordinates for this position and, on the script you have been making to move the sprite between backgrounds (refer to Figure 3-20), add the motion block `go to x:0 y:0`. Replace the values with the new coordinates.

FIGURE 3-20 Adventurer script to set location on new background

Creating an Enchanted Key to Exit the Cave and Giving Extra Health Points

Rather than making another portal sprite to move to another level or background, why not introduce a new sprite that will behave like a magic object?

1. Using the Sprites palette, click the Choose New Sprite From File icon and select Key1 from the Things folder. Rename the sprite by clicking in the name box above the centre tabs and typing `Key`.
2. Just like the script that you created to move the Adventurer sprite to the inside of the cave, the script required for this sprite will use the `wait until touching _` conditional and a new broadcast message called `new_level`, only this time the Key sprite waits until it is touched by the Adventurer sprite to trigger the action, as shown in Figure 3-21.
3. The script will work only if you add another script to the stage so that when it receives the new broadcast message for the `new_level`, it switches to the `Outside` background. Click the Stage icon in the Sprites palette and follow the steps in the preceding section ("Adding a Script to Switch the Stage") to add a new script that says: "When I receive new_level, switch to background Outside".

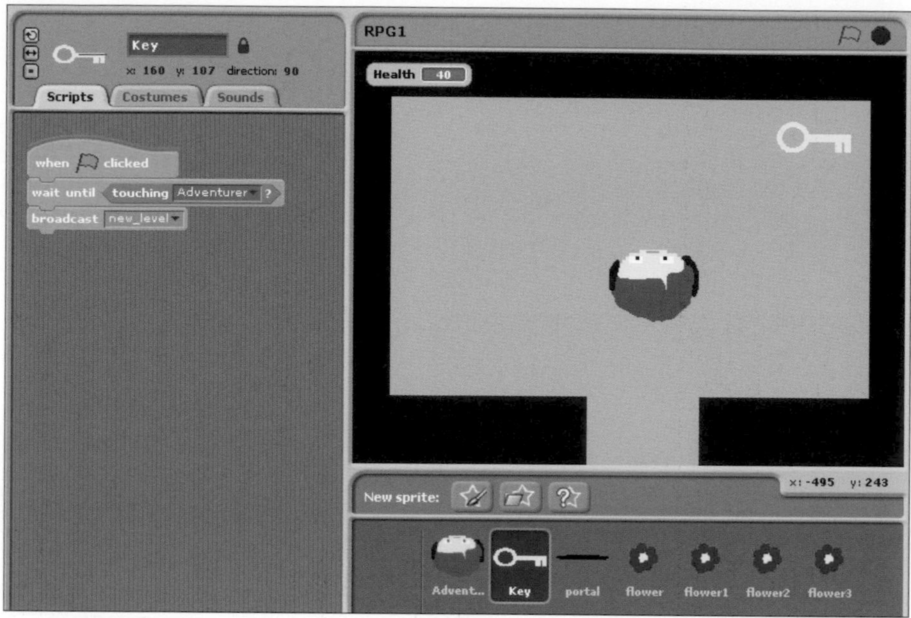

FIGURE 3-21 The enchanted key script

CHALLENGE

You can have a little fun by adding looks blocks to make the key say something when it's touched, and a variable block to increase the Adventurer sprite's health points. Try adding blocks to the script for those actions. Refer to Figure 3-22 if you need help.

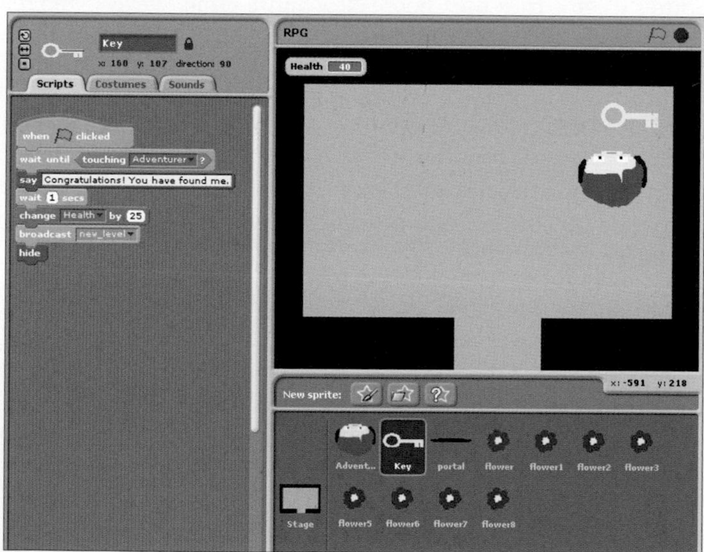

FIGURE 3-22 The enchanted key script, with blocks added for the challenge actions

Using "if" Statements to Show and Hide Sprites

As it stands now, when you play this game the new sprites that you have created so far, such as the portal sprite, remain visible even when you change backgrounds. This is a little confusing. You really want the portal to show only on the first background, `Outside`, and the key to show only on the second background, `Inside`. In this section, you learn how to add an **if...else** block to address this problem.

If and **if...else** statements are common constructs in computer programming. When you use an `if` statement, you are asking for a condition to be met, and then making something happen if the condition set is true. For example: *If* it is raining, then put up an umbrella. You can add another action for when the condition is false using the ***else*** command. For example: *If* it is raining, then put up an umbrella; ***else,*** wear sunglasses.

The script you create in the following steps tells the portal sprite to appear only when background 1—the outside of the cave—is shown, and to remain hidden the rest of the time.

1. In the portal sprite's Scripts tab, add the control block `when` 🏴 `clicked` and attach a `forever` looping control block to it.
2. Next, add the control block `if else` inside the `forever` loop and drag the operator block `0 = 0` into the `if` hexagon condition (refer to Figure 3-23).
3. Place the sensing block `of` inside the first 0 of the operator block, and add the value 1 to the second part of the same block.
4. Using the drop-down menus on the sensing block, change the first value to `background #` and the second to `stage`.
5. Finally, add the looks block `show` under the `if` condition and the looks block `hide` under `else`. Save and test your script.

CHALLENGE

What amendments to this script would you need to create to hide the key on the `Outside` background and show the key on the `Inside` background? Try making these changes to your script.

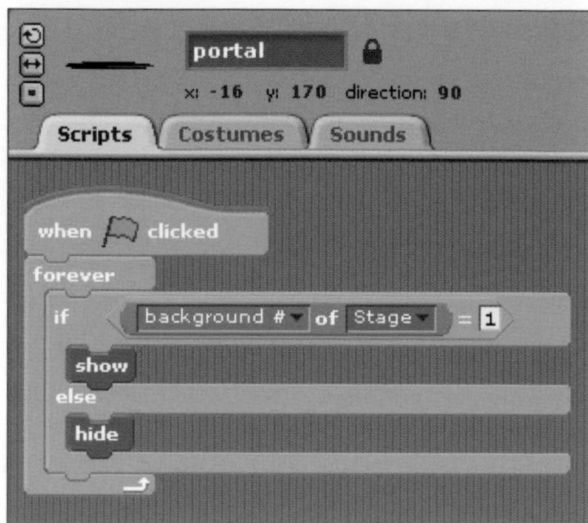

FIGURE 3-23 An `if else` script is used to show and hide sprites in Scratch.

Creating Health-Point-Stealing Sprites

The Adventurer sprite can now move around the stage and move between stage backgrounds using the broadcast message. However, as it stands, this will be a really easy game to play and anyone playing the game may tire of it very quickly! You can make the journey to the cave entrance more difficult for the player by adding obstacles that will steal health points.

1. To add some obstacles to make it more difficult for the Adventurer sprite to get around the stage, click the Paint New Sprite icon to create a new sprite. Use the tools to draw a flower as your new sprite, and name it *flower*.
2. Next, add a script to the flower sprite by selecting it from the Sprites panel and then dragging the control block `when` 🏴 `clicked` onto the Scripts tab.
3. The obstacle needs to be a constant danger for the sprite, so you need a script that is constantly running. To achieve that, add the `forever if` block. This time the condition will be *if the Adventurer sprite is touching the flower then remove a certain number of health points*. Add the sensing block `touching _`. Figure 3-24 shows the completed block.
4. Inside the `forever if` block, add the variable block `change health by 0` and change the value from 0 to -10 so that it removes health points from the player.
5. Add the looks block `say ouch! for 2 secs` after the variable block inside the `forever if` loop block.
6. Remember to add the `if else` script to hide the flower sprite after the player enters the cave, and then save and test your script.

FIGURE 3-24 Health-point-stealing flower sprite script

Don't forget to add the script to hide the flower sprite after the Adventurer sprite enters the cave. After you have added this script, you can duplicate the flower to cover the stage with more obstacles, making the game more interesting. To duplicate the flower sprite, right-click on it in the Sprites palette and click Duplicate. You can do this as many times as you like to make multiple copies.

Improving the Movement of the Adventurer Sprite Using "if" Blocks

The player controls the Adventurer sprite by using the keys on the keyboard. This works well when the sprite is on the stage using the `Outside` background, as there are no walls. However, when it enters the cave, the sprite will appear to be walking over the walls. You can use another `if` condition to help stop this from happening.

1. Click the Adventurer sprite and locate the four scripts that control movement using the arrow keys on the keyboard (refer to Figure 3-17).
2. On one of the scripts, add a control block `if` inside the `forever if` loop, above the `point in direction 90` block that is already there.
3. Add the sensing block `touching color` into the blank hexagon on the `if` loop you have just added. Select the colour of the walls by clicking the coloured square box; this action will turn the mouse cursor icon into a droplet icon, and you can select the walls with your mouse, getting the exact colour match required.
4. Next, add the motion block `move 0 steps` inside the `if` loop and set the value to -20 steps. Figure 3-25 shows the new script.
5. Add the same extra piece of script to the three remaining control scripts for each key. Don't forget to save the file and test that your script works.

FIGURE 3-25 Completed script to control movement of right key

Creating a Game Over Screen

Typically in role-playing games, when a player loses all her health points, the game ends and a Game Over screen is displayed. Follow these steps to create a Game Over screen:

1. First you need to add a new Game Over background to the stage. You can either paint a new one or duplicate one of the existing backgrounds and edit it to display Game Over across it in large letters (see Figure 3-26).
2. Next, add another script to the Adventurer sprite. Click on the sprite in the Sprites palette, and then drag the control block `when` 🏁 `clicked` onto the Scripts tab.
3. Add a `forever` control block underneath, and an `if` control block inside the `forever` block.
4. Drag the operator block `0 < 0` inside the the `if` blank hexagon, Add the variable `health` inside the left side of the < sign and type the value `0.1` in the right side.
5. Add the control block `broadcast` and create a new broadcast message called `Game Over`.

The code of this script states that if the health of the Adventurer sprite is less than 0.1, the Game Over message will be broadcast to all the sprites and the stage. You need to add the following script to the stage to listen for this broadcast message to end the game.

```
When I receive 'Game Over'
Switch to background 'Game Over'
Stop All
```

The Stop All control block will stop all the scripts in Scratch from running, ending the game.

FIGURE 3-26 Creating a Game Over screen in Scratch

Save the file and run the program to ensure it works as expected. If not, check your work and correct it if you need to.

Ideas for Improvements to Your Game

Now that you've learned how to use Scratch, you may want to continue to improve your game. Here are some further ideas to keep you going:

- Try setting some random events to happen during the game.
- Add music and sound effects to make it more exciting for the player.
- Create more sprites for the Adventurer sprite to interact with.
- Use a MaKey MaKey invention kit to create a custom game pad to match your game. You can learn more about MaKey MaKey and order a kit at `www.makeymakey.com`.

For the complete guide to Scratch, download the Scratch Reference Guide from `http://download.scratch.mit.edu/ScratchReferenceGuide14.pdf`.

Scratch Command Quick Reference Table	
Command	**Description**
Control Blocks	
`broadcast` *x*	Sends a message to all the sprites and the stage which can be used to synchronize scripts across multiple sprites and the stage.
`forever`	Repeatedly iterates actions within set.
`forever if`	Checks whether a condition is true, over and over. If the condition is true the program will run the blocks inside.
`if…else`	If the condition is true, the program will run the blocks inside the `if` section. If not, it will run the blocks inside the `else` section.
`repeat` *x*	Sets number of times for action to repeat.
`stop all`	Stops all scripts for all sprites.
`wait` *x* `secs`	Sets time before executing next command.
`when` [flag] `clicked`	Begins script when green flag icon is clicked.
`when I receive` *x*	Begins script when a set broadcast message is heard.
`When` *x* `key pressed`	Begins script when designated key is pressed.
Motion Blocks	
`change x by _`	Changes sprite's position on the stage x axis by a specified amount.
`change y by _`	Changes sprite's position on the stage y axis by a specified amount.
`go to x:_ y:_`	Moves sprite to set x and y coordinates on the stage.
`if on edge, bounce`	Turns sprite in the opposite direction if it touches the edge of the stage.
`move` *x* `steps`	Moves sprite forward or backwards *x* number of steps.
`point in direction` *x*	Points sprite in direction *x*.
`point towards` *x*	Points sprite towards another sprite or a mouse cursor.
`set x to _`	Sets sprite's position on the stage x axis to a designated place.
`set y to _`	Sets sprite's position on the stage y axis to a designated place.
`turn (clockwise)` *x* `degrees`	Rotates sprite clockwise *x* degrees.
`turn (anti-clockwise)` *x* `degrees`	Rotates sprite anti-clockwise *x* degrees.
Looks Blocks	
`change size by` *x*	Changes sprite's size by *x* amount.
`hide`	Hides a sprite from the stage.
`next costume`	Changes sprite's costume to the next costume in the list.

Command	Description
`say xxx`	Shows sprite's speech bubble saying *xxx*.
`set size to x`	Sets a sprite's size to *x* percent of its original size.
`show`	Makes a sprite appear on the stage.
`switch to background x`	Changes the background of the stage.
`switch to costume x`	Changes the costume of a sprite.
`think xxx`	Shows sprite's thought bubble thinking *xxx*.
Variables Blocks	
`Change variable by x`	Changes the variable by *x* amount.
`Make a variable`	Creates a new variable that you can name for either a single sprite or for all sprites.
`Set variable to x`	Sets the variable value to *x*.
Sensing Blocks	
`key x pressed`	If *x* key on the keyboard is pressed then reports true.
`touching color x`	If a sprite is touching a designated colour then reports true.
`touching x`	If a sprite is touching designated sprite, edge or mouse cursor, then reports true.

Achievement Unlocked: You have created a program using Scratch!

In the Next Adventure

In the next adventure, you'll learn how to program art using Turtle Graphics. In the first half, you will use Scratch. In the second half, you will be using the programming language Python, and will be introduced to the Python programming environment and some commands to enable you to draw shapes and repeat them to make patterns.

Adventure 4
Programming Shapes with Turtle Graphics

SUPPOSE YOU COULD pick up a turtle, dip his tail into coloured ink, place him on a piece of paper and make him walk around so that his tail paints a spiral shape, a pentagon or a noughts and crosses grid? This adventure introduces you to different ways that you can create shapes or line drawings using code.

You'll use a module called *Turtle Graphics* that works by directing a cursor (or *turtle*) around the screen using movement instructions; see an example of the result in Figure 4-1. This movement leaves a colour trail like a pen, which means you are able to program a computer to draw. Turtle Graphics was originally a feature of the programming language LOGO (Logic Oriented Graphic Oriented), which was designed to teach young people how to program using a logical sequence of steps by means of an onscreen cursor called a *turtle*. LOGO continues to be a very popular way to learn logic and sequencing in computer programming. Both Scratch and Python include `turtle` modules that can be used to create shapes, drawings and patterns.

This adventure draws on many of the computing concepts you have already used in previous tutorials in this book, such as sequencing, variables and loops, to create shapes and spirals in both Scratch and Python programming environments on the Raspberry Pi.

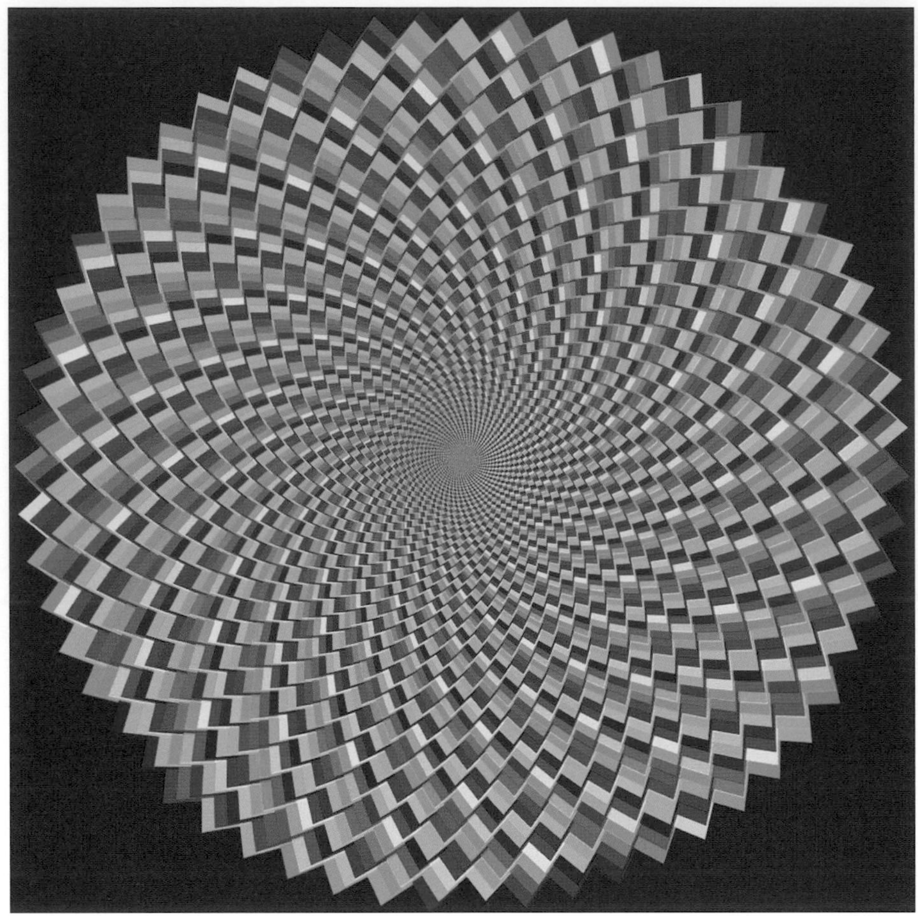

FIGURE 4-1 An example of programming art on the Raspberry Pi

Scratch Turtle Graphics

In this part of the adventure, you learn to use the basic features of Turtle Graphics in Scratch by writing a script that turns any sprite into a "pen" to draw lines and shapes on your stage.

To see a tutorial on creating shapes with Scratch, visit the companion website at `www.wiley.com/go/adventuresinrp`. Click the Videos tab and select the ScratchShapes file.

Using Pen Down and Pen Up

The `pen down` and `pen up` blocks instruct the sprite to start and stop drawing, in the same way as you touch your pen to paper to draw a line and then lift it.

The "turtle" in the following project refers to whatever sprite you choose to act as your pen. It doesn't have to look like a turtle—in fact, the sprite library doesn't include a turtle image, but you can create one using the Paint Editor if you like.

To draw some of the shapes and spirals in this adventure using Scratch, you will need lots of space on the stage. Sometimes the "turtle" can go off screen, and this can result in messy shapes! To make sure that you have plenty of space, click on the Switch to Full Stage icon above the stage on the right-hand side of the screen.

1. Open Scratch as you did in Adventure 3 by double-clicking the icon on the desktop or using the main menu to select Education➜Scratch. Once the application has loaded, maximise the size of the stage by clicking the Switch to Full Stage icon above the stage on the right hand side of the screen.
2. You can use the default Scratch Cat sprite as your "turtle". However, you may find it easier to give directions to the sprite if you have a bird's-eye (top-down) view. To change the sprite to a bird's-eye view of the Scratch Cat, right-click the Scratch Cat sprite in the Sprites palette and select Delete from the menu. Next, click Import New Sprite and browse to select Cat2 inside the Animals directory. (Refer to Figure 3-3 from Adventure 3 for a reminder of how the Scratch interface is set up.)

Keep in mind that the sprite directing the cursor in Turtle Graphics is always called a turtle, even though the image might be a cat, a person or something else.

3. Remember when starting any script in Scratch you need a trigger, so select the `When 🏴 clicked` control block and drag it onto the Scripts tab of the turtle sprite.
4. Next add the `pen down` block from the Pen blocks palette. This will begin the drawing.
5. Add the motion block `Move 0 steps` and change the value to 100.

6. Finally add the `pen up` block to end the line drawing. Figure 4-2 shows the result.

7. Select File➜Save As to name and save your file.

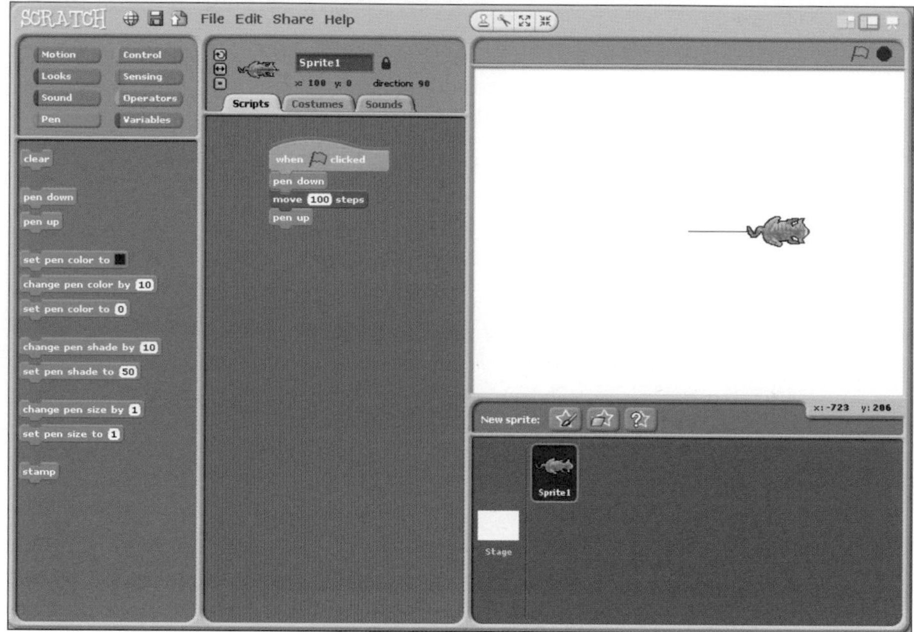

FIGURE 4-2 Using `pen down` and `pen up` to draw a line in Scratch

CHALLENGE

How could you add to the script to turn the turtle round and draw another line?

What does the `pen up` command do?

Drawing Simple Shapes

Now draw a pentagon using the script that you already created, by using the following steps.

1. Add the motion block `turn 15 degrees` underneath the `move 100 steps` block and change the value from 15 to 72.

2. So far, the script will have drawn only one side of the five-sided pentagon shape. You could add five more `move` and `turn` blocks to the sequence, or you could just add a loop to repeat, or **iterate**, the instruction five times. Add the control

block `repeat` under the `pen down` block to contain the motion blocks and change the value to 5 (see Figure 4-3).

3. Click the green flag to test that your turtle will draw a pentagon.
4. Click File➜Save As to save your changes.

The turtle can turn 360 degrees in a circle, either left or right. This helps you draw shapes. For example, to draw a square you would change the value of degrees to 90 to get the right-angled turn needed before drawing the next line.

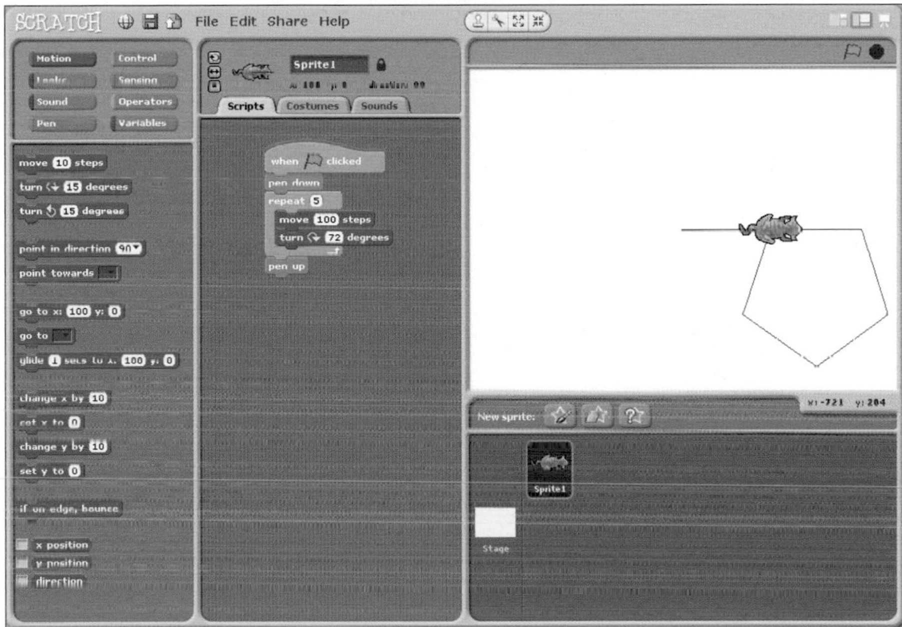

FIGURE 4-3 The Turtle pentagon script in Scratch

CHALLENGE

If the value of steps and the value of degrees to turn were set to 1, and the repeat value set to 360, what shape do you think the turtle would draw?

Now that you have created a pentagon shape, how could you go about making a hexagon shape, or an octagon shape?

Using "clear" and Setting a Start Point

You may have noticed that every time you press the 🏴 button, the image you have just drawn remains on the screen. This can be frustrating when you are testing scripts. To ensure you have a clear stage every time you run a script, add the `clear` block from the pen palette underneath the starting control block `When 🏴 clicked`, as shown in Figure 4-4. This block tells the program to remove the previous action before proceeding.

You will also notice that the turtle begins its drawing wherever it is located. This can affect your drawing, and part of it may end up offscreen if the turtle is positioned too close to the edge of the stage. To avoid this, you can add the motion block `go to x: 0 y:0` to set the start point of the pen, just like you did in Adventure 3 for the Adventurer sprite in the final game project. Remember that Scratch uses x and y coordinates, with `x:0` and `y:0` being the middle of the stage. You can also set the direction that the sprite faces before it draws your shape by using the motion block `point in direction 90` after the start coordinates. Figure 4-4 shows these blocks added to the script.

Using Variables Instead of Values

It is more logical to set **variables** for values that you wish to use several times in programming. In your pentagon drawing, you used values for the length of the side of the shape (100 steps), the angle of the turn (72 degrees) and the number of sides (repeat 5). In this part of the project, you create variables that will make it easier to create similar shapes in the future.

1. In the blocks palette, click Variables➜Make a Variable. You need to make three variables, called `Number_Sides`, `Angle` and `Side_Length`.
2. Drag the three new variable blocks onto the script and set the value of `Number_Sides` to 5, `Angle to` 72, and `Side_Length` to 100.
3. Underneath the variables blocks, add your simple shape script, but now instead of the values that you typed into the boxes, add the variable names (see Figure 4-4).
4. Now that you are using variables, you no longer need to calculate the angle of rotation. Instead, you can set the `Angle` variable to divide 360 (the number of degrees in a circle) by the number of sides that you set. To do this, drag the operators block `0 / 0` and replace the value 72 with it. Then type 360 into the left hand box, and drag the variable block `Number_Sides` into the right box.
5. If you change the number of sides to 6, the script will draw a hexagon; if you change the number of sides to 4, it will draw a square, and so on.

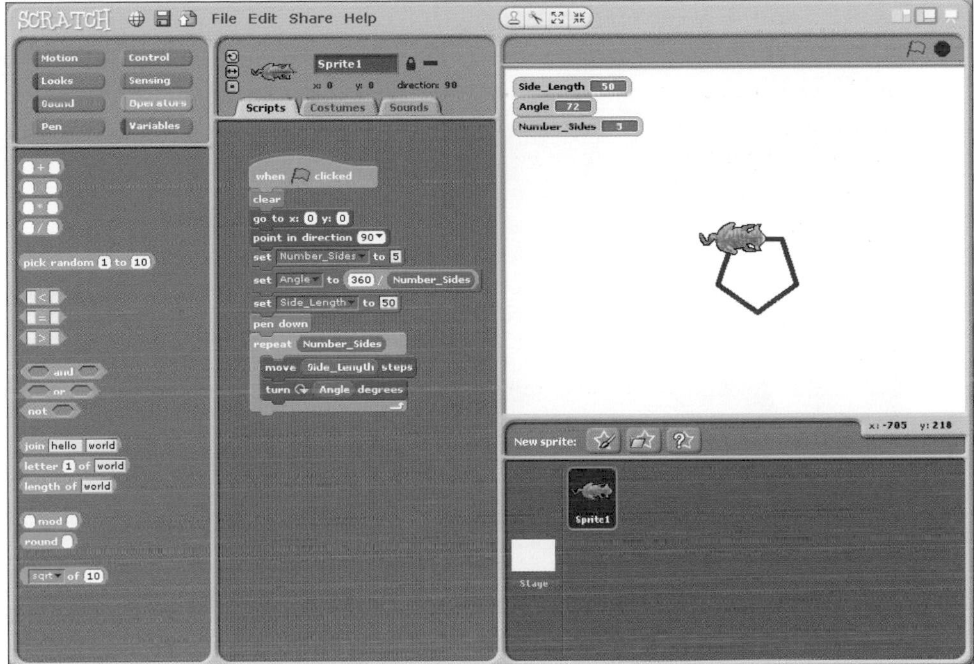

FIGURE 4-4 Using variables instead of values in Scratch

Changing the Size and Colour of the Pen

To make your drawings look more interesting, you can also change the colour of the pen and the thickness of the line.

1. Add the pen block `set pen colour to` to your pentagon script, after the `point in direction 90` block and before the `repeat` block.
2. Click on the coloured square and use the eyedropper tool to select the shade you want to use from the colour palette.
3. You can also use the `set pen size to` block to change the thickness of the line. The higher the value you set, the thicker the line will be. Add this block to the script under the `set pen colour to` block and before the `repeat` block, and change the thickness of the pen line used in the pentagon script to 5.
4. Click the green flag to run the script. Figure 4-5 shows the results.

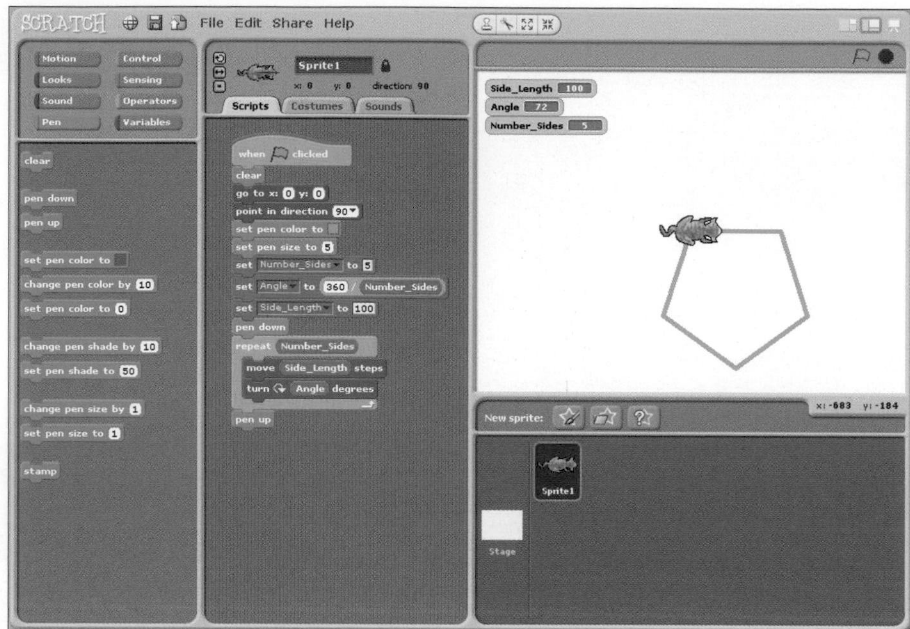

FIGURE 4-5 Setting the colour and size of the pen in Scratch

Creating Spiral Patterns

Once you have mastered drawing a single shape, you can start to think of ways to repeat the shape over and over to make a spiral pattern.

Add to the pentagon script a `repeat` control block and a `turn degrees` block, so that it looks like Figure 4-6.

To make your spiral look more colourful, you can add the pen block `Change pen shade by 10` underneath the motion block `turn 15 degrees`. This will change the colour of the pen after each pentagon shape has been drawn. Figure 4-7 shows the final script and the result.

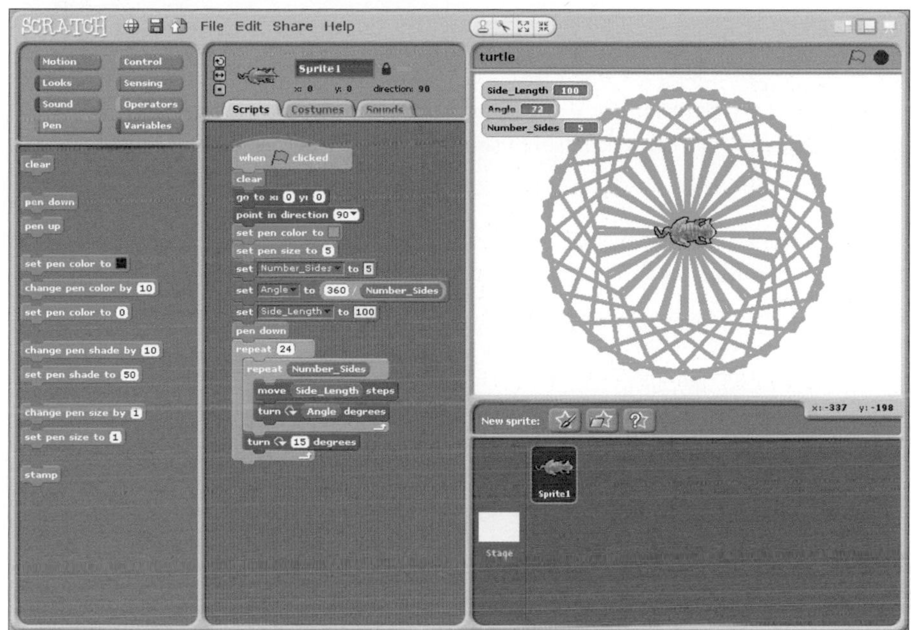

FIGURE 4-6 Creating repeating pentagon spirals

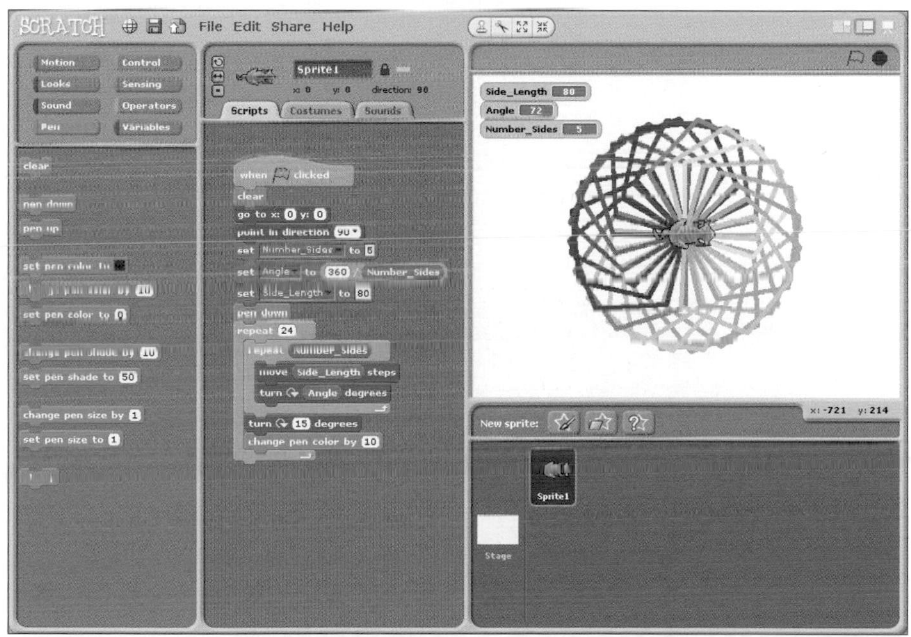

FIGURE 4-7 The results of adding the `Change pen shade by 10` block

Using User Input to Determine the Number of Sides

It is always more fun to allow a user to interact with a program you have created. In your turtle script, you can ask a user to set the value for the number of sides a shape in the spiral can have.

1. Add the sensing block `ask What's your name? And wait` underneath the start point blocks and before the set variable blocks.
2. Change the question to "How many sides would you like your shape to have?"
3. Add the sensing block `answer` to the `set Number_Sides` block, where you normally type the value. Your script should look like the one shown in Figure 4-8.
4. Now run your script. It will ask the user how many sides she wants before it draws the spiral.

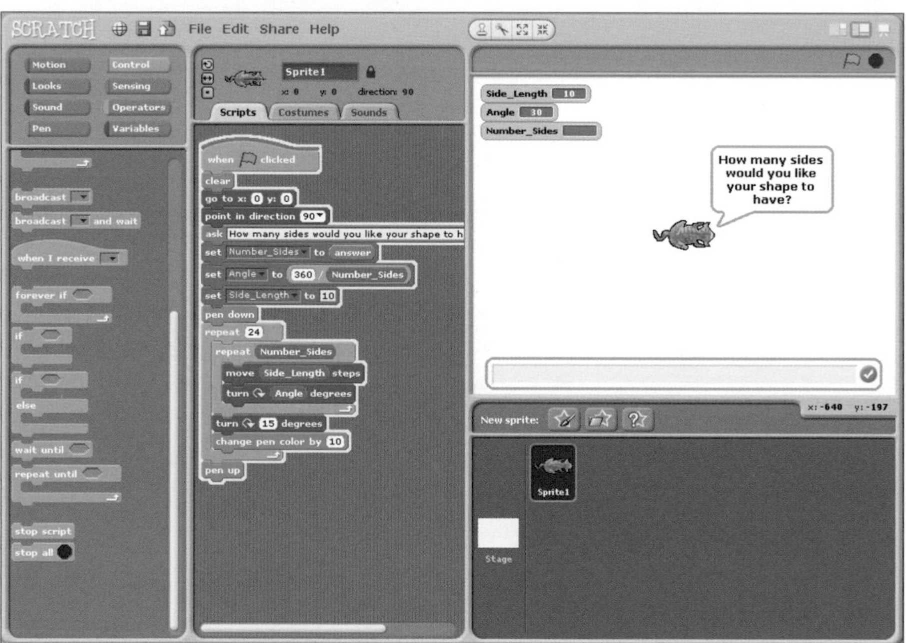

FIGURE 4-8 Adding user input to a turtle spiral script in Scratch

Python Turtle Graphics

This section gives you a quick taste of the Python programming language. Python includes a `turtle` module that you can use to create shapes and spirals in a similar way to Scratch. In this tutorial, you use the `turtle` module as an introduction to writing code in Python.

In Adventure 5, you will get a more thorough introduction to the Python programming language, the IDLE programming environment, and Python functions and modules. In this adventure, you can just follow along with the instructions, and you will begin to see how the Scratch blocks correspond to Python coding.

For a video that walks you through using the Python interface to type commands, visit the companion website at `www.wiley.com/go/adventuresinrp`. Click the Videos tab and select the PythonIntro file.

Introducing Python Modules

As you learn more about programming and continue to write code, you will discover that many of the programs you write include similar tasks and require similar blocks of code. To avoid the necessity of rewriting the same code over and over, most programming languages include reusable blocks of code, called **modules.** Python has a large number of modules containing useful code that you can reuse. You will learn more about modules in Adventure 5.

In this adventure, you use the Python `turtle` module to create graphics.

The IDLE Environment and the Interpreter Window

To use Python, you need access to the programming environment IDLE 3. To open IDLE 3, double-click the IDLE 3 icon on the desktop of your Raspberry Pi, or click on the main menu and select Programming➜IDLE 3, as shown in Figure 4-9. You can type commands directly into the IDLE window after the prompt, which is represented by three >>> characters. You type a line of code and then press Enter to run it. This window is referred to as an **interpreter** (or a *shell*), as it understands the language you are using, in this case Python, and interprets the code one line at a time.

You will learn more about the IDLE and IDLE 3 programming environments in the next adventure.

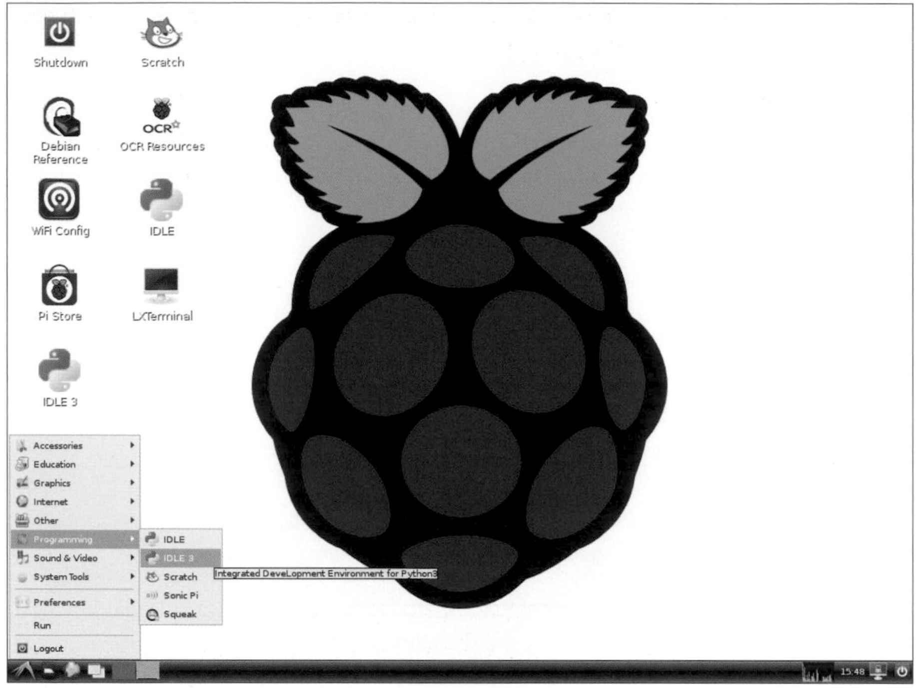

FIGURE 4-9 Opening IDLE 3 from the application launcher on the Raspberry Pi

Using the Turtle Module in Python

In the first part of this project, you will use the IDLE 3 interpreter, or shell, to add the `turtle` module for use in Python, and write the code to create a shape.

1. To use a module within a Python program, use the Python key word `import` followed by the name of the module. In the window, type the following line after the >>> prompt to import the `turtle` module:

   ```
   import turtle
   ```

   Now press Enter on your keyboard to get a new prompt.

2. At the new prompt, type the following command, and then press Enter again:

   ```
   alex = turtle.Turtle()
   ```

   This command opens the Turtle Graphics window, with an arrow cursor in the centre. The arrow cursor represents the turtle, whose movements will create your drawing.

   The = symbol in Python assigns a name on the left side to whatever is on the right side. This makes it easier to refer to it when writing lots of code. I have used the name *alex* but you can use any name.

You can change the arrow to a turtle shape, as shown in Figure 4-10, by typing the following code at the prompt:

```
alex.shape("turtle")
```

3. Just like in Scratch, you can create a pentagon shape by moving so many steps and turning so many degrees. Type in the following code, pressing Enter after each line:

```
alex.forward(100)
alex.left(72)
```

Your Python Turtle drawing will appear in a different window when you run the commands. Sometimes windows overlap and you can't see what is happening on both of them, or you may get a white screen instead of your drawing. To get over this problem, move the windows so that they are side by side when typing your commands into the shell.

These lines tell the turtle to move forward 100 steps and then turn 72 degrees to the left. How many times would you need to type these two lines of instructions or code into the Python shell to draw a pentagon? Continue repeating these lines until you have created the pentagon. Figure 4-10 shows the final code and the completed shape.

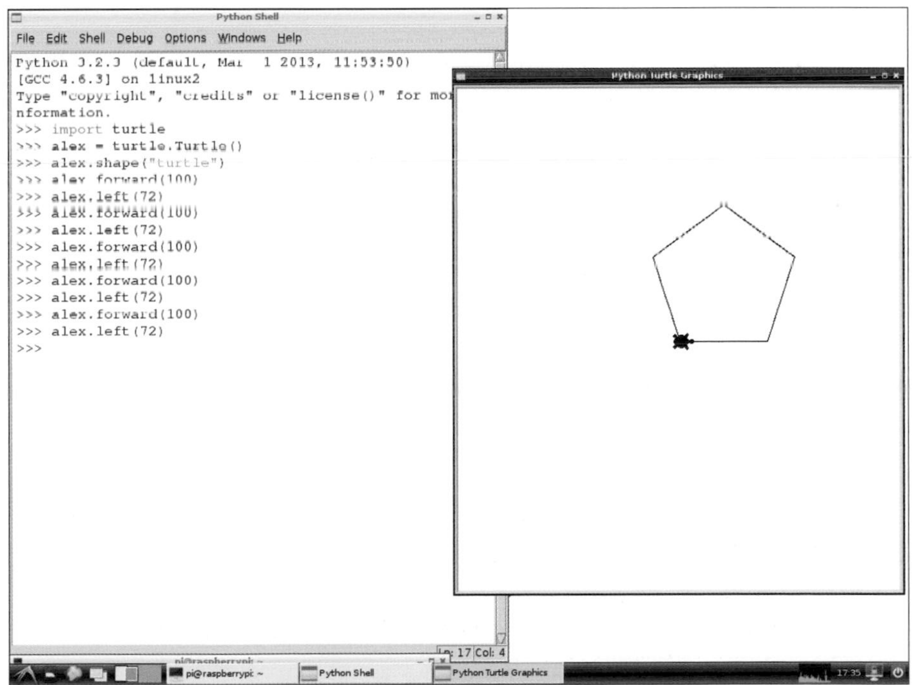

FIGURE 4-10 Drawing a pentagon in Python Turtle Graphics

You cannot save this code because you wrote it directly into the Python interpreter window or shell so that you could see it working instantly. In the following sections, you will type your sequence of steps for the turtle to follow in a text editor window.

You can learn more about using Turtle Graphics with Python by selecting the PythonTurtleShapes video from the companion website at `www.wiley.com/go/adventuresinrp`.

Using a Text Editor

As you begin to create more complex programs, it will become tiresome to type the commands straight into the Python interpreter or shell window. It makes more sense to type all your code into a text file before running it, using IDLE.

To open the text editor, click File➔New Window from the menu at the top of the Python 3 interpreter or shell. Type in all the code that you typed into the interpreter in the preceding section, and save the new file to your `Documents` directory on your Raspberry Pi as `FirstTurtle.py` (see Figure 4-11). You can run the script by clicking Run➔Run Module from the text editor toolbar.

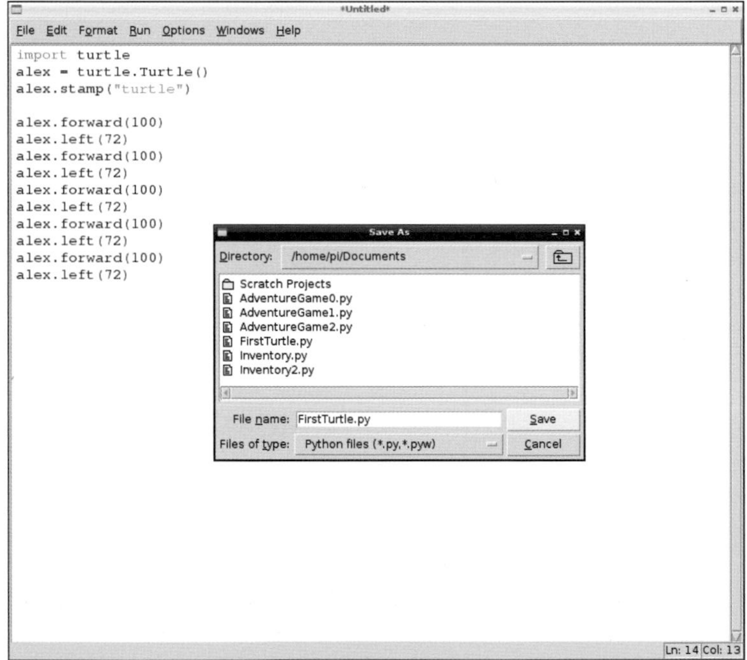

FIGURE 4-11 Using the text editor to create and save files

You should use the text editor for the remainder of this adventure.

Using "for" Loops and Lists

In your Python code so far, you have repeated the length of the line and the angle to make a pentagon shape by writing them in sequence. Repeating sequences is a common practice in computer science. You can make this code more efficient by writing the sequence once and then **looping** it five times. You have used looping before in Scratch, when you used the forever block to make an action continue repeating. As you learned in Adventure 3, each repeated instance of the looping code lines is called an **iteration**.

Quite often, you will want your code to repeat or loop. In Scratch, you use the `repeat` or `forever` blocks to iterate. In Python you can use a `for` loop.

To practice looping code, open a new text editor window and type the following code, saving the file as `FirstTurtle2.py`.

```
import turtle
alex = turtle.Turtle()
alex.shape("turtle")
```

Next add a `for` loop:

```
for i in [0,1,2,3,4,]:
    alex.forward(100)
    alex.left(72)
```

This code says, "for each instance (`i`) in the following list, move alex forward 100 steps and then turn left 72 degrees".

When you have finished typing the code, run it by selecting Run➜Run Module.

The `for` statement will repeat `forward` and `left` five times, one time for each value in the list. A list is represented in Python by square brackets. Numbered lists begin at 0 rather than 1. If you had written 0,1,2,3, inside the square brackets to form a list, then only four sides of the pentagon shape would be drawn. Likewise if you had written 0,1,2,3,4,5, then six sides of the pentagon shape would be drawn, which is one side too many! Have a go yourself to see how numbering inside Python lists work.

By using a loop to repeat a sequence of code, you have saved yourself a number of lines of code. By using iteration in your program you are thinking like a computer scientist.

Lists can contain more than numbers or integers. For example, they can contain information to change the colour of the turtle pen.

Amend your Python pentagon code to look like the following, making sure to include the letter `a` before `color`:

```
import turtle
alex = turtle.Turtle()
alex.shape("turtle")

for aColor in ["red", "blue", "yellow", "green", "purple"]:
    alex.color(aColor)
    alex.forward(100)
    alex.left(72)
```

Save the file as `FirstTurtle3.py` and run the module. You will now have a more colourful pentagon shape, as shown in Figure 4-12.

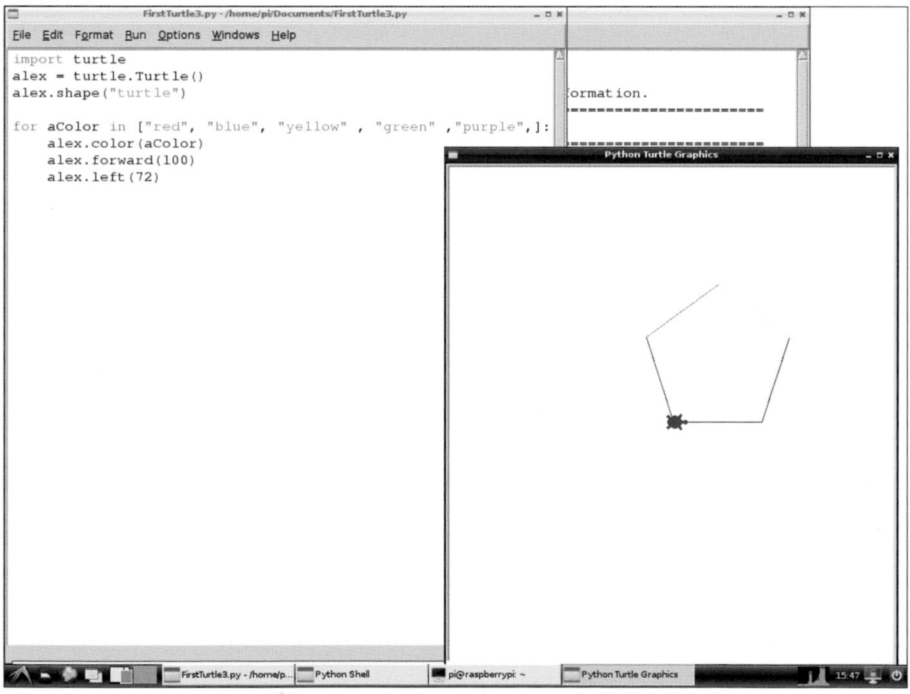

FIGURE 4-12 Using loops and lists to create turtle shapes in Python

The "range" Function

In the last few steps you used a list of numbers or integers and then colours to loop the turtle sequence in Python. Using lists is a very common coding task, especially if you are looping steps a number of times. It is so common that there is a Python **function** that you can use instead, the `range` function.

> A **function** is a piece of code that you can use over and over. You will learn more about functions in Adventure 5.

In a new text editor window, type the following code and save it as `FirstTurtle4.py`. When you have finished typing the code, select Run➔Run Module to see the code in action (see Figure 4-13).

```
import turtle
alex = turtle.Turtle()
alex.shape("turtle")

for i in range(5):
    alex.forward(100)
    alex.left(72)
```

The `range` function in this program creates a list of numbers or integers in the same way as the list you used before, `[0,1,2,3,4,]`.

DIGGING INTO THE CODE

The casing of commands used in Python code is very important, otherwise your code will not work as expected and you may get errors. You will notice in the examples in this adventure that most of the code is in lower case, except when creating the "alex" turtle. The first "turtle" in the line `alex = turtle.Turtle()` is lower case (`t`), but the second one is upper case (`T`).

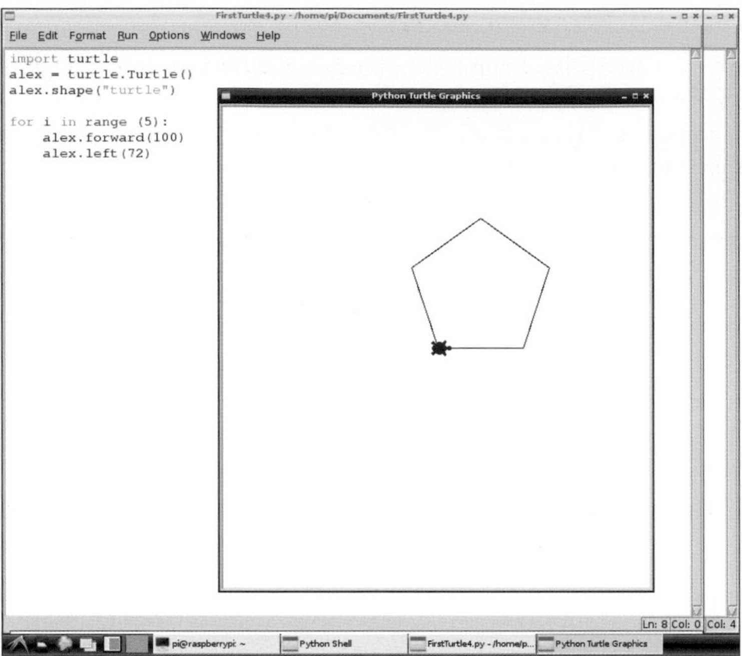

FIGURE 4-13 Using the `range` function to loop in Python

Other Python Turtle Module Commands

Once you have mastered some Python Turtle basics to create simple shapes, you can start to add extra lines of code to make your computer drawings more interesting.

Pen Up and Pen Down

Just as in Scratch, the Python `turtle` module includes code for the pen up and pen down commands so that you can move the turtle cursor around the page without leaving a line, just as if you were drawing a shape on a piece of paper with a pen. The code is written as follows, surrounding the directional code.

```
alex.pendown()
alex.forward(100)
alex.penup()
```

Setting the Pen Colour and Size

You can set the colour of the turtle using `.color` followed by the name of the colour you wish to use inside brackets:

```
alex.color("blue")
```

Similarly, you can set the size of the pen by using `.pensize` followed by the number of pixels you wish to use inside brackets:

```
alex.pensize(5)
```

Stamping

You can use `.stamp` to leave an imprint of the turtle cursor on the screen to form a pattern instead of, or as well as, using a pen line:

```
alex.stamp()
```

You will see the stamp in action in Figure 4-15.

Some Super Spirals

You can put together combinations of the Python Turtle code you have learned, in order to make some interesting shapes. Have a go yourself by typing the following two sequences into new text editor windows and saving them as `SpiralTurtle1.py` (shown in Figure 4-14) and `SpiralTurtle2.py` (Figure 4-15). You can change the `pensize` and `color` arguments to make your own creations.

The Spiral Turtle

```
import turtle
alex = turtle.Turtle()
alex.color("darkgreen")
alex.pensize(5)
alex.shape("turtle")

print (range(5,100,2))
for size in range(5,100,2):
    alex.forward(size)
    alex.left(25)
```

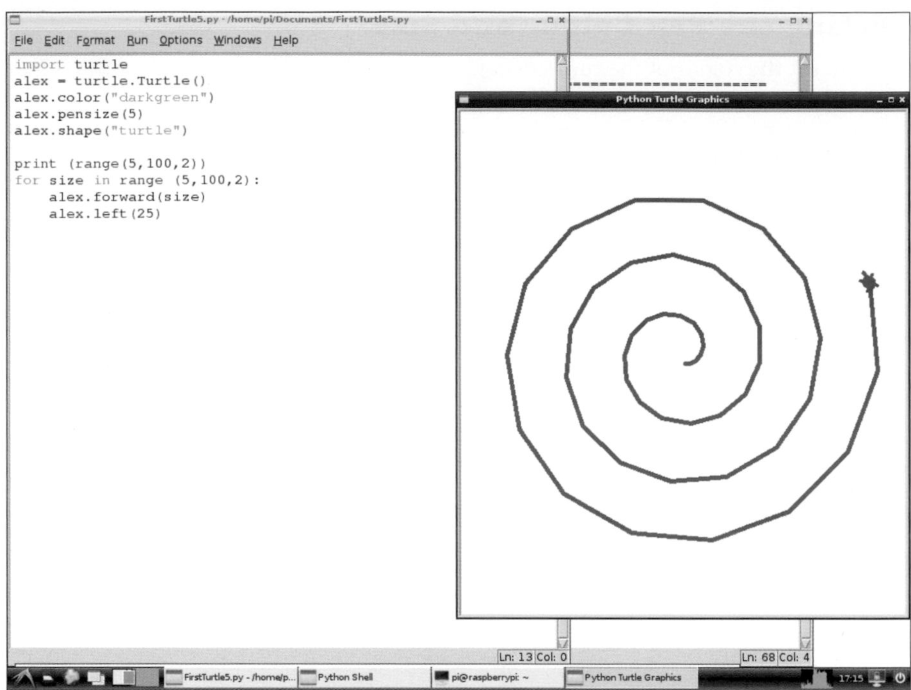

FIGURE 4-14 Using `pensize` and `color` to create `SpiralTurtle1.py`

The Spiral Turtle Stamp

```
import turtle
alex = turtle.Turtle()
alex.color("brown")
alex.shape("turtle")

print (range(5,100,2))
alex.penup()
for size in range(5,100,2):
    alex.stamp()
    alex.forward(size)
    alex.left(25)
```

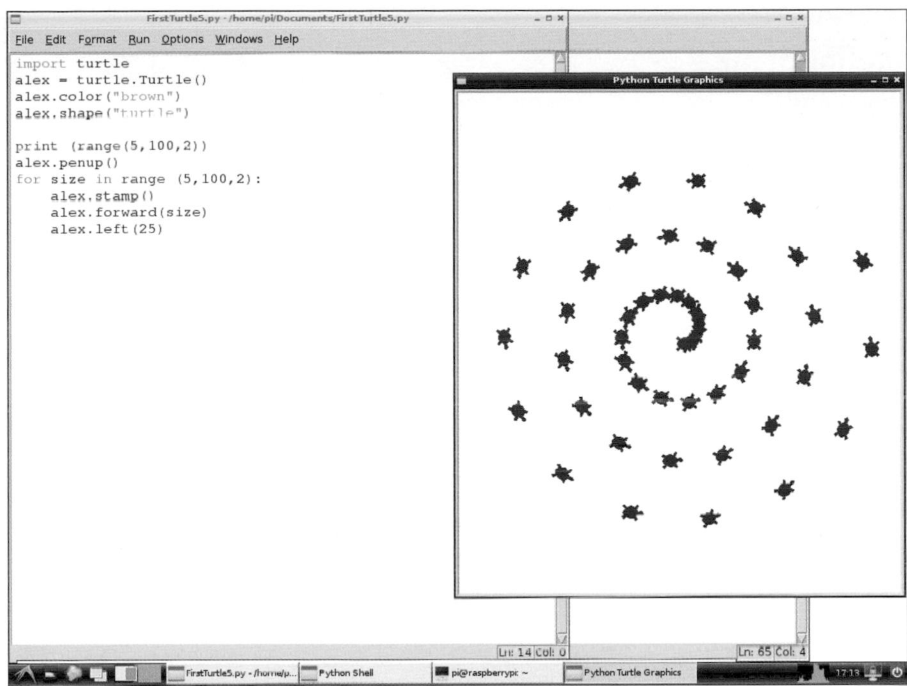

FIGURE 4-15 Using `penup` and `stamp` to create `SpiralTurtle2.py`

Further Adventures with Python Turtle

If you wish to continue creating graphics using Turtle in Python, it's worth checking out the official Python Turtle online documentation at `http://docs.python.org/2/library/turtle.html`. It includes all the Python Turtle commands that you could use. Why not experiment and see what programming art you can create?

Turtle Graphics Command Quick Reference Table

See also the Scratch Quick Reference Table in Adventure 3	
Commands	**Description**
Pen Blocks (Scratch)	
`change pen color by` *x*	Changes pen's colour by *x* amount.
`change pen shade by` *x*	Changes the pen's shade by x amount.
`clear`	Clears all pen marks and stamps from the stage.
`pen down`	Puts down a sprite's pen so that it will draw.

continued

Turtle Graphics Command Quick Reference Table (continued)	
Commands	**Description**
`pen up`	Lifts a sprite's pen so it does not draw.
`set pen color to x`	Sets a pen's colour to your choice.
`set pen shade to x`	Sets the pen's shade by x amount.
`set pen size x`	Set's a pen's line thickness to x.
`stamp`	Stamps a sprite's image on to the stage.
Turtle Module in Python	
`import turtle`	Imports the turtle module into Python. Should be at the start of any Python Turtle program.
Creating and Naming the "turtle"	
`alex = turtle.Turtle()`	Opens the Turtle Graphics window, with an arrow cursor in the centre, named *alex*. The arrow cursor represents the turtle, whose movements will create your drawing.
Move and Draw	
`forward(x)`	Moves the turtle forward by the specified distance *x*, in the direction the turtle is headed.
`left(x)`	Turns turtle left by *x* units.
`right(x)`	Turns turtle right by *x* units.
`stamp()`	Stamps a copy of the turtle shape onto the canvas at the current turtle position.
Drawing State	
`pendown()`	Puts the pen down and draws when it moves.
`penup()`	Picks the pen up and stops drawing.
`pensize(x)`	Sets the thickness of the `line` drawn to *x* pixels.
Turtle State	
`shape("turtle")`	Sets the cursor icon. Possible values for the shape are: `arrow`, `turtle`, `circle`, `square`, `triangle`, `classic`.
Colour Control	
`color("brown")`	Sets pen colour.
Additional Commands	
`for`	`for` loops are traditionally used when you have a piece of code that you want to repeat *x* number of times. Example: `for i in [0,1,2,3,4,]:`
for i in range():	A `for` loop using the `range()` function that creates a list containing numbers.
`range()`	The `range()` function generates a list of numbers in progression.

Achievement Unlocked: You can create Turtle Graphics on your Raspberry Pi!

In the Next Adventure

In the next adventure, you will learn more about how to program in Python on the Raspberry Pi. You'll use some of the same concepts you have already learned, such as iteration (loops) and conditionals (`if` statements), as well as many new constructs, to create a new game where players answer questions to determine how the game will move forward.

Adventure 5
Programming with Python

PROGRAMMING WITH SCRATCH can be a lot of fun, but as you become more skillful at creating games and graphics using this application, you may notice that there are limits to what you can achieve with Scratch. Most computer programmers use text-based languages to create computer programs, including games, desktop applications and mobile apps. Although text-based programming may seem more complicated at first, you will soon find that it is easier to achieve your goals by using code. The Python code language is used by millions of programmers worldwide, including developers at organisations like NASA, Google and CERN.

In this adventure, you'll discover what you need in order to set up Python on your Raspberry Pi. You'll write a short program, and learn to use a text editor. After that, you'll delve deeper into Python, learning about modules and their applications, how to get user input and how to use conditionals. Finally, you'll put all your new knowledge to use, creating a text-based adventure game in which your user (player) will answer questions and your game will respond based on the answers.

Although this may seem like a major departure from the graphical world of Scratch programming, the good news is that all of the programming concepts you learned in Scratch apply to other languages as well, even those that seem very different. Concepts such as using a sequence of instructions to make something happen, loops, conditionals and variables are common throughout all programming languages. By the end of this adventure, you'll be able to write some basic Python programs on your Raspberry Pi!

If you get stuck on a computing problem, you might find it helpful to use Scratch to help you visualise what is happening.

Getting Set Up for Python

The Raspbian operating system includes the programming environment called Python IDLE. This section introduces you to the programming language and environment used to create Python files and execute them.

Python Programming Language

The Raspberry Pi operating system Raspbian comes with a text-based computer programming language, Python, already installed. The *Pi* in Raspberry Pi is a nod towards this programming language, as it is considered an easy language to pick up and is used by coders all over the world.

To work with Python, you use the IDLE programming environment, or **integrated development environment** (**IDE**).

An **IDE** or **integrated development environment**, also referred to as a *programming environment,* is a software application used to write computer code in a particular language, for example Python. The application has the capability to create and edit code as well as run or execute the code. Many IDEs also provide features to help programmers check for errors in their programs and ***debug*** or resolve the errors.

The IDLE Environment

In order to create programs on the Raspberry Pi using Python, you use the Python programming environment, which is called IDLE. Notice that there are two versions of IDLE on the desktop and in the menu system: IDLE and IDLE 3 (see Figure 5-1). The projects in this book require IDLE 3, which you will remember you used in Adventure 4. Just like the English language, Python has evolved through different versions and some of the commands you will learn in this adventure will not work in older versions of IDLE.

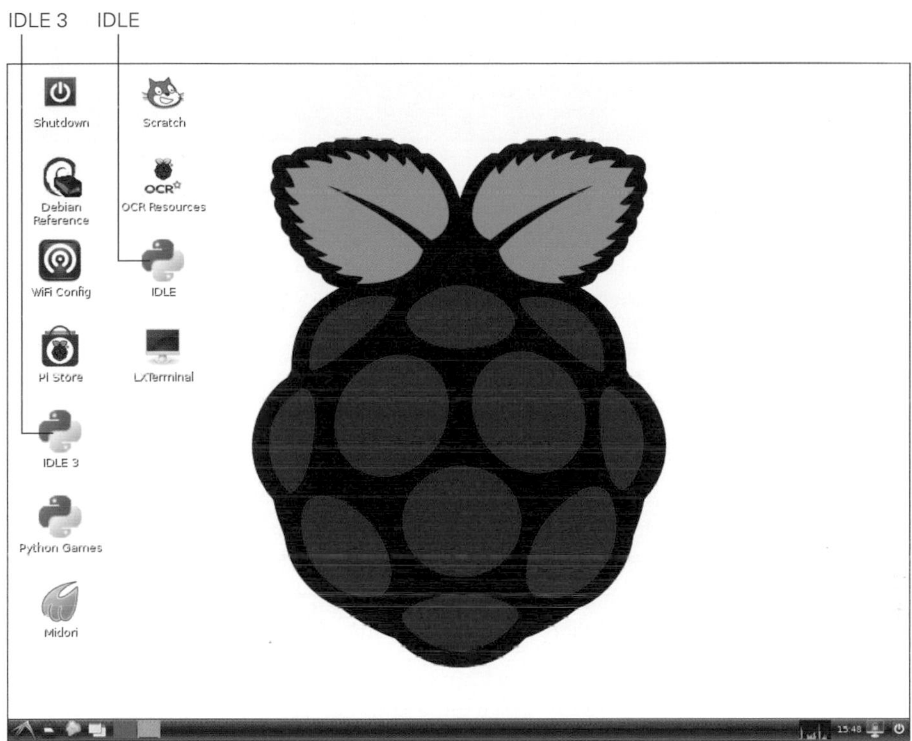

FIGURE 5-1 The Raspberry Pi desktop, with Python's IDLE and IDLE 3 programming environments both available

Programming in Python: Using a Function

To begin working with Python, double-click the IDLE 3 icon on the desktop, or open the main menu, navigate to Programming and select IDLE 3. You will be using Python 3 throughout this book rather than earlier versions, which use a different syntax. The Python shell, or command-line interface, opens and a prompt of three angle symbols (>>>) appears to indicate where you should type your code, as shown in Figure 5-2.

For your first Python program, you'll write only one line of code, using a **function,** a piece of code that tells the computer to perform a specific task. For this program, you use the `print()` function to tell the computer to print some text on the screen. Place the **string** of text you want the computer to display inside the brackets, with quotation marks around it.

SYNTAX, ERRORS AND DEBUGGING YOUR CODE

Syntax is a set of rules to check whether the code you have typed is valid Python code. In the same way as the English language has rules about how to properly combine subjects, verbs, objects and so on, each programming language has its own syntax. When you make a mistake or a typo in your code, your program may display a **syntax error** message.

A syntax error stops a program from running because the computer cannot understand the code. This usually happens because a word was misspelled or a character left out. The most common cause of syntax errors is missing out the colon at the end of loops and conditionals!

Error messages are posted to the screen to alert you to the problem, but these messages can be difficult to understand. You might want to make some typing mistakes on purpose with some simple example code, so you can see the sort of error messages Python gives you. Try leaving out a quote mark or bracket, or misspelling a command, to find out what happens.

So what do you do when you get an error message? **Debugging** is the act of locating the cause of any errors in your computer program code and fixing them. When Python displays a syntax error, the line that contains the error is repeated, with a little arrow underneath it pointing to where the error is likely to originate. Look carefully at the line to spot any misspelled words or missing characters, then correct the problem and try running the code again.

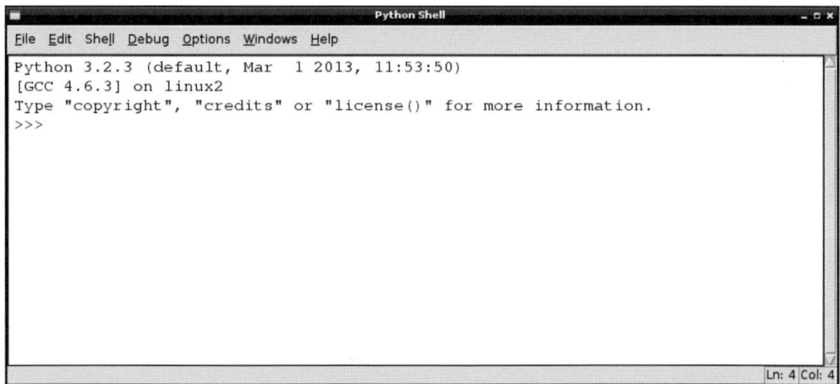

FIGURE 5-2 The Python 3 IDLE Shell

When a program gets to be more than a few lines, it becomes harder to understand and edit the code. Breaking a program's code down into small sections makes it easier to read and edit. A **function** is an example of a small section of code that does a specific task, and once it is created you can use it over and over again. An added benefit of using functions is that if you fix a bug you only have to fix it in one place.

Like most programming languages, Python includes some standard functions that the computer will already understand, like the Python 3 `print()` function that prints some text to the screen. You can also write your own functions, which you will do towards the end of this adventure.

A **string** refers to data or information entered as text (i.e., a "string" of characters).

Place your cursor directly after the >>> prompt and type the following line:

```
print("I am an Adventurer")
```

Press Enter and see what happens (see Figure 5-3).

```
Python 3.2.3 (default, Jan 28 2013, 11:47:15)
[GCC 4.6.3] on linux2
Type "copyright", "credits" or "license()" for more information.
>>> print("I am an adventurer")
I am an adventurer
>>> |
```

FIGURE 5-3 The `print()` function in action

When you press Enter, the Python Shell "interprets" your code. In this case, you gave the command to print the text between the quotation marks to the screen. Well done! You have created your first computer program in Python.

Using a Text Editor to Create a Code File

You used a text editor to create code files in Python in Adventure 4 when using the `turtle` module. As you learned in Adventure 4, it makes sense to type all your code into a text file using a text editor and save it, before you test that it works by running it using IDLE. Using a text editor has the added bonus of *syntax highlighting*, which works by adding colour to different words in your code to make it easier to read. If you use a command-line editor like nano (which you used in Adventure 2) that does not have syntax highlighting, you may find it hard to read a long program. For the projects in this adventure, you use the Python 3 IDLE text editor as you did in Adventure 4.

In the Python programming language, you can create *lists* to store data—for example, you might want a list of names of the students in your class to use in a program that sends out invitations, or a list of favourite restaurants that your program could suggest when you need an idea for dinner.

The following steps walk you through using a text editor to create a list of objects that you will use later in your adventure game. In this exercise, you will create a new file, add the code to create an inventory, and then save the file.

For a video that walks you through creating an inventory in Python, select the Inventory video from the companion website at `www.wiley.com/go/adventuresinrp`.

1. Open IDLE 3 and click File from the menu at the top. Select New Window to open an untitled text file (see Figure 5-4). Notice that this creates a new text editor file, not a shell window, and therefore does not contain a prompt.
2. To save the file, click File➜Save As. Navigate to your `Documents` directory and name the file **Inventory** before clicking Save. If you open your `Documents` directory, you can see the file is now saved there and Python has added a `.py` to the end of your file, so the complete filename is `Inventory.py`.
3. In the new file, type the following:

   ```
   inventory = ["Torch", "Pencil", "Rubber Band", "Catapult"]
   ```

   This code creates a list named `inventory`. Each string, or piece of text data, represents an item on that list.
4. Underneath the list, type the following:

   ```
   print(inventory)
   ```

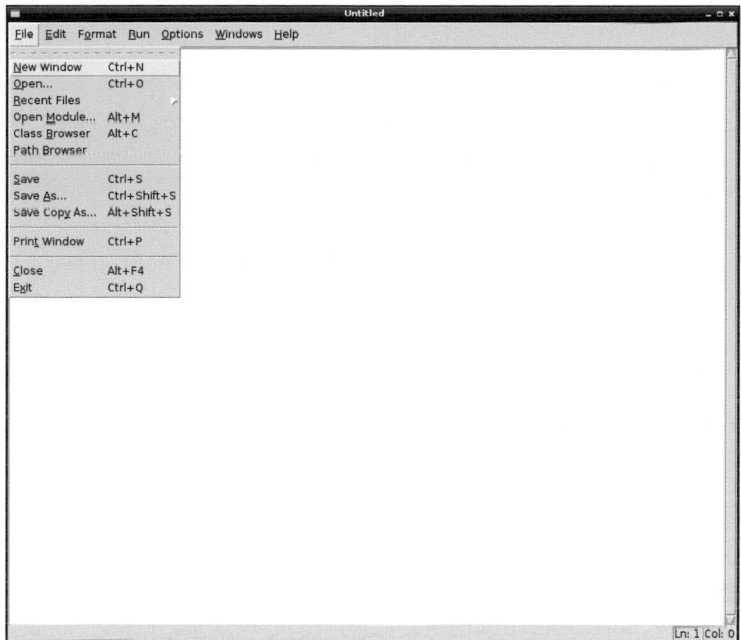

FIGURE 5-4 The Python 3 IDLE text editor and menu

5. Click File➜Save to save the file, and then run your small program by clicking Run➜Run Module. Your list is printed to the screen, as shown in Figure 5-5.

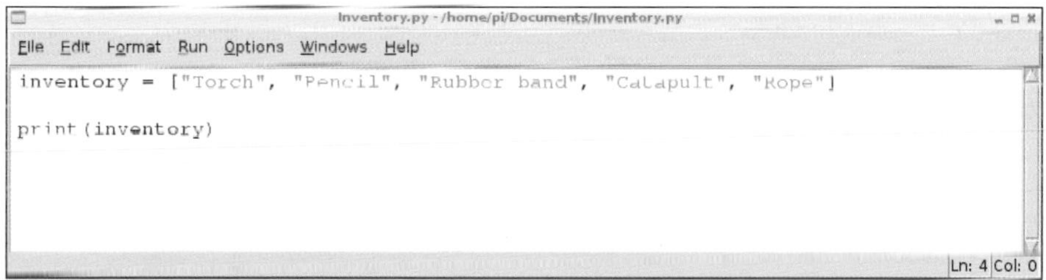


```
Python Shell
File Edit Shell Debug Options Windows Help
Python 3.2.3 (default, Mar  1 2013, 11:53:50)
[GCC 4.6.3] on linux2
Type "copyright", "credits" or "license()" for more information.
>>> ================================ RESTART ================================
>>>
['Torch', 'Pencil', 'Rubber band', 'Catapult', 'Rope']
>>> |
Ln: 7 Col: 4
```

FIGURE 5-5 Creating an inventory list in Python and using the `print()` function to display its contents

6. Now adapt the last line of code to read:

```
print(inventory[3])
```

7. Save the file using File➜Save and then run the program again.

Your program should print `Catapult` as the output. Hang on—isn't the catapult the fourth object on the list and not the third? Why did it print the third object when the command was to print the fourth?

The third object was printed because Python numbers items in a list starting at 0, rather than at 1: 0 = Torch, 1 = Pencil, 2 = Rubber Band, 3 = Catapult.

Using the Python time and random Modules

As you learned in Adventure 4, Python has a large number of **modules**—useful blocks of code that you can reuse to avoid having to rewrite the same code over and over each time you need a program that performs the same task. For example, each time you need a program that selects objects from a list randomly, you could write a new function or you could simply use the Python random module and save yourself a lot of time.

In order to use a module within a Python program, you use the Python word `import` followed by the name of the module. You can then access functions of that module in your program.

A **module** is a collection of reusable Python code that performs a specific function. It may be used alone or combined with other modules. In this adventure, for example, you use functions from the Python `time` module to add pauses.

In this section, you use the `random` module along with the inventory list you created in Python to make a program that will select an item from the list randomly.

Starting with the Python file `Inventory.py` that you created earlier, you will adapt the code to create a new, interactive program that requests user input and responds appropriately.

As you write the code, you will include **comments**. Comments are notes within your code that explain what a line or section of code in intended to do. Each comment line begins with the # symbol, which tells the computer running the program to ignore that line. If a comment wraps over several lines you need to include a # sign at the beginning of each line so that it is passed over by the IDE.

There are many good reasons for including comments inside your code. Comments can help you remember what each part of the code is doing, should you leave it unfinished for a while. In school, you may use comments to explain to your teacher what each part of your code is doing. If you are working with others, comments help them see what you have done already.

1. Begin your code with a comment line to indicate the code's purpose. Open the `Inventory.py` file that you created earlier and type the following line at the top (above the inventory list that is already in the file):

   ```
   # Adventures in Raspberry Pi Python - Inventory
   ```

   Note the # symbol at the start of the line, identifying it as a comment.

2. Next, use the `import` command to import the two Python modules you need, `time` and `random`. You can add a comment to explain this step if you like, as shown in the following code:

   ```
   # You will need the random module and the time module.

   import random
   import time
   ```

3. Press Enter to leave a blank line so that your code will be easier to read and then use the `print()` function to display two strings of text on the screen:

   ```
   # Enter a blank line here

   print("You have reached the opening of a cave")
   print ("you decide to arm yourself with a ")
   ```

4. Next, use the `sleep()` function from the time module to make the program wait for two seconds before asking the player a question by adding the **argument** `(2)` as shown.

   ```
   time.sleep(2)
   ```

An **argument** is a piece of information given to the function that it may use to perform its task. The argument goes inside the brackets that follow the function name. In the code in step 5, for example, with the `time.sleep()` function you use the argument `(2)`, which is the number of seconds you want the program to wait before implementing the next line.

5. Now you want the player to think of any item and type it in as her answer. The following code will display the line `Think of an object` and wait for the player to input an answer. The player can type anything for her answer; for example, she might type **banana**. The program will then use the `print()` function to display `You look in your backpack for banana` (or whatever object the player typed).

The ⮐ character at the end of a code line means that line and the next one should all be typed as a single line; do not add a line break or extra spaces between them.

```
quest_item = input("Think of an object\n")

print("You look in your backpack for ", quest_item)

time.sleep(2)

print("You could not find ", quest_item)
print("You select any item that comes to hand from the ⮐
  backpack instead\n")
time.sleep(3)
```

The `\n` at the end of the string in the first line doesn't get printed to the screen; instead, an extra new line is printed. This is helpful for breaking up the text and making it easier to read.

A function may produce a *return value,* which can be stored in a variable like any other value. For instance, the `input()` function will return the string that the player types in, or the `random.choice()` function will return an item from the list it is given as an argument.

6. Next comes the inventory list. You created this line earlier, so just leave it as written:

```
inventory = ["Torch", "Pencil", "Rubber band", "Catapult"]
```

7. In the last part of the inventory program code, you use the `choice()` function from the `random` module to pick an object from the inventory list and display it to the user of the program. Type the following line below your inventory list:

```
print(random.choice(inventory))
```

Functions can take a number of arguments and return a result. Here you pass an argument to the `time.sleep()` function, to tell the program how many seconds to wait, and then print the result of `random.choice`.

Figure 5-6 shows the completed code.

Inventory2.py - /home/pi/Documents/Inventory2.py

File Edit Format Run Options Windows Help

```
# Adventures in Raspberry Pi Python - Inventory

import random
import time

print("You have reached the opening of a cave you decide to arm yourself with an

time.sleep(2)

quest_item = input("Think of an object\n")

print("You look in your backpack for ", quest_item)

time.sleep(2)

print("You could not find ", quest_item)
print("You select any item that comes to hand from the backpack instead\n")
time.sleep(3)

inventory = ["Torch", "Pencil", "Rubber band", "Catapult", "Rope"]

print(random.choice(inventory))
```

Ln: 16 Col: 0

FIGURE 5-6 Using modules in Python 3 to create an Inventory program

Check that your program works by saving the file as `inventory1.py` in the `Documents` folder on the Raspberry Pi and then clicking Run➔Run Module from the toolbar. Enter input when the program prompts for it. You should see results similar to those shown in Figure 5-7.

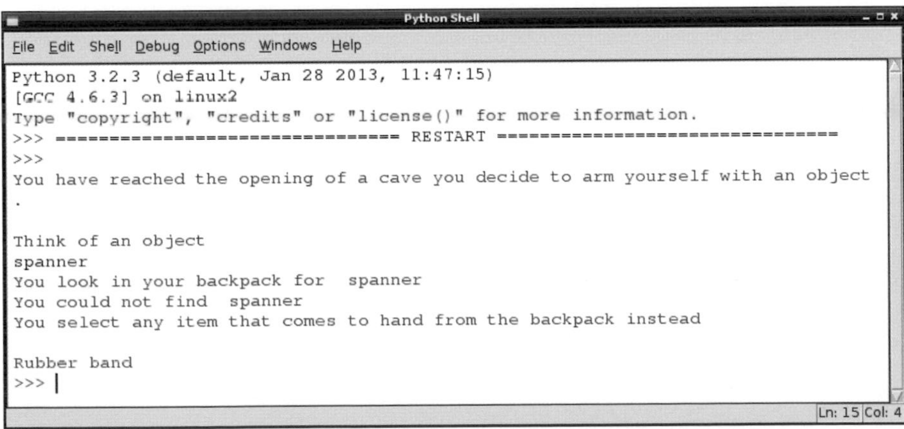

Python Shell
File Edit Shell Debug Options Windows Help
Python 3.2.3 (default, Jan 28 2013, 11:47:15)
[GCC 4.6.3] on linux2
Type "copyright", "credits" or "license()" for more information.
>>> ================================ RESTART ================================
>>>
You have reached the opening of a cave you decide to arm yourself with an object
.
Think of an object
spanner
You look in your backpack for spanner
You could not find spanner
You select any item that comes to hand from the backpack instead
Rubber band
>>>
Ln: 15 Col: 4

FIGURE 5-7 Getting a random item from the inventory list, using modules

What might happen if a user inputs the item **torch** when asked to think of an item? Do you think that the program will print:

A. You could not find torch

B. Found torch from your backpack

C. A torch! This will shed some light on the matter!

The answer is A. The program prints whatever you type in the string. It does not currently look inside the inventory list.

Can you think of a way to improve this program so that it checks to see if the item is already in the list?

Python Text Adventure Game

Text adventure games are fun to create because they are stories written by yourself that your friends and families can interact with. All you need is a bit of imagination and, of course, some programming skills.

In this tutorial, you will create your own adventure game that uses text to direct the player through the game. The program will ask the player to make decisions on what to do next. This may be as simple as finding out the direction in which she wants to turn next.

Visit the companion website at `www.wiley.com/go/adventuresinrp` and select PythonTextAdventure to see a video of this project.

Getting User Input

As the text adventure game relies on the player (user) to interact with the game to make decisions, you will need to use the `input()` function.

```
direction1 = input("Do you want to go left or right? ")
```

This line of code asks the player to answer the question, "Do you want to go left or right?" The program will wait for the player to type in an acceptable response—one that the program can understand.

Using Conditionals

Once the player has responded, you want something to happen based on her answer. You therefore need to use **conditionals**. You used conditionals in your Scratch adventure game in Adventure 3 to control the movement of the adventurer sprite, using the `forever if` control block.

Remember that creating a conditional is like asking a question where there are two or more outcomes. For example, you could ask the question "Is it raining?" If the answer is yes, you should put on a raincoat; if the answer is no, you should go out without a jacket. The key word used here is "`if`".

You will use `if` in Python 3 to create your game conditions. Open a new Python IDLE 3 text editor window and save the file as `AdventureGame.py`.

1. The first step is to import the modules that you will need for the program. As in the inventory program, you will need the `sleep()` function from the `time` module, so import that module with the following code:

   ```
   import time
   ```

2. Later in this game, you may wish to give your player health points that could go up or down depending on which directions she takes in the adventure. The number of remaining health points is stored in a variable. To include that feature, type the following line:

   ```
   hp = 30
   ```

3. Now use the `print()` function to tell your player where she is located in the game, and then use the `sleep()` function to wait one second before moving on.

   ```
   print("You are standing on a path at the edge of a ⮐
     jungle. There is a cave to your left and a beach ⮐
     to your right.")

   time.sleep(1)
   ```

4. As in the inventory program, you will want to get input from the player of your game. In this case, you want to know if she wishes to turn left or right, and the player's answer is then labelled as `direction1`.

   ```
   direction1 = input("Do you want to go left or right? ")
   ```

5. Next, create conditions depending on the player's answer. You will need one condition if the player chooses `left` and another if she chooses `right`. You may remember using conditionals in Scratch in Adventure 3. In Python, you use if, `elif` (else if) and `else` to check conditions:

```
if direction1 == "left":
  print("You walk to the cave and notice there is an ⮐
    opening.")

elif direction1 == "right":
  print("You walk to the beach but remember you do ⮐
    not have any swimwear.")

else:
  print("You think for a while")
```

`if`, `elif` and `else` are the Python words used to check conditions. In the preceding code, if the player types **left**, the program prints the statement, "You walk to the cave and notice there is an opening"; else if (`elif`) the player types in **right**, the program prints a different piece of text. Finally, if the player types in any answer that is not `left` or `right` (`else`), the program prints, "You think for a while". Figure 5-8 shows this code in the text editor.

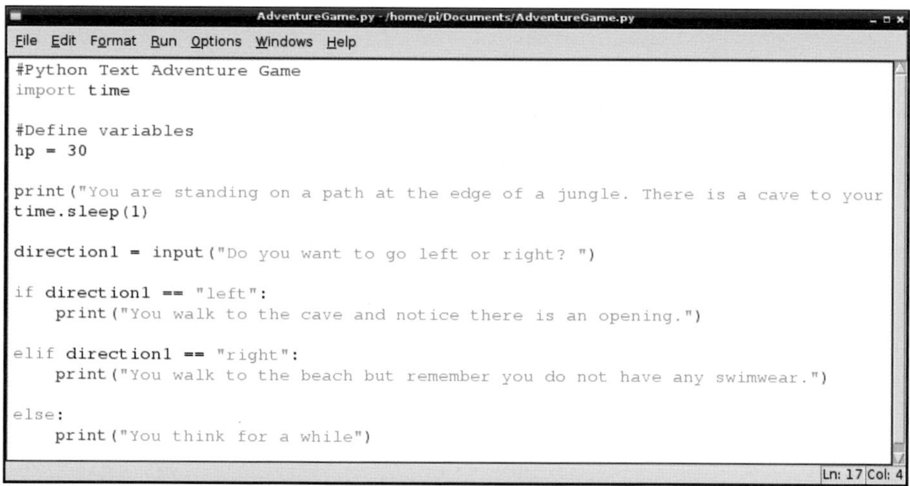

FIGURE 5-8 Using conditionals in a Python adventure game

DIGGING INTO THE CODE

In Adventure 3, you created conditions for the Scratch role-playing game using an `if…else` block like the one in Figure 5-9. In Scratch, the blocks for each part of a condition are automatically indented slightly for you within the `if…else` block. You can easily see which parts of the condition need to be met by how far they are indented. In Python code, you have to add indents to show which lines of code are part of the conditional. Python code also uses the colon (`:`) to show where you might need to indent. Take a look at Figure 5-9 to compare indentation in the `if…else` statements in Scratch and Python.

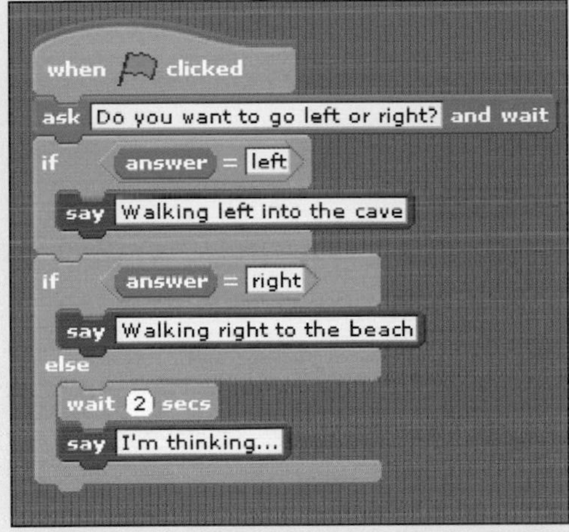

conditional.py - /home/pi/conditional.py

File Edit Format Run Options Windows Help

```
direction = input("Do you want to go left or right? ")

if direction == "left":
    print("Walking left into cave")

elif direction == "right":
    print("Walking right to the beach")

else:
    print("Thinking...")
```

FIGURE 5-9 Using `if…else` statements in Scratch (top) and Python (bottom)

6. Test to see if your code works by first saving the file as `AdventureGame.py` in `Documents` on the Raspberry Pi, and then running it by selecting Run➜Run Module. You should see a display similar to Figure 5-10.

```
Python Shell
File Edit Shell Debug Options Windows Help
Python 3.2.3 (default, Mar  1 2013, 11:53:50)
[GCC 4.6.3] on linux2
Type "copyright", "credits" or "license()" for more information.
>>> ================================ RESTART ================================
>>>
You are standing on a path at the edge of a jungle. There is a cave to your left an
d a beach to your right
Do you want to go left or right? left
You walk to the cave and notice there is an opening.
>>> |
```

FIGURE 5-10 Using Run Module to test conditionals in Python adventure game

What happens if the player types `LEFT` or `RiGhT` instead of `left` or `right`? Will the condition still be met?

To make sure that the player types in the correct lower case response that you require to meet the conditions, you can use a lower case function so that if the player types in capital letters, the program will turn the text into lower case, which is a recognised response to the `if`, `elif`, `else` conditions.

```
direction1 = direction1.lower()
```

Add this line *before* the first `if` statement used, and *after* asking the player to input a direction. See the final game code towards the end of this adventure for reference.

Using a while Loop

So far, the player has not been required to input specific answers in order for the game to move on. If the player does not input anything at all, the game simply stalls; and if the player types an unrecognized answer, the game says, "You think for a while". You want the player to input one of the responses that you have defined, `left` or `right`, to move on to the next location. You can ensure she inputs one of the desired responses by adding a `while` loop to your code. This will loop the user input question until the player types in a response that you were looking for—**left** or **right**—to move on. For example:

```
# Loop until we get a recognised response
while True:
  direction1 = input("Do you want to go left or right? ")
  direction1 = direction1.lower()
  if direction1 == "left":
    print("You walk to the cave and notice there is an ⮐
      opening.")
```

```
    break # leave the loop
  elif direction1 == "right":
    print("You walk to the beach but remember you do not ⮐
      have any swimwear.")
    break # leave the loop
  else:
    print("You think for a while")
```

In this code, shown also in Figure 5-11, you can see in bold text the Python words `while True:` added before the user input question, and `break` added within the conditionals for left and right. The `while True:` condition will loop the question over and over until the player enters either **left** or **right** so that the game does not end if the player types anything else.

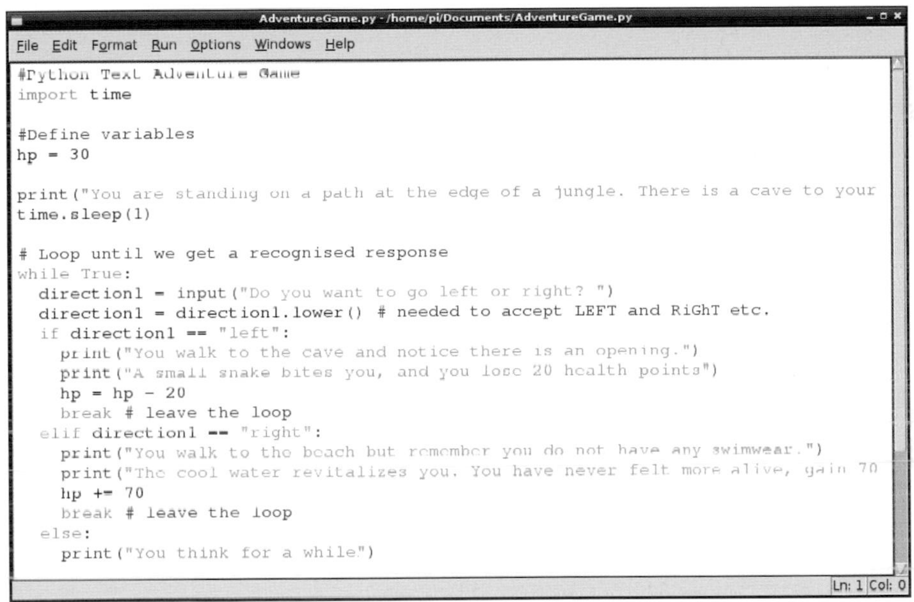

FIGURE 5-11 Using a `while` loop in the Python adventure game

Indentation refers to how far from the margin a line of code is typed. Indentation of code in Python is very important, especially when you begin to add more structure to your code by using conditionals and loops. In Adventures 3 and 4, you used conditionals and loops in Scratch. When you added a `forever` loop, you placed individual blocks inside it. These blocks inside the loop were indented from the rest of the statement. It is similar in Python. After you type `while True:` the next line should be indented, otherwise your code may not work. The same is true of the conditionals `if`, `else` and `elif`.

Using a Variable for Health Points

In the text adventure game so far, you have created a variable for health points (`hp = 30`), like the variable you created in the Scratch adventure game in Adventure 3. Here you have given an initial value that will change as the player plays the game. The value you have given is 30, but this could be any value of your choosing.

Now code can be added that will change the `hp` value based on the decisions made by the player. You name a variable using the form `name = value`, as in the following example:

```
hp = 30
```

Here are two ways to change the value of the `hp` variable in Python 3:

To subtract 10, use `hp = hp - 10` or `hp -= 10`

To add 10, use `hp = hp + 10` or `hp += 10`

You can use the following symbols to program calculations:

- Subtract
+ Add
* Multiply
/ Divide
< Less than
> Greater than

The following symbols produce a value that is True or False, so they are useful in conditionals:

== Equals
!= Not equals
<= Less than or equal to
> Greater than
>= Greater than or equal to

To make the game more interesting for the player, you can add some code to the end of what you have already written to tell her how many health points she has after each move:

```
# Check health points after the player has made a move
print("You now have ", hp, "health points")
if hp <= 0:
  print("You are dead. I am sorry.")
```

The last two lines add a conditional so that if the value of the hp variable is less than or equal to 0, the statement "You are dead. I am sorry." is displayed and the game ends.

Putting It All Together

Now put all the elements together in your text adventure game by typing the following program into a new Python 3 IDLE text editor window:

You can download the completed AdventureGame1.py code file from the companion website at www.wiley.com/go/adventuresinrp but, as I mentioned earlier, you will learn more by typing in the code as you read through the steps.

Python Text Adventure Game

```
# Python Text Adventure Game

import time

# Create health point variable
hp = 30

# Tell player their location and wait 1 second
print("You are standing on a path at the edge of a jungle. ⮐
  There is a cave to your left and a beach to your right.")
time.sleep(1)

# Loop until we get a recognised response
while True:
  direction1 = input("Do you want to go left or right? ")
  # Convert to lower case to accept LEFT and RiGhT etc.
  direction1 = direction1.lower()
  if direction1 == "left":
    print("You walk to the cave and notice there is an opening.")
    print("A small snake bites you, and you lose 20 health ⮐
      points.")
    hp = hp - 20
```

continued

Python Text Adventure Game (continued)

```
    break # leave the loop
  elif direction1 == "right":
    print("You walk to the beach but remember you do not ⮐
      have any swimwear.")
    print("The cool water revitalizes you. You have never ⮐
      felt more alive, gain 70 health points.")
    hp += 70
    break # leave the loop
  else:
    print("You think for a while")
    time.sleep(1)

# Check health points after the player has made a move
print("You now have ", hp, "health points")
if hp <= 0:
  print("You are dead. I am sorry.")

print("Your adventure has ended, goodbye.")
```

Test to see if your code works by saving the file as `AdventureGame1.py` in your `Documents` directory on the Raspberry Pi and then running it (see Figure 5-12). (Be sure to add the `1` in the filename to keep this file separate from your original `AdventureGame.py` file.)

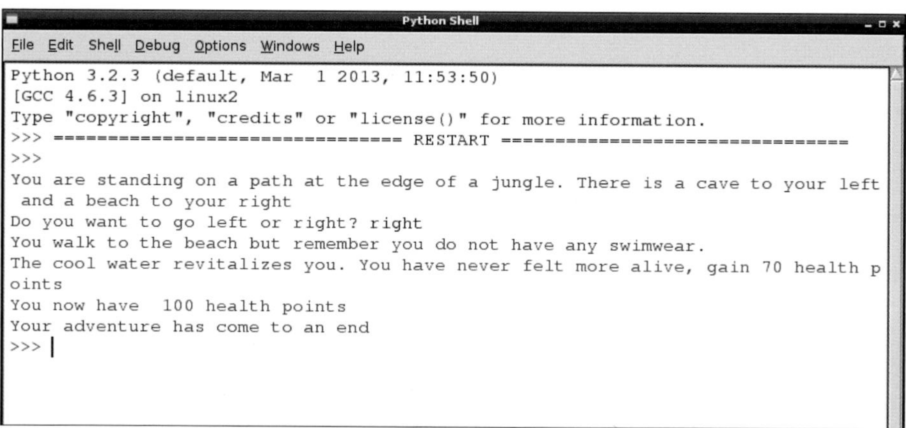

FIGURE 5-12 Using Run Module in Python to play `AdventureGame1.py`

Defining Functions

Although the game works, you will find it difficult to scale it up to include more locations and directions, such as going into the cave and then deeper into the cave, especially if the game relies on input from players to make decisions. You could add more conditionals by copying and pasting those you have already created but your code will get messy and out of control very quickly. It will also be difficult to locate any bugs, or make changes without introducing even more bugs!

The best solution is to create your own functions. Until now you have been using pre-existing functions from other Python modules such as `time` and `random`, but you can also create your own. Writing your own functions is easy; for example, this is how you would write a function called multiply that multiplies its two arguments and returns the result:

```
def multiply(m, n):
  return m * n
```

Just like the functions you used earlier in this adventure, these can take a number of arguments and return a result. They are a very useful way of organising your code. You can use various ways to reorganise your code into different functions. This process is called **refactoring** and is a logical process when developing computer programs. One way of reorganising the adventure game you have created so far is to create and use two functions: `get_input()` and `handle_room()`. These functions are described in the following sections.

Refactoring is a way of restructuring code you have already written to make it more efficient and easy to read, and to avoid bugs. If you find yourself copying and pasting large sections of code, this is usually a good indicator that you need to refactor your code!

The get_input Function

The `get_input()` function will keep asking the player to enter input (using the text in the prompt argument) until it matches one of the accepted inputs. For example:

```
get_input("Do you want to go left or right? ", ["left", "right"])
```

This function will keep asking the player the same question until she types one of the accepted inputs, which in this case are **left** and **right**.

The handle_room Function

The handle_room() function will contain the main logic for changing locations in the adventure game. The function will take the current location as its argument, and then use conditionals to decide what to do based on that location. For most locations, the function will ask the player to input a direction. The specific input determines which location the player will move to next.

Creating a Main Game Loop

Up to this point, you wrote all of your game logic in the while loop. With the following code, you move most of the logic into separate functions, avoiding repetitive code. The new loop calls the handle_room() function to perform a task appropriate for the current room, and then updates the location variable with the new room. This is a little more advanced than the code you have written so far. It will require you to check and double-check that your indentation is correct and you have not made any syntax errors!

Open a new text editor window and save the file as AdventureGame2.py in your Documents directory. Follow the steps below to add functions to your adventure game.

You can download the completed AdventureGame2.py code file from the companion website at www.wiley.com/go/adventuresinrp but, as I mentioned earlier, you will learn more by typing in the code as you read through the steps.

1. Begin by creating the health point variable as before; it is important to do this at the start as it is a *global* variable, meaning it can be accessed by the functions you will define:

```
# Create health points variable
hp = 30
```

2. Next, define the first of the functions, get_input(). The word def introduces a function definition. This function will ask for input from the player with the given prompt, and as it contains a while loop it will keep retrying until the player types one of the words in the accepted list, **left** or **right**. The in keyword allows you to check easily whether a value is *in* a list or not.

```
def get_input(prompt, accepted):
  while True:
    value = input(prompt).lower()

    if value in accepted:
```

```
      return value
    else:
      print("That is not a recognised answer, ⮐
        must be one of ", accepted)
```

3. Now define the function `handle_room()`, which takes the current location, performs an action based on that location, and then returns the new location. For example, if the location is `start`, the game will ask which direction the player wants to go and use that answer to move the user to a new room.

Remember to indent your code correctly here, as three levels of indentation are being used.

```
def handle_room(location):
  global hp


  if location == "start":

    print("You are standing on a path at the edge of a ⮐
      jungle. There is a cave to your left and a beach to ⮐
      your right.")
    direction = get_input("Do you want to go left or right? ",
      ["left", "right"])

    if direction == "left":
      return "cave"
    elif direction == "right":
      return "beach"

  elif location == "cave":
    print("You walk to the cave and notice there is an ⮐
      opening.")
    print("A small snake bites you, and you lose 20 ⮐
      health points.")
    hp = hp - 20

    answer = get_input("Do you want to go deeper?",
      ["yes", "no"])
    if answer == "yes":
      return "deep_cave"
    else:
```

```
    return "start"

  elif location == "beach":
    print("You walk to the beach but remember you do ⮐
      not have any swimwear.")
    print("The cool water revitalizes you. You have never ⮐
      felt more alive, gain 70 health points.")
    hp += 70

    return "end"

  else:
    print("Programmer error, room ", location, " is ⮐
      unknown")
    return "end"
```

4. Now add a loop to the game that loops until the player reaches the special end location that ends the game.

```
location = "start"
# Loop until we reach the special "end" location
while location != "end":
  location = handle_room(location) # update location
```

5. As the game also relies on the player having health points, at each turn the program needs to check how many health points the player has and determine that the player is not dead, because this would end the game.

```
  # Check we are not dead each turn
  print("You now have ", hp, "health points.")
  if hp <= 0:
    print("You are dead. I am sorry.")
    break

print("Your adventure has ended, goodbye.")
```

Each time around, the loop checks that the health points are greater than or equal to zero (checking that the player is not dead!) so that the game can continue. The loop will also end if the location returned by handle_room is end, a special room name indicating the end of the game. Figure 5-13 shows the refactored code using functions in the Python adventure game.

CHALLENGE

Compare the code of `AdventureGame2.py` to `AdventureGame1.py` and note the changes. Do you think refactoring the code was a good idea?

How can you add more locations to the code you have created so far for the adventure game?

How many different times must you run the program to try all possible paths through the code to make sure that it works?

Can you add the inventory list to the text adventure game so that the player can make decisions about using objects?

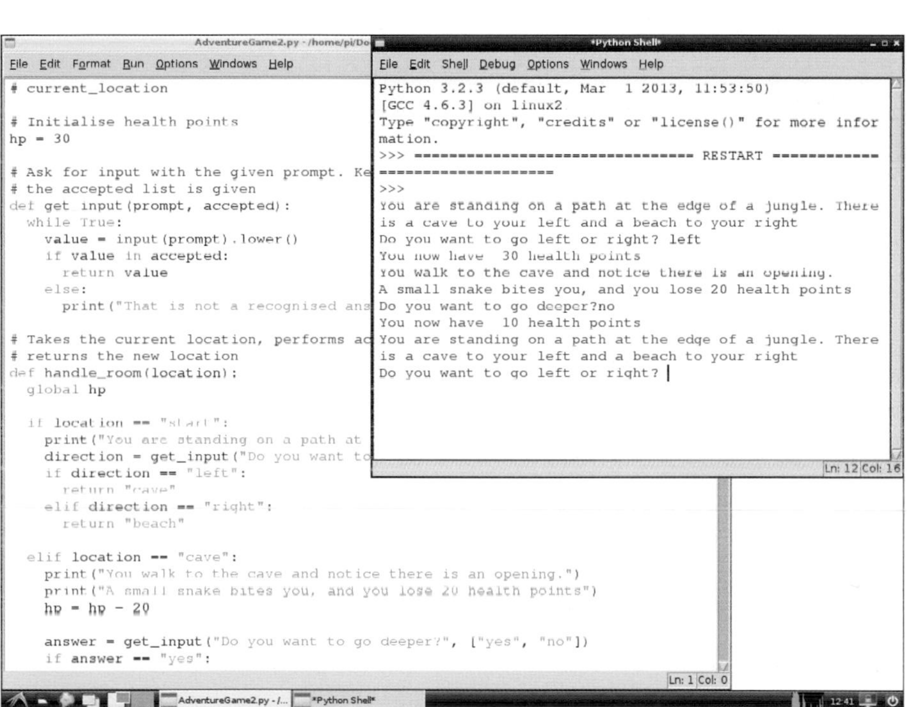

FIGURE 5-13 The Python Adventure Game in action, using the newly defined functions

Continuing Your Python Adventure

If you want to learn more about programming in Python on your Raspberry Pi, you can find a wide assortment of resources. Here are a few to try:

- For more detailed information on Python basics, I recommend *Python Basics* by Chris Roffey (Cambridge University Press, 2012).
- The official Python documentation is available at `http://docs.python.org/3`.
- Visit `http://inventwithpython.com` for links to online PDFs that teach you how to invent your own computer game with Python.

Python Command Quick Reference Table	
Command	**Description**
`#`	The `#` symbol is used at the beginning of a code line to indicate the line is a comment, not part of the program's instructions to the computer.
`\n`	Returns a new line in a string.
`break`	Breaks out of a `for` or `while` loop.
`def`	Allows you to define a function of your creation.
`elif`	Short for 'else if', the `elif` syntax allows you to create multiple conditions that make something happen when they return a value of `true`.
`for`	`for` loops are traditionally used when you have a piece of code which that you want to repeat x number of times.
`if`	Sets a condition which, if true, makes something happen.
`if…else`	Sets a condition which, if true, makes one set of things happen, or if false makes a different set of things happen.
`import`	Imports modules and libraries to add more functionality to your code.
`input()`	A function that asks for user input and converts it into a string.
`inventory = ["Torch", "Pencil", "Rubber Band", "Catapult"]`	An example of a list in python. Lists can contain values or strings that are separated by commas and encased in square brackets.
`name = value`	An example of a variable.
`print()`	A function that prints anything inside the brackets.
`print(inventory[3])`	An example of using the `print()` function to print item number 3 in the inventory list.
`random`	A Python module that returns a random value.

Command	Description
`return`	The `return` keyword is used when a function is ready to return a value.
`time`	Python module that provides various time-related functions, such as `sleep`.
`while`	A `while` loop continually repeats if a given condition is true.

Achievement Unlocked: You can program in Python on your Raspberry Pi!

In the Next Adventure

The next chapter introduces you to the computer game Minecraft—more specifically, you'll use the Minecraft Pi version created for use on the Raspberry Pi. This special version of the game allows you to use Python programming code to manipulate the Minecraft world in some way. For example, you will learn how to post messages to the chat window, add different blocks to create structures, and teleport across the Minecraft world in which your player is located.

Adventure 6
Programming Minecraft Worlds on the Raspberry Pi

MINECRAFT IS A computer game that allows you to build any computer world you like, by using virtual building blocks (see Figure 6-1). You can let your imagination run riot—there are no limits! The game was created by Markus Persson (who also goes by the gamer tag *Notch*). Players collect (or *mine*) blocks from the world around them, using nothing but a trusty axe, while avoiding monsters who might be set on eliminating them. You can learn more about Minecraft and register to play an online demo version at `https://minecraft.net`.

FIGURE 6-1 Minecraft

Downloading and Installing Minecraft

Minecraft is available to download onto the Raspberry Pi as the Minecraft Pi application. It is similar to the Minecraft Pocket Edition. As with all extra applications, you will need to connect your Raspberry Pi to the Internet in order to download it. It's likely that Minecraft Pi will be pre-installed in future versions of the Raspbian operating system, enabling you to run it by using the menu system or by clicking on the desktop icon. If your version of Raspbian does not include Minecraft Pi, you will need to follow these steps to download and install it onto your Raspberry Pi:

For a video that walks you through setting up Minecraft Pi, visit the companion website at `www.wiley.com/go/adventuresinrp`. Click the Videos tab and select the MinecraftPiSetup file.

1. Open the LXTerminal by double-clicking the icon on the desktop.
2. To download Minecraft, type:

```
cd ~
wget https://s3.amazonaws.com/assets.minecraft.net/pi ⮐
  /minecraft-pi-0.1.1.tar.gz
```

The tilde character (~) after `cd` takes you to the home directory of the user who is currently logged in. If you have logged in as the user Pi, the first line will change directory to `/home/pi`. When you first open LXTerminal after logging into your Raspberry Pi, you will automatically be located in your home directory and so this first line is not necessary.

It will take a few seconds, depending on your Internet connection speed, for the download to start. A progress bar will appear in the terminal window for you to check how long the download will take, as shown in Figure 6-2. When it has reached 100% you can move on to Step 3.

3. The file that you have downloaded is a `.tar.gz` file, an archive file similar to a `.zip` file, so you need to extract the game files. Type the following code to extract the game files from the `.tar.gz`:

```
tar -zxvf minecraft-pi-0.1.1.tar.gz
```

This command will extract the Minecraft Pi files into your home directory on the Raspberry Pi. You will only need to do this once—to load Minecraft Pi in future, you only need to use Step 4.

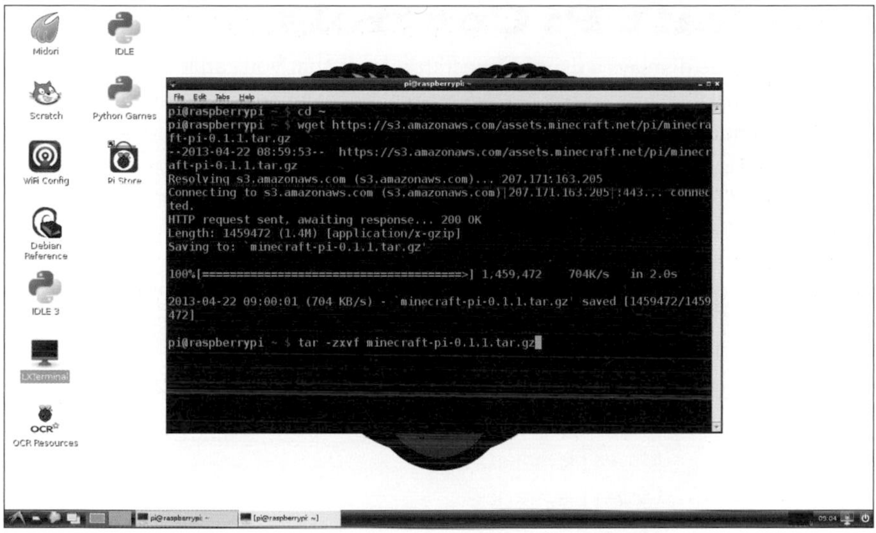

FIGURE 6-2 Minecraft Pi downloading and extraction commands via the LXTerminal on Raspberry Pi

4. To run Minecraft Pi, type these lines:

```
cd mcpi
./minecraft-pi
```

You may remember using the `cd` command in previous adventures to change directories or folders from the command line. You use it here to move from `/home/pi` into the directory `/home/pi/mcpi` where the `minecraft-pi` game is located. Run the command `./minecraft-pi` to start the game. You'll see a screen similar to Figure 6-1.

DIGGING INTO THE CODE

Are you wondering about some of the commands and terms in the code? Here's a short breakdown of some of the new bits.

- A `.tar.gz` file is an archive file, containing other files. `tar` is also an application that allows you to extract the files from within the archive.
- `-zxvf`, used in Step 3, are extra flags to the `tar` command that change the way it extracts the files inside the archive. You can get a list of flags to any command by checking the online manual; for example, type `man tar` to see all the options for the `tar` command.
- The `wget` command is used to get content, such as an archive file (`.tar`) from a web server where it is stored. The name `wget` comes from *World Wide Web* plus *get*.

Minecraft Pi Controls

Clicking Start Game displays a list of Minecraft worlds that you can join. On your first go, however, this list will be empty. Click Create New to generate a Minecraft world in *build* mode. Minecraft has two modes, *survival* and *build*. In build mode, you are able to construct objects without having to avoid monsters who may end your life. Play around a bit and familiarize yourself with the controls for playing Minecraft in build mode, shown in Table 6-1.

Table 6-1 Minecraft Pi Controls

Key press/mouse movement	Action
W	Moves player forwards.
A	Moves player left.
S	Moves player back.
D	Moves player right.
Spacebar	Makes player jump. Tap the spacebar twice to make the player fly.
Tab	Releases the mouse so you can click on other windows.
Esc	Returns you to the menu.
Move the mouse	Allows you to see around the player and point the player in a particular direction.
Left mouse click	Breaks the blocks around you.
Right mouse click	Places a block.

Being able to play Minecraft is one fun aspect of Minecraft Pi, but what is more exciting is being able to use Python code to manipulate the Minecraft environment. Time to dive in.

Minecraft Pi has programming libraries for Java and Python but not Python 3, which you have been using so far in this book.

In previous adventures you have used the Python 3 shell—IDLE 3. In this adventure, however, you will create and run your Python Minecraft programs from the command line using the LXTerminal and the text editor nano. This is slightly more advanced, and you will find it slightly quicker than running all your Python programs in IDLE.

Your First Minecraft Pi Python Program

Now that you have installed Minecraft Pi for the Raspberry Pi, it's time to see what adventures you can have with code in the Minecraft world. In this project, you will run a Minecraft game and write a Python script from the command line in LXTerminal to test that your connection to the game works. You'll do this by displaying a message in the game.

To see a tutorial for this part of the Minecraft Pi Python program, visit the companion website at `www.wiley.com/go/adventuresinrp`. Click the Videos tab and select the FirstMinecraftPi file.

1. Begin by opening LXTerminal and running Minecraft Pi—if it is not already open—by typing the following lines:

   ```
   cd mcpi
   ./minecraft-pi
   ```

2. When Minecraft Pi has loaded, click on Start Game and select a world from the list that is displayed. (If you have not yet created any worlds, click Create New to enter build mode, as instructed earlier.)
3. Navigate back to the LXTerminal window with your mouse, and open a new tab by clicking File➔New Tab. You need an open tab so that you can type commands into LXTerminal while Minecraft Pi is running.
4. To make sure that you are in the right folder or directory to begin writing your code, type this command in your new LXTerminal tab window:

   ```
   cd api/python
   ```

5. To create your first Minecraft Pi program, open the nano text editor by typing this command:

   ```
   nano testmcpi.py
   ```

   This will open a text editor from the command line.
6. Type the following code into the nano text editor file:

   ```
   import mcpi.minecraft as minecraft
   ```

   As in previous Python programs you have created, here you are importing a module that you will need in your program—in this case, the `minecraft` module. Now type the following command (being sure to use the correct capitalization):

   ```
   mc = minecraft.Minecraft.create()
   ```

This line connects your program to Minecraft and allows you to start interacting with it. Remember, you must have Minecraft running and be in a game for your program to work.

7. Next, create a message string using the following code:

```
msg = "I am starting my Minecraft Pi Adventures"
```

Then type the following line to post your message to the Minecraft chat window:

```
mc.postToChat(msg)
```

8. Press CTRL+X to exit, and press Y (for yes) to save what you have written. The message `File name to write: testmcpi.py` will appear. Press Enter to confirm that you want to write to this file. You will then be returned to the command line in LXTerminal.

9. Now run your script by typing the following line in the LXTerminal tab window:

```
python testmcpi.py
```

You will see your message displayed in the Minecraft game window open on your screen, as shown in Figure 6-3.

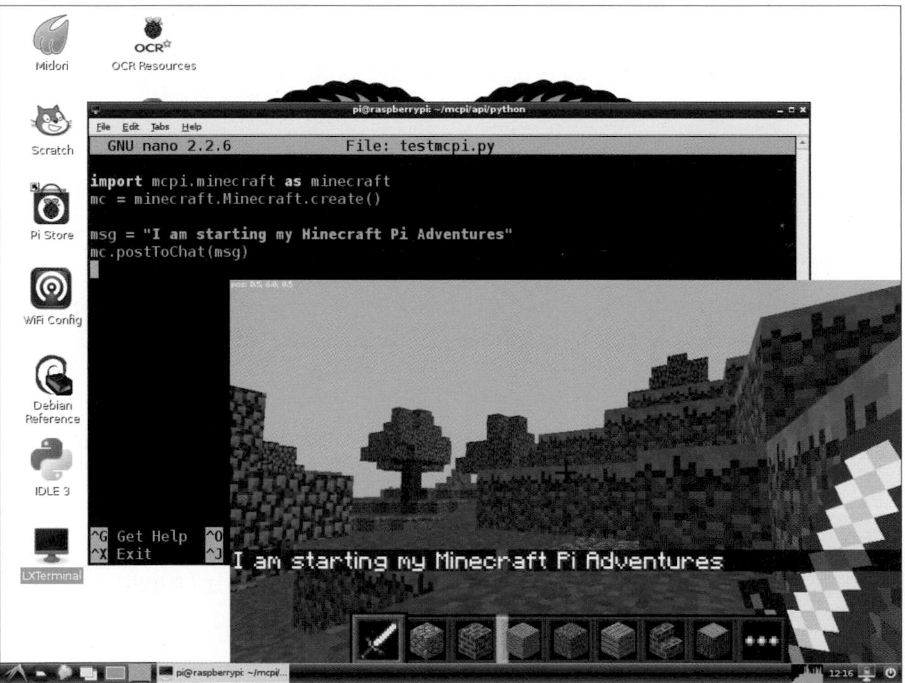

FIGURE 6-3 Your first Minecraft Pi Python program

Using Coordinates in Minecraft Pi

You can see how easy it is to make something interesting happen in the Minecraft game environment using Python code. Minecraft gives the appearance of three dimensions. To achieve this, Minecraft Pi uses x, y and z coordinates to generate a 3D environment, with x representing forward and back, y representing up and down and z representing left and right (see Figure 6-4).

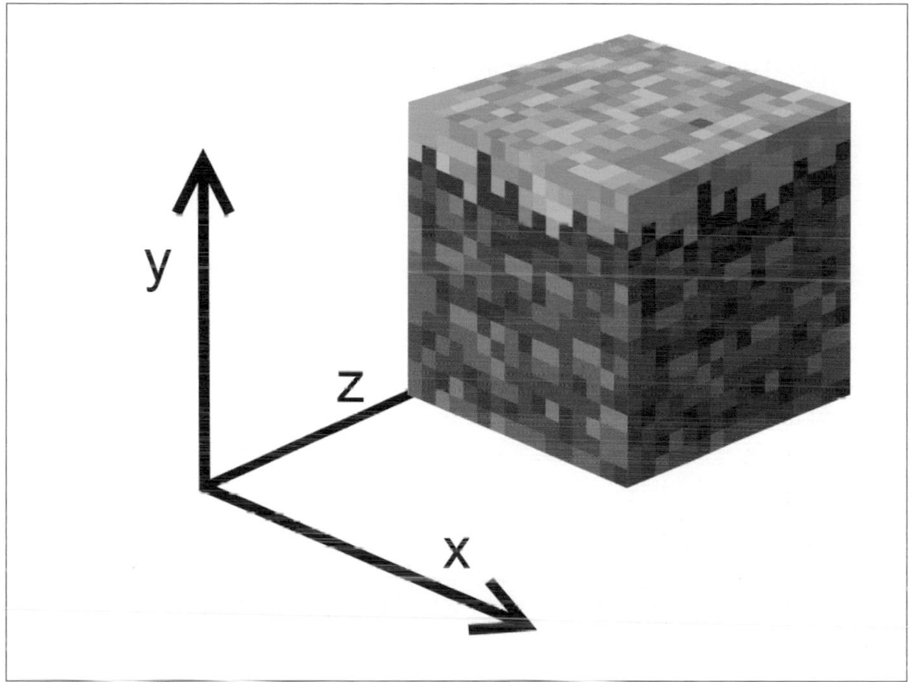

FIGURE 6-4 x, y and z coordinates

Finding the Player's Location

To understand coordinates within Minecraft, in this part of the adventure you will find out the current coordinates of your player and then transport her to a different location by changing the coordinates. Begin by writing a program to locate your player.

1. In an LXTerminal window, type the following commands to create a new nano text editor file called `location.py`:

```
cd mcpi/api/python
nano location.py
```

2. In the new text file, first import the modules you will need in this program by typing the following code:

```
import mcpi.minecraft as minecraft
import time

mc = minecraft.Minecraft.create()

time.sleep(1)
pos = mc.player.getPos()
```

In the last line, you use the command `getPos` or *get position* of your Minecraft player. Next, you want to display that information in the Minecraft chat window so you can see it in the game. To do that, type the following code:

```
mc.postToChat("You are located x=" +str(pos.x) + ", y=" ⮐
  +str(pos.y) +", z=" +str(pos.z))
```

`pos.x` will give the x coordinate, `pos.y` will give the y coordinate, and `pos.z` will give the z coordinate.

3. Press CTRL+X on the keyboard to exit the nano text editor, ensuring that you press y (for yes) and Enter to save your code.

4. Run the program by typing the following command:

```
python location.py
```

The coordinates for the player's location are displayed in the chat window (see Figure 6-5).

DIGGING INTO THE CODE

`postToChat` requires a string, and `pos.x` is a number. `str()` converts the number into a string, and Python allows you to add different strings together to make one long string.

Changing the Player's Location

Now that you can easily detect your player's position within Minecraft, why not change her location? Amend `location.py` by typing **nano location.py** to open the file and adding the following lines of code at the end of your program:

```
time.sleep(2)
mc.postToChat("Get ready to fall from the sky!")

time.sleep(5)
mc.player.setPos(pos.x, pos.y + 60, pos.z)
```

When you run this code, the player will suddenly change position. The last line of code—`mc.player.setPos(pos.x, pos.y + 60, pos.z)`—adds 60 only to the y axis (up and down). The result is that the player is suddenly transported from her current position to the middle of the sky—and because the player has nothing to stand on, she starts to fall! In the next section, you'll discover how to give your player something to stand on.

FIGURE 6-5 Using `getPos` and `setPos` to locate and move a player in Minecraft Pi

Placing a Block

Traditionally, Minecraft is played by building structures such as shelters, homes and other buildings. In fact, you can build whole cities if you are good at the game and have spent lots of time farming and creating the different levels of material blocks. However, if you use a version of Minecraft that you can manipulate with code, you don't need to spend hours building a structure; you can simply program it to happen.

Before you start this section, it is important that you create a new world in Minecraft Pi by clicking on the Create New button after starting the game from the title menu. This will place the player at the home position. If you do not do this, you might not be able to see the blocks you create in the next section.

1. In the LXTerminal window, type the following commands to create a new nano text editor file called `placeblock.py`:

```
cd mcpi/api/python
nano placeblock.py
```

2. You need to import the `block` module from Minecraft Pi that allows you to use the Minecraft block names. Type the following code into the nano text editor window:

```
import mcpi.minecraft as minecraft
import mcpi.block as block
mc = minecraft.Minecraft.create()

mc.setBlock(1, 10, 1, block.STONE)
```

   The three numbers in the last line refer to the x, y and z coordinates (see Figure 6-4). This is followed by the block type you wish to use—`STONE` in this example (Figure 6-6). The result in Minecraft Pi will be a single block of stone hanging in the sky above the player.

3. Press CTRL+X to exit nano, ensuring that you press y and Enter to save your work. Test your code to see what happens.

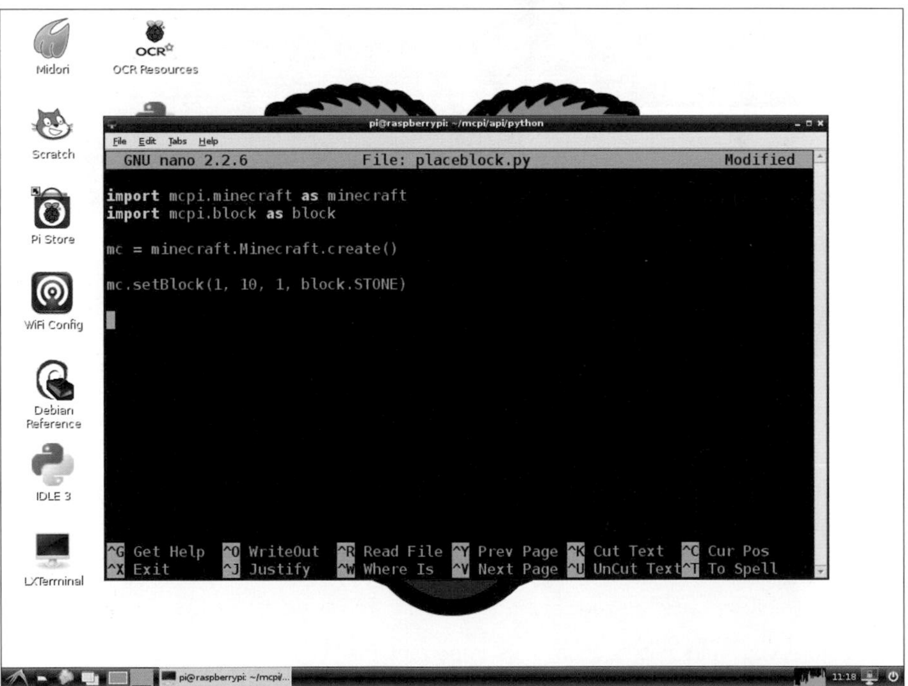

FIGURE 6-6 Using `setBlock` in Minecraft Pi

CHALLENGE

See if you can navigate to a new location, make a note of the coordinates and then place some different blocks using the `setBlock` command. You can find the full list of blocks supported in Minecraft Pi in the file `block.py`, which is located in `~/mcpi/api/python/mcpi/`.

Placing Multiple Blocks

Placing one block at a time is still going to be time-consuming and not very helpful if you want to build a bigger structure. But with the addition of one letter, you can place more than one block at a time.

So far, with `setBlock` you have been using one set of coordinates to tell the game where to place a single block. The `setBlocks` command (note the added `s` at the end) works in much the same way as `setBlock`. You start with a set of x, y and z coordinates that indicate where in the Minecraft world you want the blocks to be placed. Then the second set of x, y and z coordinates represent the number of blocks needed to make the shape you want to create:

```
setBlocks(x1, y1, z1, x2, y2, z2, blocktype)
```

For example, to generate a cube you would type:

```
setBlocks(0, 0, 0, 10, 10, 10, block.MELON)
```

The first three numbers are the location for where the blocks should be placed. The last three are the number of blocks. So the preceding code would place 10 `MELON` type blocks on the x axis, 10 on the y axis and 10 on the z axis, forming a cube (see Figure 6-7).

However, if you try to use this script you may not be able to find your cube of melons, as Minecraft Pi will set the blocks from the center location (`0, 0, 0`) of the world. Depending on the terrain, this could be inside a mountain!

It makes more sense to place the blocks where the player is located, so that you can find a nice empty spot for your cube. To do this, you need to get the player's position using the following code:

```
pos = mc.player.getTilePos()
```

DIGGING INTO THE CODE

Until now, you have used the position of the player as a starting point for interacting blocks; this allows you to find out what block the player is standing on or place blocks around the player. However, this poses a problem if you want to place multiple blocks. The x, y and z coordinates returned by the `getPos()` function are decimals (also known as *floats*), as your player can be in the middle of a block in Minecraft—but to interact with blocks you need to use whole numbers (aka *integers*). So instead, use the function `getTilePos()`, which returns the block (or tile) that the player is standing on.

CHALLENGE

Try changing the values for the block coordinates and see what cubes and cuboids (rectangular cubes) you can make. See Figure 6-7 if you need some guidance.

How might you use `setBlocks` to build a wall?

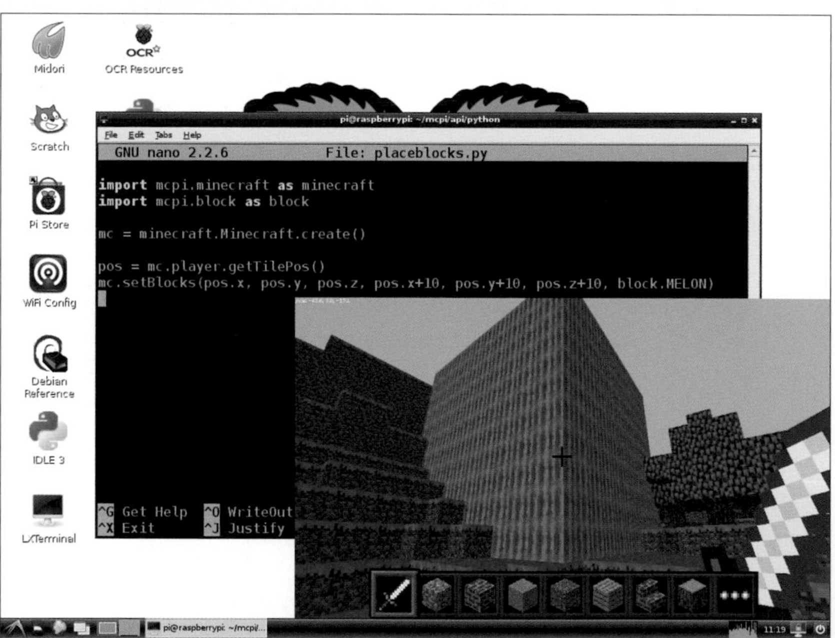

FIGURE 6-7 Using `setBlocks` to make a cube in Minecraft Pi

You can then use setBlocks, adding the coordinates of the player's location to indicate where you would like the blocks to be placed:

```
mc.setBlocks(pos.x, pos.y, pos.z, pos.x + 10, ⮐
  pos.y + 10, pos.z + 10, block.MELON)
```

You may find that you end up inside this cube because the first set of coordinates is the player's position! You could change the location coordinates in the same way:

```
mc.setBlocks(pos.x + 5, pos.y + 5, pos.z, pos.x + 10, ⮐
  pos.y + 10, pos.z + 10, block.MELON)
```

Try this yourself by modifying your existing code, and see if you can get it to work.

Creating a Diamond Transporter

When you are playing Minecraft in build mode, it takes a lot of time to move from one side of the world to the other. You can speed things up by creating a diamond block transporter to whisk you from location to location. To do this, you will use set Block, getPos and setPos.

To see a tutorial for diamond transporter program, visit the companion website at www.wiley.com/go/adventuresinrp. Click the Videos tab and select the DiamondTransporter file.

1. In the LXTerminal window, type the following code to create a new nano text editor file called transporter.py:

```
cd mcpi/api/python
nano transporter.py
```

2. Import the modules that you will need:

```
import mcpi.minecraft as minecraft
import mcpi.block as block
import time
```

3. Set up the connection to Minecraft and post a message to the screen:

```
mc = minecraft.Minecraft.create()
mc.postToChat("A Transporter Adventure")time.sleep(5)
```

The time delays are important in this code, so that you can move the player around the Minecraft world before the transporter blocks are placed.

4. Place a diamond block as the first transporter location, underneath the player's position:

```
transporter1 = mc.player.getTilePos()
mc.setBlock(transporter1.x, transporter1.y - 1, ⮐
  transporter1.z, block.DIAMOND_BLOCK)
mc.postToChat("1st Transporter created")
time.sleep(2)
```

5. Display a message on the screen to tell the player to move and find the second location where he wants to be able to transport to and from:

```
mc.postToChat("Find another location in 30 seconds")
time.sleep(30)

transporter2 = mc.player.getTilePos()
mc.setBlock(transporter2.x, transporter2.y -1, ⮐
  transporter2.z, block.DIAMOND_BLOCK)
mc.postToChat("2nd Transporter created")
time.sleep(2)
```

6. Create a `while true` loop to continually check the player's position. If the player is positioned on the first transporter diamond block location, her location will be changed to where the second diamond block is located. If the player is positioned on the second transporter diamond block location, her location will be changed to where the first diamond block is located.

```
while (True):
  time.sleep(1)
  pos = mc.player.getTilePos()

  if(pos.x == transporter1.x) and (pos.y == ⮐
    transporter1.y) and (pos.z == transporter1.z):
        mc.player.setPos(transporter2.x, transporter2.y, ⮐
          transporter2.z)
  if(pos.x == transporter2.x) and (pos.y == ⮐
    transporter2.y) and (pos.z == transporter2.z):
        mc.player.setPos(transporter1.x, transporter1.y, ⮐
          transporter1.z)
```

Figure 6-8 shows the code, and Figure 6-9 shows the diamond transporter in position.

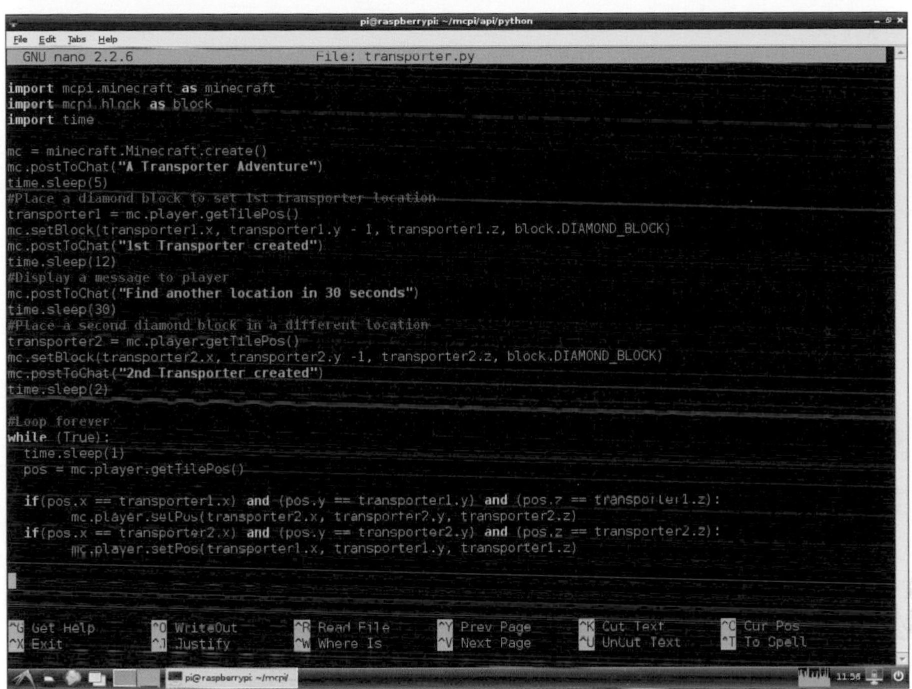
pi@raspberrypi: ~/mcpi/api/python
File Edit Tabs Help
GNU nano 2.2.6 File: transporter.py
import mcpi.minecraft as minecraft
import mcpi.block as block
import time
mc = minecraft.Minecraft.create()
mc.postToChat("A Transporter Adventure")
time.sleep(5)
#Place a diamond block to set 1st transporter location
transporter1 = mc.player.getTilePos()
mc.setBlock(transporter1.x, transporter1.y - 1, transporter1.z, block.DIAMOND_BLOCK)
mc.postToChat("1st Transporter created")
time.sleep(12)
#Display a message to player
mc.postToChat("Find another location in 30 seconds")
time.sleep(30)
#Place a second diamond block in a different location
transporter2 = mc.player.getTilePos()
mc.setBlock(transporter2.x, transporter2.y -1, transporter2.z, block.DIAMOND_BLOCK)
mc.postToChat("2nd Transporter created")
time.sleep(2)
#Loop forever
while (True):
time.sleep(1)
pos = mc.player.getTilePos()
if(pos.x == transporter1.x) and (pos.y == transporter1.y) and (pos.z == transporter1.z):
mc.player.setPos(transporter2.x, transporter2.y, transporter2.z)
if(pos.x == transporter2.x) and (pos.y == transporter2.y) and (pos.z == transporter2.z):
mc.player.setPos(transporter1.x, transporter1.y, transporter1.z)
^G Get Help
^X Exit
^O WriteOut
^J Justify
^R Read File
^W Where Is
^Y Prev Page
^V Next Page
^K Cut Text
^U UnCut Text
^C Cur Pos
^T To Spell

FIGURE 6-8 Code for the diamond transporter program for Minecraft Pi

FIGURE 6-9 The diamond transporter, ready for action!

CHALLENGE

Can you improve the transporter program in the following ways?

- Modify the code so that a player can set the second transporter location when and where she wants it. Instead of using a timer, you could use input!
- Modify the code so that it can post to chat with a countdown number every five seconds, so that the player knows how long she has left to move.

Sharing and Cloning Minecraft Pi Programs

When the Minecraft community meets the Raspberry Pi community, good things happen. Many people enjoy sharing the programs they have made for Minecraft Pi so that you can clone them or make copies of them to use on your own Raspberry Pi. You can find shared Minecraft Pi programs on the Minecraft Pi forum (`www.minecraftforum.net/forum/216-minecraft-pi-edition`) or the Raspberry Pi forum (`www.raspberrypi.org`). Many programmers who share their code use an online repository such as GitHub (`https://github.com`) so that you can easily download their code, try it out and help improve it. Why not have a go at downloading Martin O'Hanlon's Minecraft Cannon program? This program places a cannon where your player is positioned in Minecraft Pi. You use the LXTerminal command line to move the cannon up or down before firing blocks. Check out the video at `www.youtube.com/watch?v=6NHorP5VuYQ` to see it in action.

1. Open an LXTerminal window. If your Raspbian image is not up to date you may not be able to install the required applications, so first update your application packages by typing the following command into the terminal:

   ```
   sudo apt-get update
   ```

2. Next, type the following line:

   ```
   sudo apt-get install git-core
   ```

   This command installs an application called `git-core` that lets you clone the code that Martin has placed on a repository called *github*.

3. After `git-core` is installed, type the following code to have `git-core` create a clone of the Cannon program on your Raspberry Pi:

   ```
   cd ~
   git clone ⮐
     https://github.com/martinohanlon/minecraft-cannon.git
   ```

```
cd minecraft-cannon
```

4. Once you have navigated to the `minecraft-cannon` directory, type the following command to start the Minecraft cannon program:

```
python minecraft-cannon.py
```

Now you're ready to play with the cannon! To control the cannon, shown in Figure 6-10, you can use the following commands in LXTerminal window:

- `start`—Start up the cannon
- `rotate` [0-360 degrees]—Rotate the cannon between 0 and 360 degrees
- `tilt` [0-90 degrees]—Tilt the cannon upwards between 0 and 90 degrees
- `fire`—Fire the cannon
- `exit`—Exit and clear the cannon

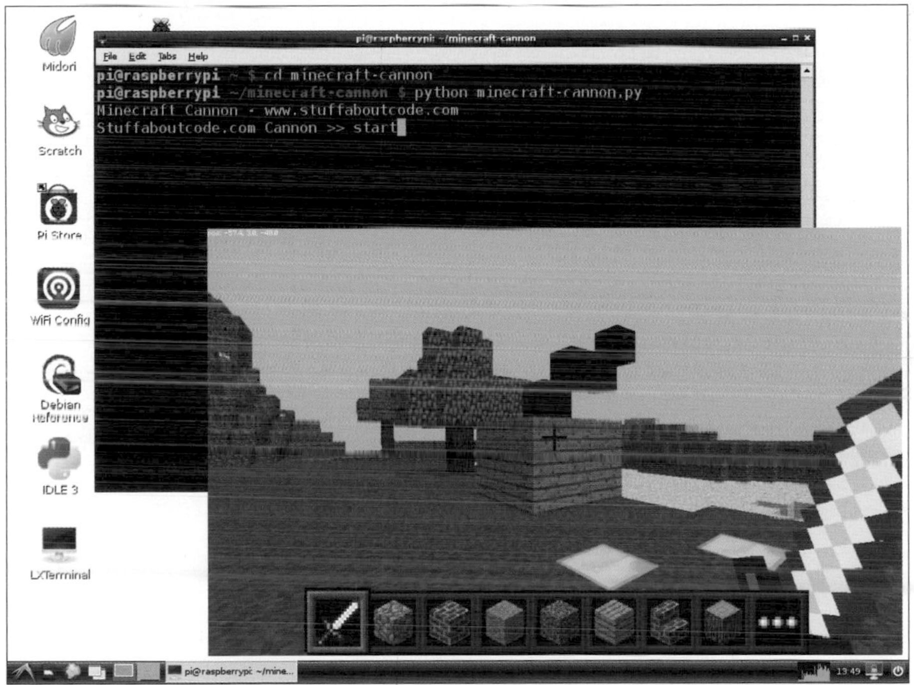

FIGURE 6-10 Minecraft Pi cannon

Further Adventures with Minecraft Pi

Minecraft Pi allows you to be really creative. As well as finding programs created by other people, you can find online tutorials to generate things like rainbows, bridges and other games like Snake inside your Minecraft world. Here's a list to get you started:

- Make a colourful rainbow with this tutorial: `www.minecraftforum.net/topic/1638036-my-first-script-for-minecraft-pi-api-a-rainbow`
- You can't go wrong following Martin O'Hanlon's Minecraft Pi tutorials on his website, *Stuff about="code"*: `www.stuffaboutcode.com/p/minecraft.html`
- Advance your programming skills using Craig Richardson 's Python *Minecraft Pi Book* (`http://arghbox.files.wordpress.com/2013/06/minecraftbook.pdf`) and API cheat sheet (`http://arghbox.files.wordpress.com/2013/06/table.pdf`)

Minecraft Pi Command Quick Reference Table

Command	Description
`cd mcpi`	Changes directory to `mcpi`.
`import mcpi.minecraft as minecraft`	Imports the Minecraft modules.
`mc = minecraft.Minecraft.create()`	Connects to Minecraft Pi by creating the Minecraft object.
`./minecraft-pi`	Opens Minecraft Pi from the LXTerminal or command line.
`pos = mc.player.getPos()`	Returns the players position with floats.
`pos = mc.player.getTilePos()`	Returns the players position with integers.
`postToChat(msg)`	Posts a message to chat in Minecraft Pi.
`setBlock`	Sets a block at coordinates.
`setBlocks`	Sets blocks between two sets of coordinates.
`setPos`	Sets the position of a player.
`wget`	Used to get content, such as an archive file (`.tar`) from a web server where it is stored.

Achievement Unlocked: Why dig when you can code with Minecraft Pi?

In the Next Adventure

In the next adventure, you'll transform your Raspberry Pi into an electronic synthesizer as you learn how to program music using an application called Sonic Pi!

Adventure 7
Coding Music with Sonic Pi

THE RASPBERRY PI can be many things—a standalone computer, a games machine and even a music synthesizer. The way we as humans interact with computers has changed over the years. Computers are no longer just devices on which to create text files or play computer games. They are also communication devices, transporters and musical instruments!

Creating music using computers is not a new idea. Computer music has its roots in electronics, and a growing number of musicians are turning to code to create new sounds. *Chiptune* is a style of music that uses sound chips from old computers and consoles from the 1980s and 1990s, like the Nintendo Game Boy. Pixelh8 (`www.pixelh8.co.uk/music/`) and 2xAA (`http://brkbrkbrk.com`) are chiptune artists and computer programmers, who program their music before it is performed. Other computer music programmers prefer to code their music live, feeling the atmosphere around them and responding to it with sound. They are called *live coders*. The band Meta-eX (`http://meta-ex.com`) are an example of a live coding group who perform at events, creating their code live on a big screen so the audience can see it as it happens (see Figure 7-1).

Your Raspberry Pi has a headphone/speaker jack port so that you can listen to sounds. You also have a keyboard and mouse that allow you to type code. In this adventure, you will put those features to good use by creating music with code using an application called Sonic Pi (`http://sonic-pi.net`). You will become a computer music programmer!

FIGURE 7-1 Live coding band Meta-eX's screen during a performance

Getting Started with Sonic Pi

To create music in this adventure you will use an application designed to be used on the Raspberry Pi called *Sonic Pi*. Sonic Pi was created by Dr Sam Aaron, a live coder of music, and is based on his more complex music system called *Overtone*. Sonic Pi may already be installed automatically as part of NOOBS Raspbian.

For a video that walks you through setting up Sonic Pi on your Rasperry Pi, select the SettingUpSonicPi video from the companion website at `www.wiley.com/go/adventuresinrp`.

To check whether Sonic Pi is installed on your Raspberry Pi, click on the main menu and navigate to Education➜Sonic Pi. If Sonic Pi is not on the menu, it is not already installed and you will need to download the application using the following instructions.

Make sure that you are using the most up to date NOOBS Raspbian operating system available.

1. In an LXTerminal window, first type the following command to update your application packages:

   ```
   sudo apt-get update
   ```

2. Next, type the following command to download and install Sonic Pi.

   ```
   sudo apt-get install sonic-pi
   ```

Once Sonic Pi is installed, it will appear on the main menu under Education. If it does not, simply reboot your Raspberry Pi and it will appear. Figure 7-2 shows the installation command being executed.

```
pi@raspberrypi ~ $ sudo apt-get install sonic-pi
Reading package lists... Done
Building dependency tree
Reading state information... Done
The following packages were automatically installed and are no longer required:
  libblas3gf liblapack3gf
Use 'apt-get autoremove' to remove them.
The following NEW packages will be installed:
  sonic-pi
0 upgraded, 1 newly installed, 0 to remove and 43 not upgraded.
Need to get 140 kB of archives.
After this operation, 512 kB of additional disk space will be used.
Get:1 http://archive.raspberrypi.org/debian/ wheezy/main sonic-pi armhf 1.0 [140
 kB]
Fetched 140 kB in 0s (678 kB/s)
```

FIGURE 7-2 Using `apt-get install` to download and install Sonic Pi

To be able to hear the sounds, you will need to connect your Raspberry Pi to a sound device. This can be headphones/earphones or speakers connected to the Pi using the jack port, or an HDMI TV or monitor with built-in speakers, connected with an HDMI cable.

The Sonic Pi Interface

Once Sonic Pi is installed, it will appear on the main menu under Education (see Figure 7-3). As Sonic Pi is a new application designed and created especially for the Raspberry Pi, you may not have encountered it before. You'll find it helpful to get to know the interface and what each panel is used for first, before creating your music. You may need to resize the application window to see the whole interface.

The elements of the Sonic Pi interface are identified in Figure 7-3:

- **The programming panel**—The main panel in Sonic Pi, on the left side. This is where you type your code to make music.
- **The output panel**—The upper panel on the right side. This is where you will see information about your program as it runs.

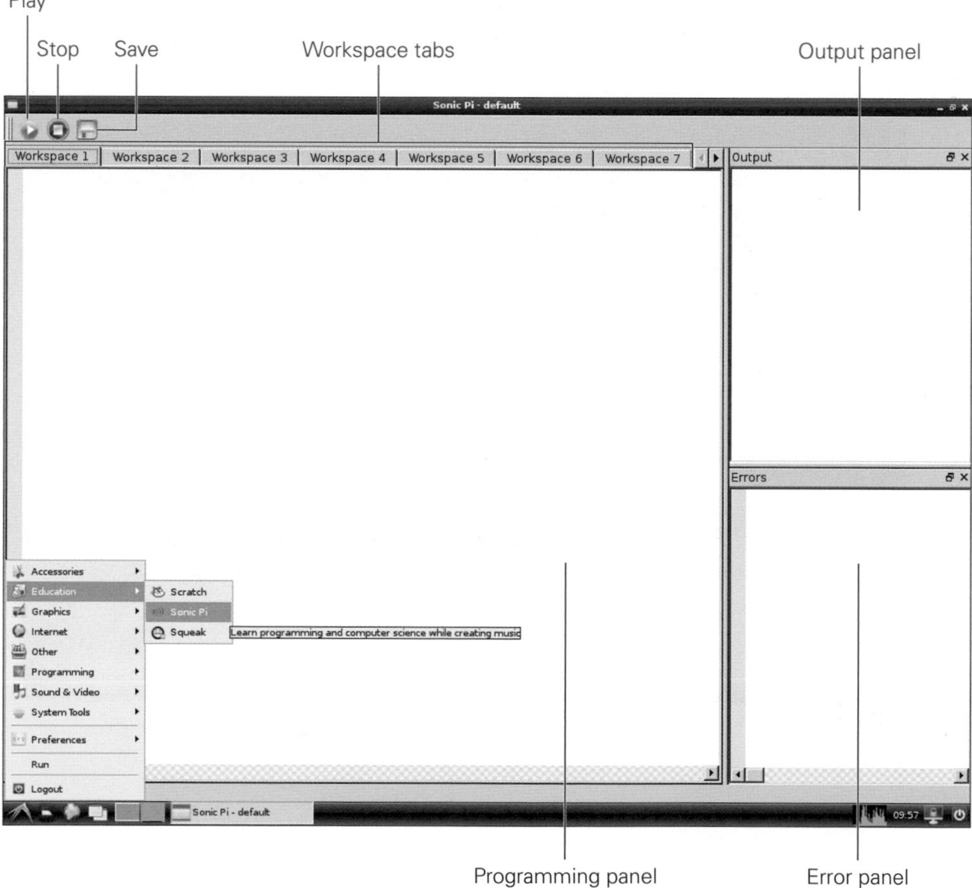

FIGURE 7-3 The Sonic Pi interface

- **The error panel**—The lower panel on the right side. This is where errors will be displayed if there is a problem with your program, or a bug—for example, if you have made a syntax error or perhaps mistyped a word.
- **Workspaces**—You can use different workspaces to create and save your code. In this adventure, you will use a different workspace for each exercise. You can move between workspaces using the tabs along the top of the programming panel.
- **Play and Stop buttons**—Click these buttons to start and stop your music scripts.
- **Save button**—Sonic Pi will automatically save what you write in the programming panel. However, if you want to save your code into a text file to store it elsewhere, you can use the Save button at the top of the application to do so.

Creating Your First Sounds with Sonic Pi

Now that you are familiar with the Sonic Pi interface, it's time to start making some noise! In this first project you'll learn how to play single notes, chords, how to add timings, and play *Twinkle Twinkle Little Star*.

Visit the companion website at `www.wiley.com/go/adventuresinrp` and select FirstSounds to see a video of this project.

1. To play your first note, open Workspace 1 and type the following:

   ```
   play 60
   ```

   Now click the Play button in the top left hand side of the application. Not only will you hear your note playing but you will see the following information displayed in the output panel, as shown in Figure 7-4:

   ```
   playing pretty_bell with: ["note", 60]
   ```

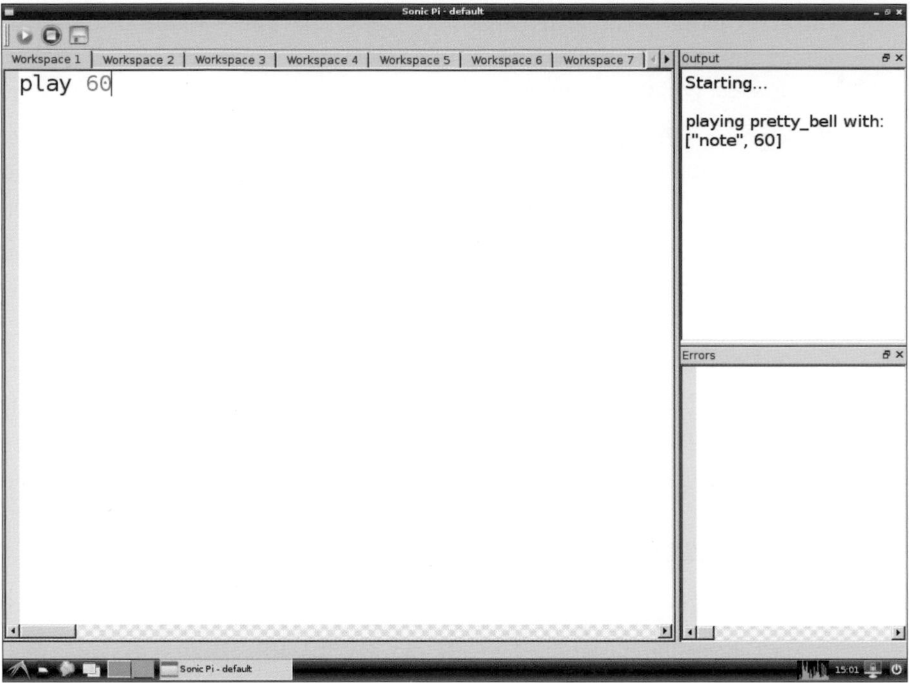

FIGURE 7-4 Creating sounds using Sonic Pi

2. The error panel should remain empty, because the application was able to run your code. Change your line of code so that it looks like this:

```
pley 60
```

Click the Play button. You will not hear anything, as Sonic Pi found a syntax error in your code because you misspelled `play`. You will see in the error panel that some information has appeared (as in Figure 7-5). Sonic Pi is letting you know there is an error.

3. Fix the error by changing `pley` to `play`. Now try playing a few notes one after the other in sequence by typing the following underneath your first note:

```
play 67
play 69
```

Click the Play button. It will sound like the notes are being played almost at the same time, like a chord. This is no good if you want to play *Twinkle Twinkle Little Star*, as all music is played to a beat. You need to introduce delays between each of the notes in the sequence.

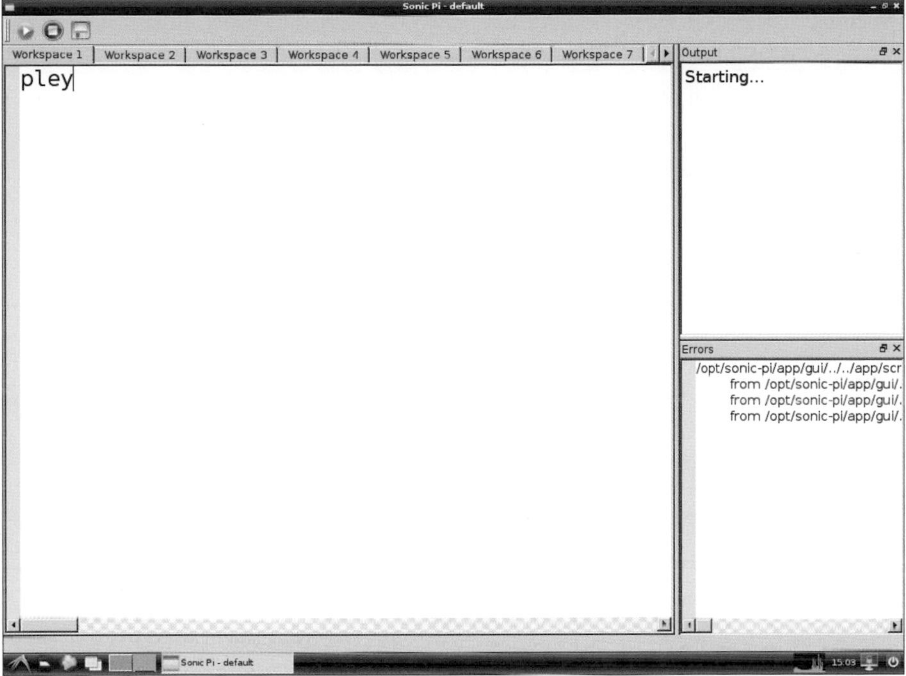

FIGURE 7-5 A syntax error in Sonic Pi

4. Add delays to your code by typing `sleep 0.5` in between each of the play instructions like this:

```
play 60
sleep 0.5
play 67
sleep 0.5
play 69
```

   Click the Play button. You will hear the notes play with half a second delay between them.

The numbers used after `play` in Sonic Pi represent notes. Each note is a key on a piano (`http://computermusicresource.com/midikeys.html`). The `play 60` is actually a C, and `play 69` is a G. These numbers are **MIDI** keyboard note numbers.

The numbers used after `sleep` represent timings: `1` is a second, and `0.5` is half a second.

DIGGING INTO THE CODE

You may notice that Sonic Pi does not use the same sort of programming language that you have used in previous adventures. It actually uses a different programming language called Ruby. Ruby uses the same computing concepts as Scratch and Python, such as conditionals, iteration, and data structures.

A **MIDI** keyboard, or Musical Instrument Digital Interface, is a musical instrument that can communicate with a computer. Piano sheet music notes and MIDI keyboard notes are the same, only sheet music notes are represented by letters G, C, A, and so on, whereas MIDI keyboard notes are represented by numbers. (In fact, MIDI note numbers are in semitone steps. G, A, B are tones whereas 67, 68, 69 are semitones.)

Twinkle Twinkle Little Star

You have the building blocks to generate a simple tune with notes C, G and A—or in this case `60`, `67` and `69`—along with delays in between those notes using `sleep` (see Figure 7-6).

Amend your code so that it looks like the following, and click Play:

```
play 60
sleep 0.5
play 60
sleep 0.5
play 67
sleep 0.5
play 67
sleep 0.5
play 69
sleep 0.5
play 69
sleep 0.5
play 67
```

Remember that Sonic Pi will run through each line in your code in sequence. You could go on and write the next part of the tune, but you will end up with a long list of `play` and `sleep`, which could get confusing to read, especially if you mistype a line and create a bug.

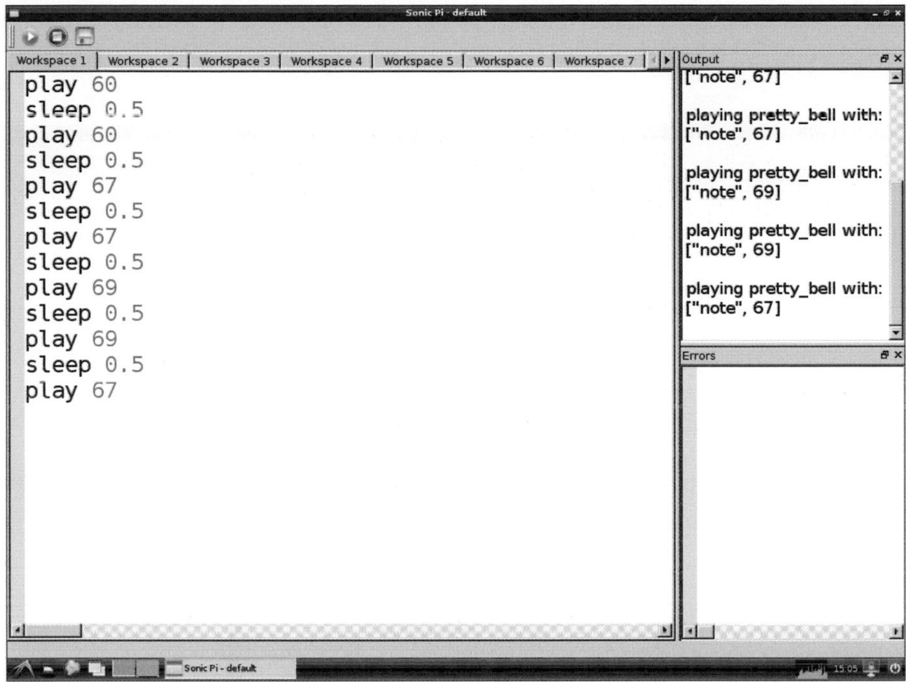

FIGURE 7-6 Using `play` and `sleep` to play *Twinkle Twinkle Little Star* in Sonic Pi

It makes more sense to rewrite this code using a **data structure**. In this case you can use a list like the ones you created in Python in Adventures 4 and 5. To create a list in Ruby, you use square brackets and separate the items in the list with commas in much the same way as in Python.

In computer science, a **data structure** is a particular way of storing and organizing related pieces of information. For example, in a list or array like `play_pattern [60, 67, 69]`, the list enclosed by square brackets in this line of code is an example of a data structure.

Type the following example list into Workspace 2 and click Play:

```
play_pattern [60,60,67,67,69,69,67]
```

You will notice that the same tune will play, but the delays between the notes are quite slow. To speed up the timing you can set the tempo. At the top of Workspace 2, above the line of code you have just written, type this line:

```
with_tempo 150
```

Click Play and the delay between the notes will decrease, giving the effect of speeding up the tune. The value `150` in this code is the beats per minute (BPM).

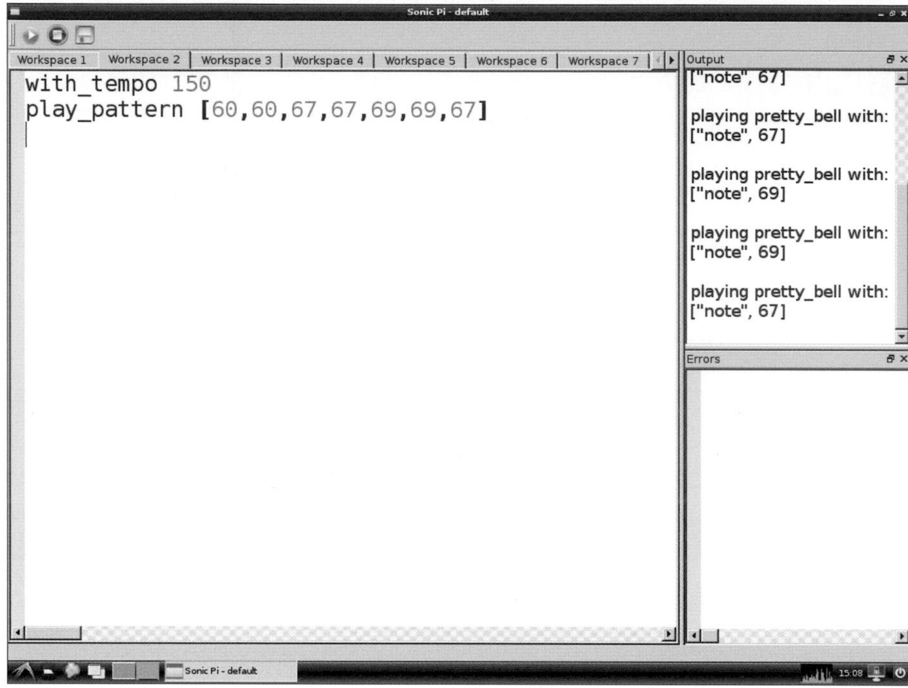

FIGURE 7-7 Using a list in Sonic Pi to play notes

Repeating Lines in a Loop

Musical tunes are sometimes made up of repeating notes or phrases. For example, in *Twinkle Twinkle Little Star*, the third and fourth lines, "up above the world so high" and "like a diamond in the sky", use the same notes. In your Sonic Pi code you could type these lines out twice, like this:

```
play_pattern [67,67,65,65,64,64,62]
sleep 0.5
play_pattern [67,67,65,65,64,64,62]
```

Or instead you could use a loop:

```
2.times do
  play_pattern [67,67,65,65,64,64,62]
  sleep 0.5
end
```

CHALLENGE

Can you recreate the rest of *Twinkle Twinkle Little Star* in code by translating the following musical notes into MIDI note numbers? Refer to the table at `http://computermusicresource.com/midikeys.html` to match the notes to the correct numbers.

Each line could be put into a `play_pattern [ ]` data structure:

C C G G A A G (You have already written this part of the song)

F F E E D D C

G G F F E E D

G G F F E E D

C C G G A A G

F F E E D D C

Can you translate another song into MIDI notes and recreate it using Sonic Pi?

For one more challenge, try introducing variables to define the notes. For example:

```
C=60
D=62
play_pattern[C,C,G,G,A,A,D]
```

All the code between `do` and `end` is repeated; in this case, `2.times` tells the program to play it twice. You will see that the colour of the words `do` and `end` have automatically changed to blue and are bold, as in Figure 7-8. Programs that use colours for syntax highlighting in this way make it easier for you to read your code. In this example it is important that the code you want to repeat is between `do` and `end`, so Sonic Pi highlights those words to show you this.

You could change the value `2` to make the loop repeat more times. For example, if you wanted to play the line five times you would type `5.times do`, followed by the code you want repeated, and then `end`.

Your *Twinkle, Twinkle* tune might not sound the way you expect it to sound. Can you figure out what you may need to add to improve it?

It is good practice to indent your code when you create loops in code. This will make it easier to read, especially if you are searching for a bug to fix to make your music play. All code between `do` and `end` should be indented. Press the spacebar on your keyboard twice to indent each line two spaces.

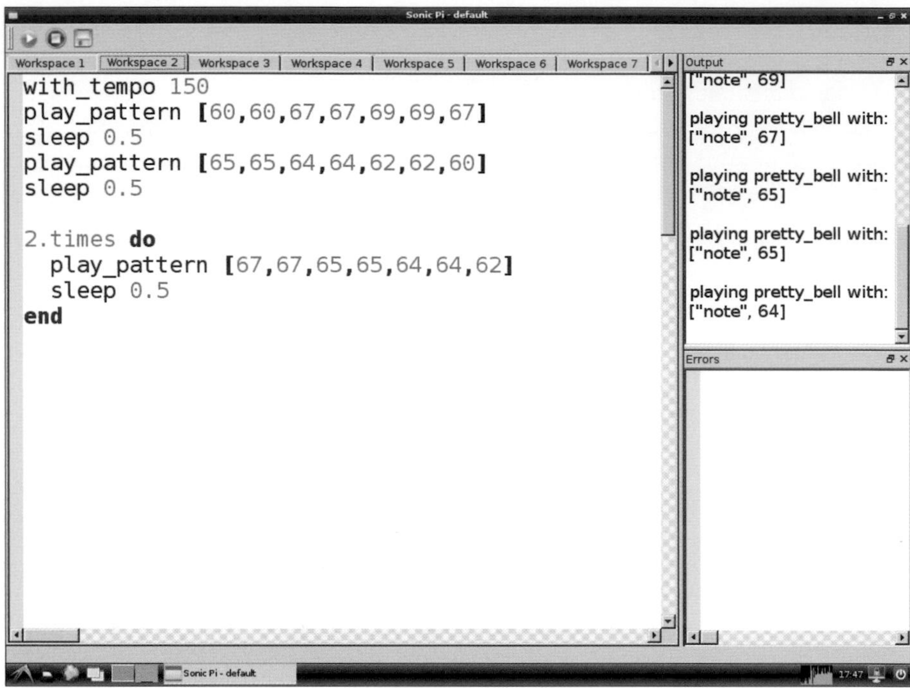

FIGURE 7-8 Using repeating loops in Sonic Pi

First Electronic Track

It's time to take a step up from nursery rhymes and start making some cool sounding electronic beats using Sonic Pi. In this project you will create a complete track in the style of the electronic artists mentioned earlier. Use a new Workspace to try the following exercises and adapt them to create a cool tune.

Visit the companion website at `www.wiley.com/go/adventuresinrp` and select ElectronicMusicTrack for a video of this project.

Using Different Synthesizer Sounds

So far you have used the default Sonic Pi synthesizer sound, called pretty_bell. You can change the sound by using the `with_synth` command, followed by the name of the synth (`fm`, in this example) in quotation marks:

```
with_synth "fm"
```

This line of code must be placed above the instructions to play a note, a pattern or a sleep, like this:

```
with_synth "fm"
5.times do
  play 49
  sleep 1
end

with_tempo 150
with_synth "pretty_bell"
2.times do
  play_pattern [67,67,65,65,64,64,62]
  sleep 0.5
end
```

Figure 7-9 shows the use of different synths in Sonic Pi.

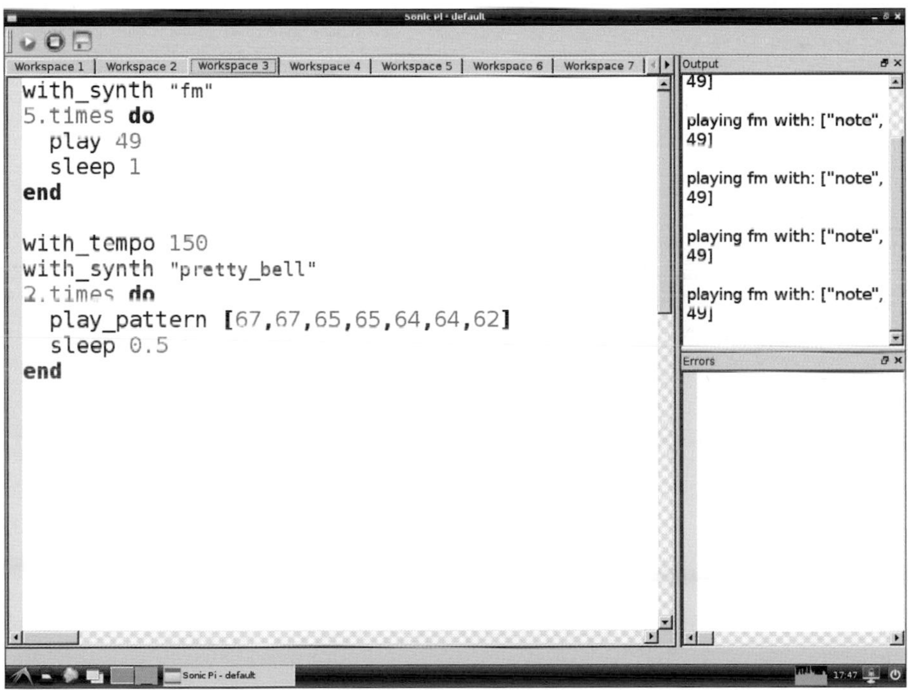

FIGURE 7-9 Using different synthesizer sounds in Sonic Pi

In this example, you would hear the MIDI note 49 play five times using the fm sound, and then the list of notes played twice using the pretty_bell sound.

The following list includes some different synths in Sonic Pi you can try out.

- pretty_bell
- dull_bell
- fm
- beep
- saw_beep

More sounds will be added to the Sonic Pi application in time, so be sure to watch for them and keep your Pi application packages updated using `sudo apt-get update`.

Creating a Surprising Tune

So far, you have run your music program in sequence and then using a repeating loop. To add an element of fun, you could add a junction using a conditional. You used conditionals in Adventures 3 and 5 in both Scratch and Python. Setting conditions allows different paths to be followed, as if you were at a junction.

Type the following example script into your current Workspace to try it out (see Figure 7-10):

```
10.times do
  if rand < 0.5
    play 42
  else
    play 30
  end
  sleep 0.25
end
```

The first line is the start of the repeating loop. Everything after `do` and before `end` will be played 10 times. The second line is the start of the conditional statement. The condition used here is like flipping a coin: `rand` stands for random, and it will return a random value between 0 and 1. If the value returned is less than 0.5 then this statement is true and the MIDI note 42 will be played. If the value returned is not less than 0.5, then the statement is false and MIDI note 30 will be played instead. Only one of the `play` steps will be run. To complete the condition, `end` is used. Each time the loop plays, a new value for `rand` is generated.

What do you think happens if the `rand` returns the value 0.5? Is the statement true or false?

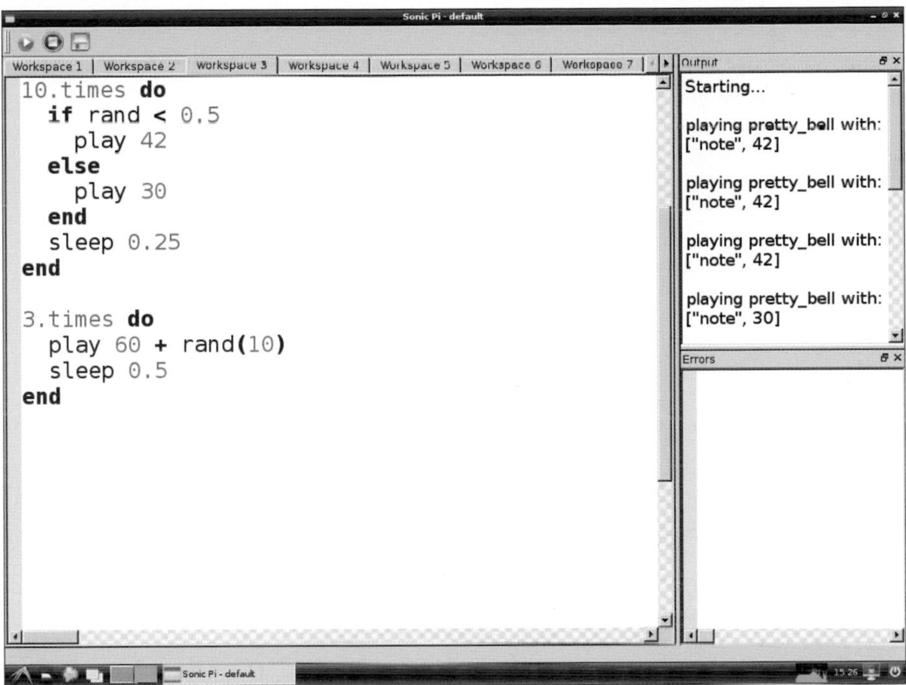

FIGURE 7-10 Using conditionals and random in Sonic Pi

Using "rand" to Play Random Notes

You can use `rand` in other interesting ways outside of a conditional too. For example, you could use it to play a random note in a sequence.

Underneath the conditional sequence, after the final end line, type the following:

```
3.times do
  play 60 + rand(10)
  sleep 0.5
end
```

The first line is the start of the repeating loop. Everything after `do` and before `end` will be played three times. The next line uses a calculation to determine what note it will play. The code `play 60 + rand(10)` will play a random note between 60 and 69 because you are adding a random number between 0 and 10 to 60 to make a random note each time; for example, 61, 68, 63. Changing the value of `play 60` sets the lowest note, whilst changing the value of `rand(10)` changes the range of the highest note.

This will make the music sound more interesting, especially if it is inside a loop, as each time it is played a different note could be heard between the MIDI note numbers you specify.

Using Algorithms

You don't always need to write brand new lines of code to add functionality to your programs. You can use built-in **algorithms** instead, as in this code:

```
play_pattern [60,72,65,80].sort
```

This code is an example of a sorting algorithm you can use in Sonic Pi. When the program is run, the algorithm will sort the numbers in the list into ascending order from lowest to highest.

You can also use `.reverse` to reverse the numbers in a list and `.shuffle` to randomly shuffle the numbers in a list as shown in the following code:

```
3.times do
  if rand < 0.5
    play_pattern [60,62,65]
  else
    play_pattern [60,62,65].reverse
  end
  sleep 1
end
```

In this code, shown in the Sonic Pi interface in Figure 7-11, `.reverse` has been used inside a conditional, so that if the random value returned by `rand` is less than 0.5 then the notes 60, 62 and 65 will play in order. If any other value is returned then the notes will be played in reverse.

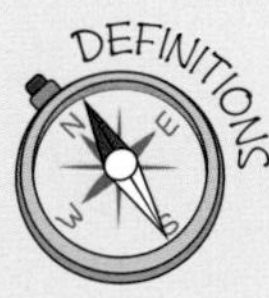

An **algorithm** is a set of rules to be followed to calculate or solve a problem. Common algorithms are those used for sorting information or data, as can be seen by the sorting algorithm animations at `www.sorting-algorithms.com`. Rather than writing a sequence of code to sort the MIDI notes that you used in a list in Sonic Pi, for example, you could use an existing sorting algorithm, `.sort`.

Running Two Scripts at the Same Time

Electronic synthesized music usually has a repeating beat that you can nod your head or dance along to, with a tuneful melody playing at the same time. This is similar to the way pianists typically play with two hands on a piano. One hand plays one set of notes of a song, usually in a lower octave, while the other hand plays a different set of notes.

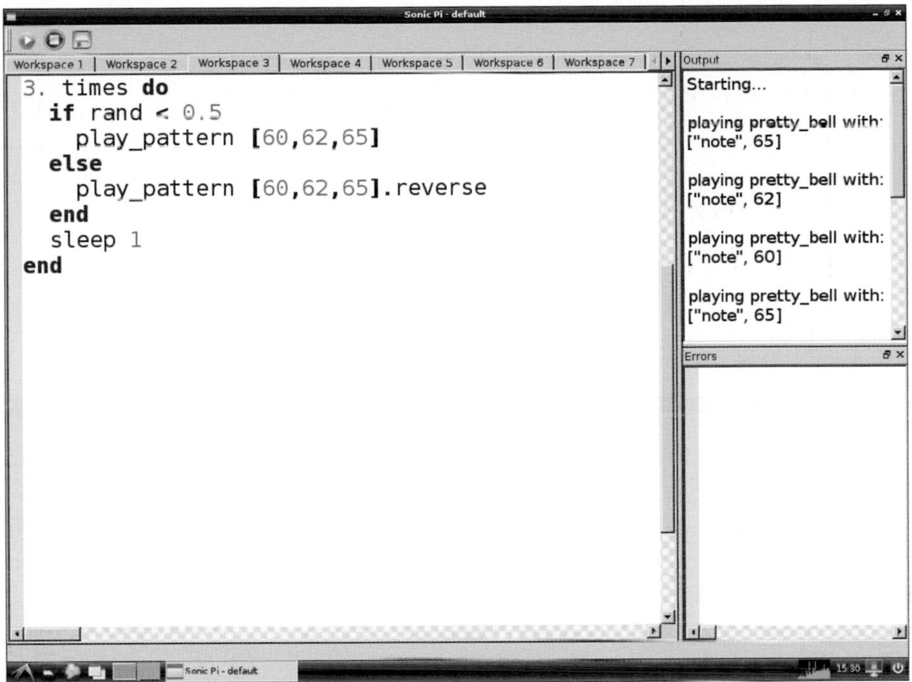
Sonic Pi - default
Workspace 1
Workspace 2
Workspace 3
Workspace 4
Workspace 5
Workspace 6
Workspace 7
3. times do
if rand < 0.5
play_pattern [60,62,65]
else
play_pattern [60,62,65].reverse
end
sleep 1
end
Output
Starting...
playing pretty_bell with: ["note", 65]
playing pretty_bell with: ["note", 62]
playing pretty_bell with: ["note", 60]
playing pretty_bell with: ["note", 65]
Errors

FIGURE 7-11 Using algorithms to change the order of notes in lists

In Sonic Pi you can use *threads* to run more than one script simultaneously, in much the same way as you can do in Scratch. To run multiple tunes at the same time, encase the first tune between `in_thread do` and `end`. For example:

```
in_thread do
  with_synth "saw beep"
  10.times do
    if rand < 0.5
      play 37
    else
      play 49
    end
    sleep 2
  end
end
```

Next, wrap a second tune between `in_thread do` and `end`, and place this code after the first block, as in Figure 7-12. Although this section of code is beneath the first in sequence, it will be played at the same time as the first thread, just as two hands can play the piano simultaneously.

```
in_thread do
  with_synth "pretty_bell"
  20.times do
    play 49
    sleep 1
  end
end
```

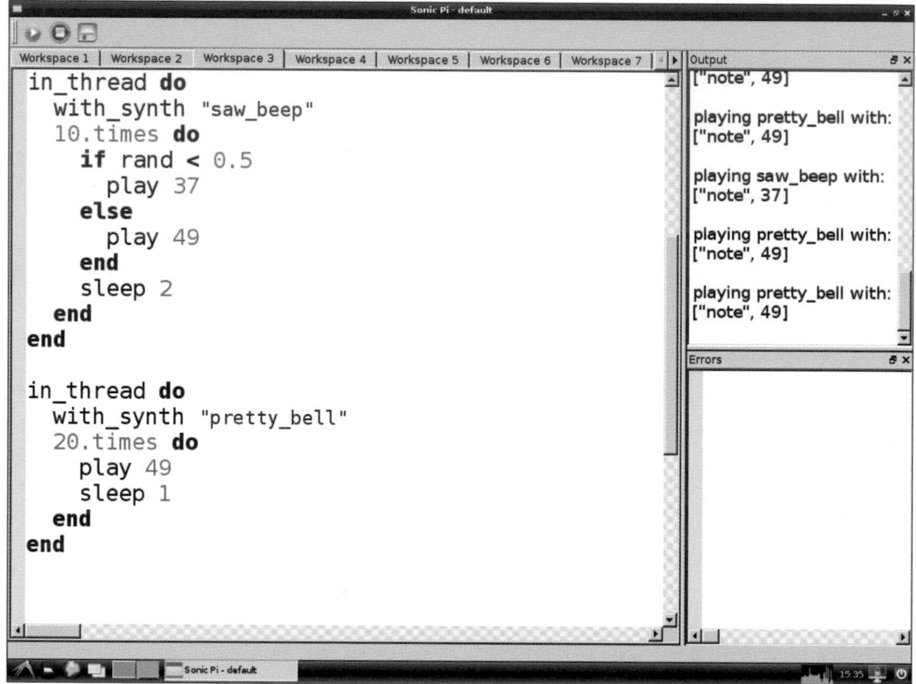

FIGURE 7-12 Playing multiple tunes at the same time using threads

Using the Mouse to Control Sound

There are other elements of computerised sound that you can use to create more interesting sounding music. For example, you may wish to add a background sound that never ends and that reacts to the movement of the mouse.

To use a background sound that never ends, type the following line at the top of your script:

```
play_pad "woah", 56
```

This will play the sound woah, which sounds very electronic, as a *pad* or background noise. The value 56 refers to the MIDI note. You can change the value and it will change the note of the sound.

You can also control this continual sound by moving your mouse left and right, to add an element of live coding and performance to your computer music. Underneath the first line, type:

```
control_pad "note", 57
```

Click Play, and move your mouse left and right, up and down. You will notice the sound change as you move it.

There are currently three pads available in Sonic Pi:

- `saws`
- `woah`
- `babbling`

You can add more pads at a later date.

Figure 7-13 shows a script using `play_pad` and `control_pad`.

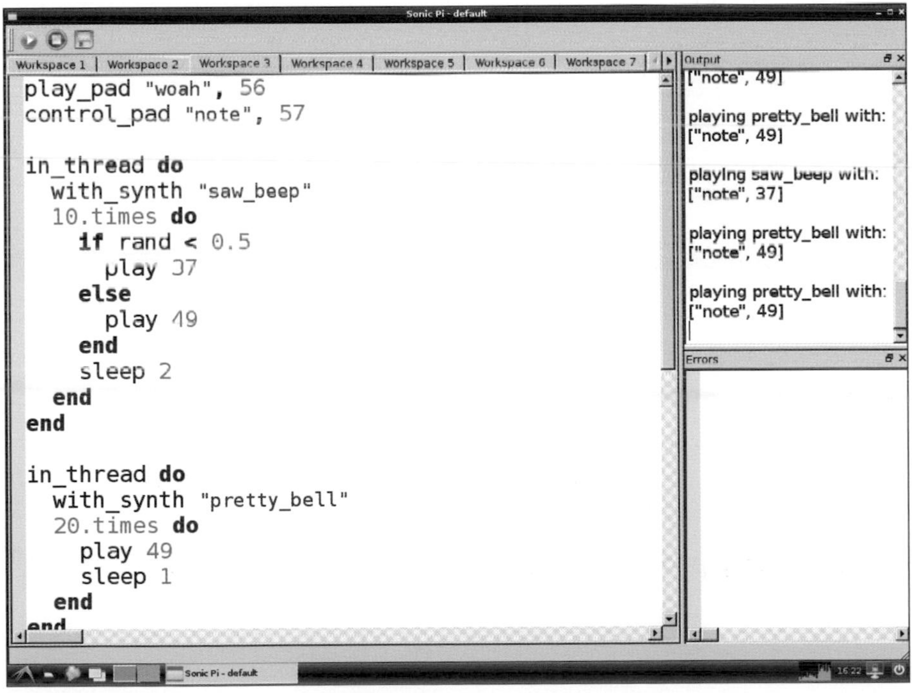

FIGURE 7-13 Adding pads in Sonic Pi

Further Adventures with Sonic Pi

If you have enjoyed learning how to make music using Sonic Pi and the programming language Ruby, you can continue having fun with it by looking at these resources:

- Sonic Pi website (`http://sonic-pi.net`)
- Kids Ruby (`www.kidsruby.com`)
- Live Coding Music (`http://toplap.org/category/music`)
- Official Ruby Documentation (`www.ruby-lang.org/en`)

Sonic Pi Command Quick Reference Table	
Command	**Description**

`in_thread do`
…
`end`
	Runs any code between `do` and `end` at the same time as another `in_thread` block.

`play x`	Plays note *x*.
`play_pad "woah", x`	Plays an ongoing sound effect or pad at note *x*.
`play_pattern [60,60,67,67,69,69,67]`	Plays a pattern of notes inside a list.
`rand`	Returns a random number.
`.reverse`	An algorithm that reverses the order of notes in a list.
`.shuffle`	An algorithm that shuffles the order of notes in a list.
`sudo apt-get install sonic-pi`	Downloads and installs the Sonic Pi application from the Raspberry Pi command line.
`with_synth "fm"`	Sets the synth sound; in this example, the fm sound.
`with_tempo 150`	Sets the speed at which notes inside a list will be played.

`x.times do`
…
`end`
	Runs any code between `do` and `end` *x* number of times.

Achievement Unlocked: Head bopping, toe tapping, creator of coded computer music with Sonic Pi!

In the Next Adventure

In the next adventure, you'll see that you can use Raspberry Pi as more than just a tool for programming. With a little knowledge of electronics you are able to create circuits, control lights and even use marshmallows as input buttons to control computer games—all thanks to the GPIO pins on the Raspberry Pi!

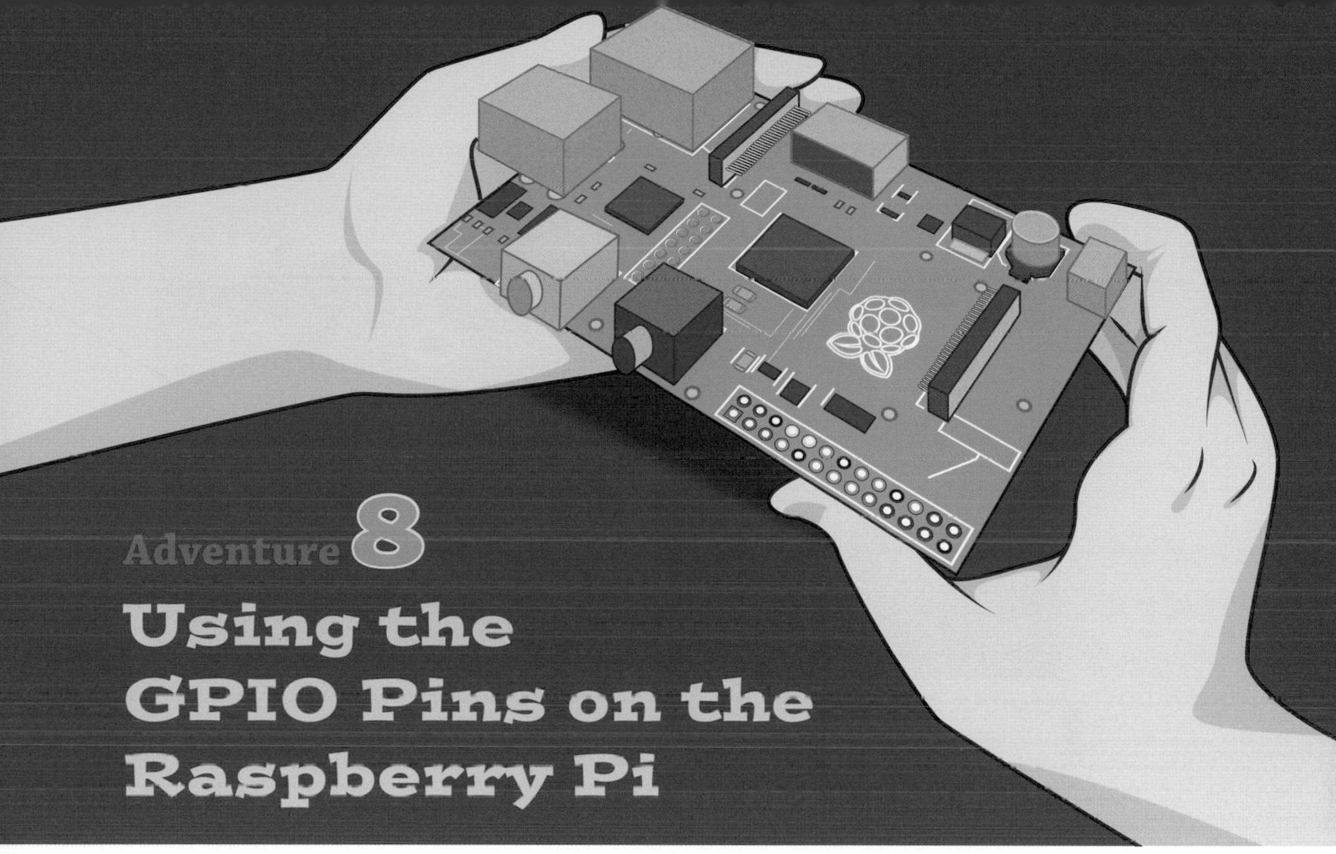

Adventure 8
Using the GPIO Pins on the Raspberry Pi

THE GENERAL PURPOSE INPUT OUTPUT (GPIO) pins on the Raspberry Pi are what make it really special. The behaviour of these pins can be controlled or programmed—by you! You can use the pins to sense and control physical objects in the real world, like lights and switches. The pins are located on the main board of the Raspberry Pi, shown in Figure 8-1.

In this adventure, you'll learn some basics of electronics and then discover how to **output** to a light-emitting diode (LED), making it light up using your Raspberry Pi. For the final project in the adventure, you'll hook up a marshmallow (yes, a real marshmallow) to **input** a signal to your Raspberry Pi to play a Scratch marshmallow game that senses the press of a button.

FIGURE 8-1 The General Purpose Input Output (GPIO) pins on a Model B Raspberry Pi

Input refers to the raw data or information that can be entered into a computer system like a Raspberry Pi before it is processed. An example of an input device is a push button or a microphone. The Raspberry Pi has pins that can be connected to these and other devices.

Output refers to the data or information that is communicated to you as it exits a computer system like a Raspberry Pi after it has been processed. An example of an output device is a speaker or monitor screen.

Using a Raspberry Leaf Diagram

Raspberry Pi projects using GPIO pins give you the opportunity to use electronics concepts and techniques to make something happen electronically, such as making an LED light up. Many of the pins have different purposes, and the instructions in this adventure tell you which pin to use for each connection.

There are two *revisions* of the GPIO pin layout. Later in this adventure you will learn how to find out whether your Raspberry Pi is a Revision (Rev) 1 or a Rev 2. It is important to know this before you begin any exercises in this adventure, as the instructions here are based on Rev 2. Figure 8-2 shows the layout of the pins on a Raspberry Pi Rev 2 board. You should refer to this diagram when connecting cables to the pins, and when writing your code to program them.

Raspberry Pi Revision 2

3.3V	1	2	5V
I2C1 SDA	3	4	5V
I2C1 SCL	5	6	GROUND
GPIO4	7	8	UART TXD
GROUND		10	UART RXD
GPIO 17	11	12	GPIO 18
GPIO 27	13	14	GROUND
GPIO 22	15	16	GPIO 23
3.3V	17	18	GPIO 24
SP10 MOSI	19	20	GROUND
SP10 MISO	21	22	GPIO 25
SP10 SCLK	23	24	SP10 CE0 N
GROUND	25	26	SP10 CE1 N

FIGURE 8-2 Raspberry Pi GPIO layout, Revision 2 board

You can find this diagram, along with a diagram of the Rev 1 board, at `www.hobbytronics.co.uk/raspberry-pi-gpio-pinout`.

If you have a Rev 1 Raspberry Pi, you can still follow the steps, but ensure that you refer to the layout diagram for your board and use the pin numbers from that diagram in your programs, and not those specified in the instructions.

To make it easier to tell which pin is which, Dr Simon Monk has created a *Raspberry Leaf* template with a label for each pin—you can cut these out and place them over the pins. It is a good idea to download, print and cut out a Raspberry Leaf to help you know which pins to use in the projects in this adventure. You can download the template from the Adventure in Raspberry Pi website or from Dr Monk's electronics website (`www.doctormonk.com/2013/02/raspberry-pi-and-breadboard-raspberry.html`). Dr Monk's site has templates for both the Rev 1 and Rev 2 boards; be sure to download the correct version for your board. Figure 8-3 shows the Raspberry Leaf for the Rev 2 board.

3.3V	O	O	5V
2 SDA	O	O	5V
3 SCL	O	O	GND
4	O	O	14 TXD
GND	O	O	15 RXD
17	O	O	18
27	O	O	GND
22	O	O	23
3.3V	O	O	24
10 MOSI	O	O	GND
9 MISO	O	O	25
11 SCKL	O	O	8
GND	O	O	7

FIGURE 8-3 The Raspberry Leaf for the Rev 2 board

You should take great care when connecting cables to the GPIO pins on your Raspberry Pi. There are two reasons for this. First, you should be cautious to protect yourself from harm. Second, the Raspberry Pi is a 3.3V device, and if you plug in anything at a higher voltage than that it will damage the processor and possibly render your board useless.

It is also very important that you connect any external components to the correct pins on the Raspberry Pi, so it is essential that you refer to the correct GPIO revision layout diagram.

Electronic Basics

You are delving into a new world of electronics by using the Raspberry Pi's GPIO pins. If you have never created any electronic circuits before, following the tutorials in this adventure will be a good place to learn basic electronics. To get started, you should become familiar with the electronic concepts and components in the following list.

- **Current** is the rate at which electrical energy flows past a point in a circuit. It is the electrical equivalent of the flow rate of water in pipes. Current is measured in amperes (A). Smaller currents are measured in milliamperes (mA).
- **Voltage** is the difference in electrical energy between two points in a circuit. It is the electrical equivalent of water pressure in pipes, and it is this pressure that causes a current to flow through a circuit. Voltage is measured in volts (V).
- **Resistors** are electrical components that resist current in a circuit. For example, LEDs can be damaged by too much current, but if you add the correct value resistor in series with the LED in the circuit to limit the amount of current, the LED will be protected. Resistance is measured in *ohms*. You need to pick a resistor with the correct value to limit the current through a circuit; the value of a resistor is shown by coloured bands that are read from left to right. The exercises in this adventure will use some resistors and explain how to read the value.
- A **diode** is a device that lets current flow in only one direction. A diode has two terminals, called *anode* and *cathode*. Current will flow through the diode only when positive voltage is applied to the anode, and negative voltage to the cathode.
- A **light-emitting diode** or **LED** is a diode that lights up when electricity passes through it. An LED is an example of an output device. LEDs allow current to pass in only one direction. They come in a variety of colours, and have one short leg and one long leg, which helps you to determine which way round they need to be placed in a circuit for current to flow through them. The exercises in this adventure will use some LEDs.
- A **capacitor** is used to store an electric charge. The capacity that this component has is measured in farads (F). A farad is a very large quantity, so most of the capacitors you see will be measured in microfarads.
- A **breadboard** is a reusable device that allows you to create circuits without needing to solder all the components. Breadboards have a number of holes into which you can push wires or jumper cables and components to create circuits. The two columns of holes on either side of the breadboard, between red and blue lines, are for power. The column next to the red line is for positive connections and the column next to the blue line is for negative connections (see Figure 8-4 for an example of a breadboard). The exercises in this adventure use a breadboard.
- **Jumper cables** can be used to connect the GPIO pins on the Raspberry Pi to a breadboard or other components. They are reusable and do not require

soldering. They come in different formats: female-to-male; female-to-female; and male-to-male.

- A **circuit diagram** shows you which electronic components, represented by symbols, are connected to complete a circuit and in what order they should be placed. The exercises in this adventure include circuit diagrams to help you understand how the circuit works and to show you the order in which the components need to be placed for current to flow through.

Figure 8-4 shows a half size breadboard, a variety of jumper cables, an LED, a push button and some resistors.

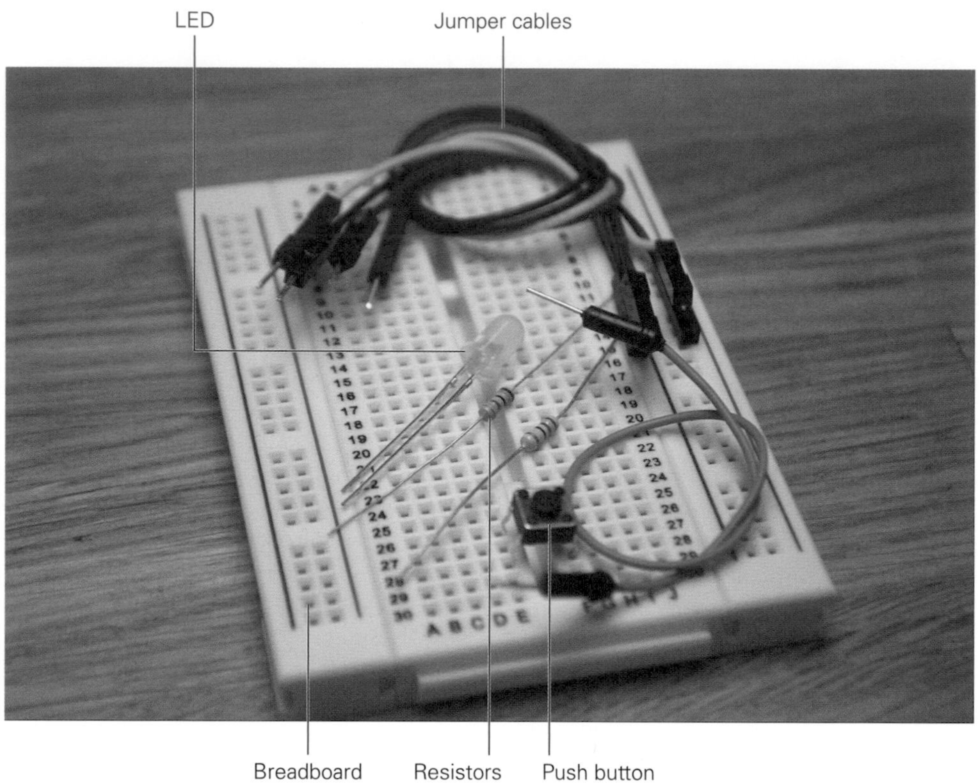

FIGURE 8-4 Electronic components

Using the Python Library to Control GPIO

To use Python to control the GPIO pins, you first need the Python GPIO library installed onto your Raspberry Pi. A library is a collection of already written code that you can use. For example, libraries contain modules that you can use in your code, like the `sleep` function from the `time` module that you used in previous adventures. In this adventure, you use the GPIO library to sense and control the pins. To check whether you have it, open an LXTerminal window from the desktop and type the following command:

```
sudo apt-get install python-RPi.GPIO
```

The Python library to control GPIO should be preinstalled on your Raspberry Pi. If you are using an early distribution of Raspbian or another Pi operating system, however, you may need to download and install it. To do so, follow the onscreen instructions, as shown in Figure 8-5.

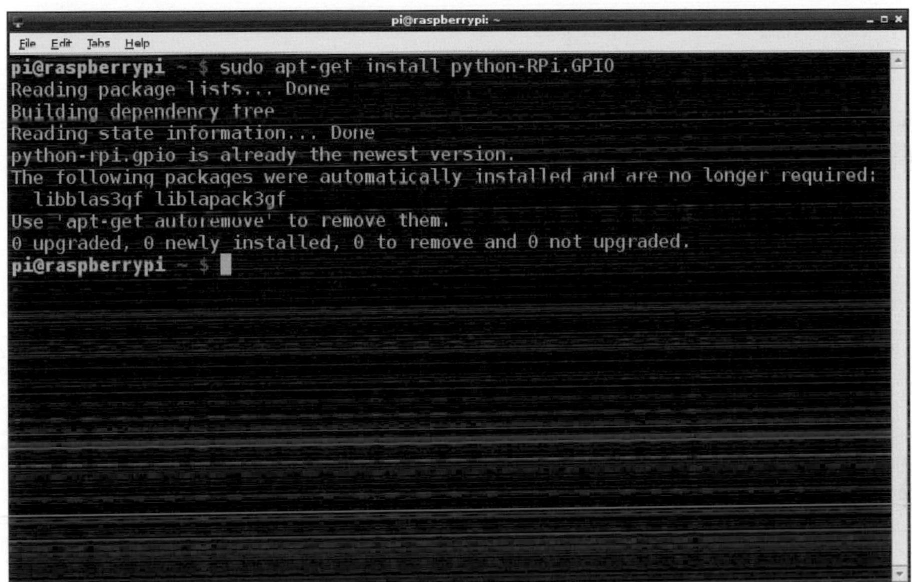

FIGURE 8-5 Downloading and installing the Python GPIO Library on the Raspberry Pi

Do You Have a Rev 1 or a Rev 2 Board?

As I have mentioned, there are two versions of the Raspberry Pi GPIO pin layout: the original Rev 1 and the newer, improved Rev 2. Before you start the exercises in this adventure, you need to find out which version your Raspberry Pi has. There is a simple way to do this.

In the LXTerminal window opened from the Raspberry Pi Desktop, type this code:

```
sudo python
import RPi.GPIO as GPIO
GPIO.RPI_REVISION
```

Using `sudo` in the command `sudo python` runs Python as the `root` or super user so that it can gain access to the GPIO hardware, which is not accessible to a normal user.

The first line runs the Python interpreter in interactive mode, while the second line uses `import` to use the RPi.GPIO library. The last line will determine what revision of Raspberry Pi you are using. Figure 8-6 shows this code and the output. The Raspberry Pi in this figure has returned the value of `2`, meaning that it is a Raspberry Pi Rev 2 board.

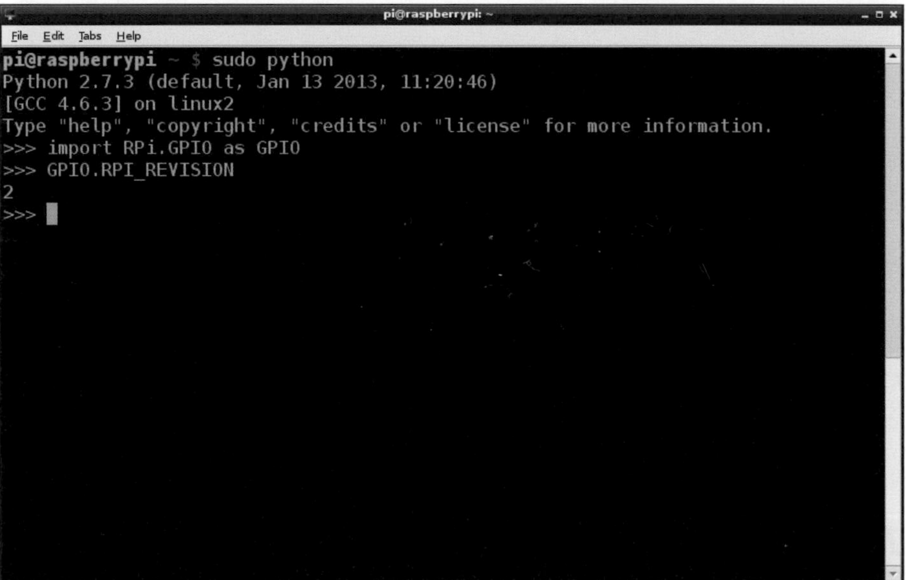

FIGURE 8-6 Using `GPIO.RPI_REVISION` in LXTerminal to find out which Raspberry Pi revision you have

To close the Python shell, type:

```
quit()
```

Making an LED Blink

Now that you have the Python library installed, you can use the GPIO pins to make something physical happen. In this project you will control an LED and make it blink.

Along with your Raspberry Pi you will need the following items, shown in Figure 8-7:

- A breadboard
- Two jumper cables
- An LED
- A 330 ohm resistor

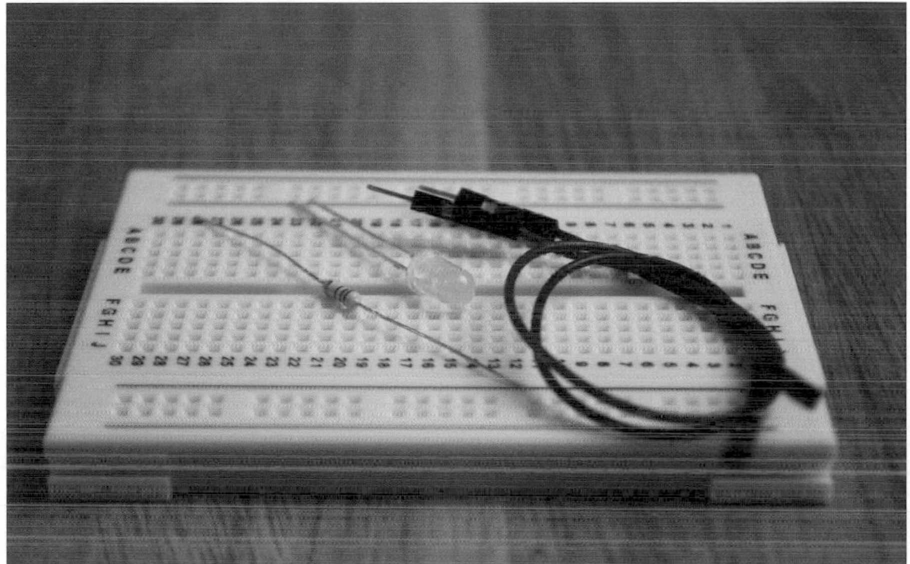

FIGURE 8-7 Components for exercise to make an LED blink

You can purchase the components that you need from the following shops:

Adafruit—`www.adafruit.com/`

CPC Farnell—`http://cpc.farnell.com`

RS Components—`http://uk.rs-online.com/web`

SKPang—`www.skpang.co.uk`

Creating the LEDblink Python Code

The first part of the project is to write the code that will make your LED blink.

For a video that walks you through the LEDblink project, visit the companion website at www.wiley.com/go/adventuresinrp. Click the Videos tab and select the LEDblink file.

1. Open Python IDLE 3 to program the GPIO pins, and select File➜New Window to create a blank text editor window to write your Python code to control the GPIO pins.

   Type the following code into your text editor window:

   ```
   import RPi.GPIO as GPIO
   import time
   ```

   These two lines import the modules and their functions that you will need to control the GPIO pins on the Raspberry Pi, and to create timed delays between the LED turning on and off. (You used the `time` module in Adventure 5 to wait for user input in the inventory program and the text-based adventure game.)

2. Underneath those lines, set the mode of pin numbering you are going to use, either BCM or BOARD (see the "Digging into the Code" sidebar for more details). You are then able to set up the individual pins on the Raspberry Pi.

   ```
   GPIO.setmode(GPIO.BCM)
   GPIO.setup(24, GPIO.OUT)
   ```

   In this project, you are outputting to an LED. Therefore you need to set up the pin that the LED connects to on the Raspberry Pi as an output. To do this, use the command `GPIO.setup(`*`the GPIO number`*`, GPIO.OUT)`.

3. Next, use a `while True` loop to set the output of GPIO 24 to `True`, which will turn on the LED followed by a pause for one second. Then set the output of GPIO 24 to `False`, followed by another one-second pause. When this is looped over and over, the LED will repeatedly turn on (true) and off (false) with a one-second delay between each.

   ```
   while True:
     GPIO.output(24, True)
     time.sleep(1)
     GPIO.output(24, False)
     time.sleep(1)
   ```

4. Save the file as `LEDblink.py` in `Documents`.

DIGGING INTO THE CODE

You might be wondering about the `setmode` and `BCM` in the first line of the Step 2. There are two ways—*modes*—of numbering the GPIOs within RPi.GPIO—`BCM` and `BOARD`. It is important that you set the mode (`setmode`) you wish to use in your Python code. `BOARD` means that the numbers passed into the GPIO functions refer to the pin numbers of the header on the Raspberry Pi. `BCM` means that numbers passed into the GPIO functions refer to what the BroadCoM chip uses for its GPIOs (which are different from the actual pin numbers on the RPi header).

The exercises in this adventure use the `BCM` numbers, which is why you needed to include `GPIO.setmode(GPIO.BCM)` at the start of your GPIO program. To use the `BOARD` mode, you would write `GPIO.setmode(GPIO.BOARD)`.

Connecting the LEDblink Components

Before running your program to make the LED blink, you need to assemble the electronic components and connect them to the Raspberry Pi GPIO pins. Figure 8-8 shows the Raspberry Pi on the left and a breadboard on the right. Use this diagram and the following steps to help you connect the right cables and components in the circuit.

As noted earlier, these instructions are written for a Rev 2 board. If you have a Rev 1, you must adjust the instructions based on the Rev 1 layout diagram. You could cause permanent damage your Raspberry Pi if you connect circuits to the GPIO pins incorrectly.

1. Start by plugging a female-to-male jumper cable from GPIO pin 24 of your Raspberry Pi to the A10 hole on your breadboard (the red cable in Figure 8-8). It helps to use different coloured wires. The jumper cable will easily fit onto the pins of your Raspberry Pi on one end, and into the holes on the breadboard. Make sure that you gently push them down as far as they will go to make a secure connection.
2. Next, plug another female-to-male jumper cable from a ground pin, sometimes represented as GND on Raspberry Pi GPIO diagrams (the blue cable). On a Rev 2 Raspberry Pi board, the third pin from the top on the outside strip is a ground pin (see Figure 8-8). Remember to use Dr Monk's Raspberry Leaf so that you know which pins are which!

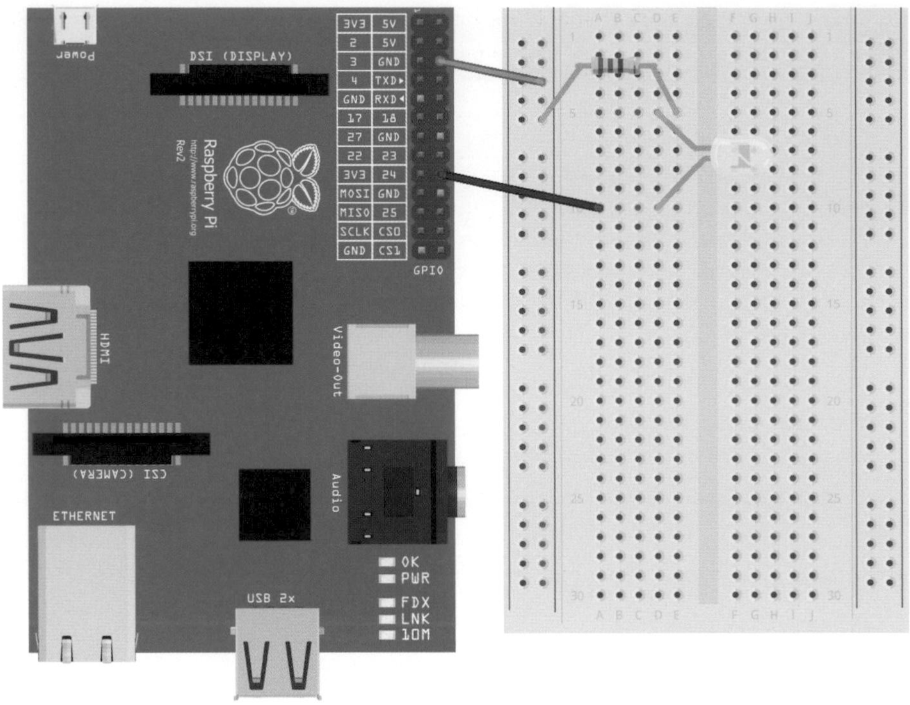

Made with Fritzing.org

FIGURE 8-8 Circuit diagram to connect components to Raspberry Pi for a blinking LED

3. Plug the other end of the jumper cable into a hole in the second column, between the red and blue lines on the breadboard. Remember that these two columns between the red and blue lines are for power—one for positive (red) and one for negative (blue). You want to plug your jumper cable into the blue negative column, three rows down.

4. Now add a 330 ohm resistor by pushing one of its legs into E5 and the other leg into a hole in row five of the blue negative power column on the breadboard. It does not matter which way round the resistor is placed.

   Remember that LEDs can only pass current in one direction. For the LED to work, you must make sure that you place the longer leg into the same row (D10) as the jumper cable connecting to GPIO 24. The short leg must be placed into a hole on the same row as the resistor (D5). Refer to Figure 8-8 for guidance.

Running LEDblink.py as the Super User root

The program will not run unless you run it as the super user `root` on the Raspberry Pi. In previous adventures, when you created Python programs you selected File➔Run

Module in the Python shell screen. If you do this for the `LEDblink` program, you will get an error message explaining that you do not have the correct permissions to run this program. The hardware of the Raspberry Pi is only accessible to the super user (root) and not the user account you logged in as. Using `sudo` temporarily gives you super user privileges so that you do not need to log out and back in to run a program. Instead, you need to open an LXTerminal window and type the following command to move into the folder or directory where you have saved your Python program:

```
cd Documents
```

Then type the following line to run the program:

```
sudo python3 LEDblink.py
```

Is that cool or what!

To interrupt the program and return to the command line in LXTerminal, press CTRL + C on the keyboard. Figure 8-9 shows the code.

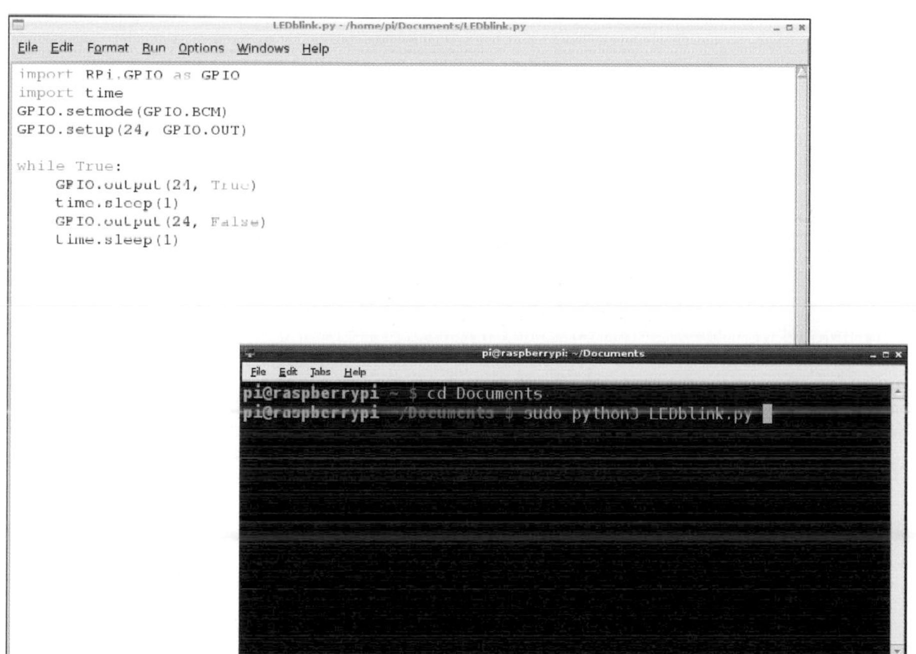

FIGURE 8-9 Programming in Python 3 on Raspberry Pi to make an LED blink

Using a Button to Turn on an LED

So far, you have controlled an LED, which is an output device. In this exercise you will add an input device in the form of a button that will start the light sequence when pushed.

For this project, you need your Raspberry Pi plus the following items:

- A breadboard
- Six jumper cables
- A simple push button
- An LED
- A 330 ohm resistor to protect the LED
- A 10k ohm resistor for use with the push button

For a video that walks you through the LEDbutton project, select the buttonLED video from the companion website at `www.wiley.com/go/adventuresinrp`.

Creating the buttonLED Python Code

In Python IDLE 3, amend your `LEDblink` program to include the following lines (highlighted in bold):

```
import RPi.GPIO as GPIO
GPIO.setmode(GPIO.BCM)
import time

GPIO.setup(23, GPIO.OUT)
GPIO.setup(24, GPIO.IN)
```

CHALLENGE

Why did you add `time.sleep(0.1)` to the `while` loop in the `buttonLED.py` program? What might happen if you remove it? Have a go to find out!

As before, you will set a GPIO for output (GPIO 23). You also need to set a GPIO pin to detect *input*. Use GPIO 24 for this purpose.

```
while True:
  if GPIO.input(24):
    GPIO.output(23, True)
  else:
    GPIO.output(23, False)
  time.sleep(0.1)
```

In the previous project, you used a `while True` loop to repeatedly turn an LED on and off with a one-second interval. In this project, you only want the LED to turn on when the button is pushed; therefore, you need to introduce a condition. You use `if` to set the condition: *if the button (GPIO.input(24)) is pressed, then turn the LED (GPIO.output(23)) on (or true).* But this is only one part of the condition. You also need to set the conditions for the button not being pushed; what should the LED do then? For this part of the condition, you use `else`: *else the LED should be off (or false).*

Save the file as `buttonLED.py` in `Documents`.

Connecting the buttonLED Components

As with the program for making an LED blink, before you run your button LED program you need to assemble the electronic components and connect them to the Raspberry Pi GPIO pins. If you use the component configuration from the previous exercise, you will only need to add a few extra parts. Figure 8-10 shows the Raspberry Pi on the left and a breadboard on the right. Follow this diagram to help you connect the right cables and components in the circuit.

1. Leaving the original circuit complete, take a small button switch and place it across the ride in the centre of the breadboard, with two legs in holes on column E and two legs in holes in column F on rows 21 and 23, as shown in Figure 8-10.
2. When the button is in place, take a 10k resistor and push one end into D21 next to one of the button legs. Place the other end of the resistor into a hole in the blue (negative) power column of the breadboard.
3. Next take a male-to-male jumper cable (green cable) and place one end into A23 on the same row as the other leg of the button on column E. Place the other end into the red (positive) power column of the breadboard.
4. Connect a male-to-female jumper cable (yellow cable) from A21 on the breadboard to GPIO pin 24 on the Raspberry Pi.
5. Finally, add a male-to-female jumper cable (black cable) from the red column near the top of the breadboard to the top GPIO pin 3V3, which will power the circuit.

If you have a Rev 2 Raspberry Pi, you can compare your configuration to the one shown in Figure 8-10.

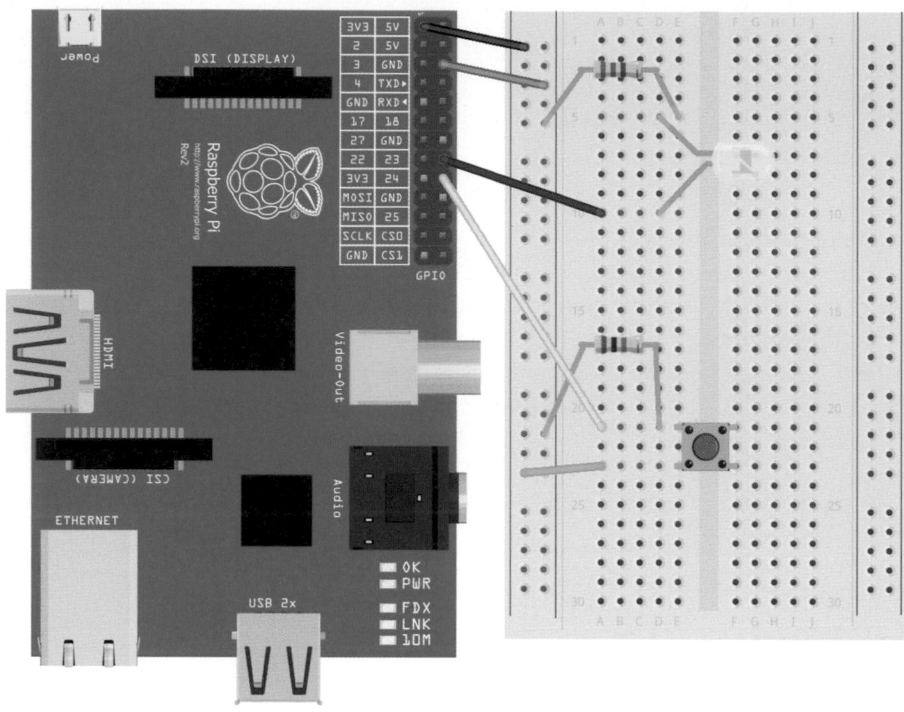

FIGURE 8-10 Circuit diagram to connect components to Raspberry Pi for button LED

Running buttonLED.py as the Super User root

As before, your program will not run unless you are logged in as the super user `root` on the Raspberry Pi. Using the LXTerminal window, run your program by typing this command:

```
sudo python3 buttonLED.py
```

When you press the button, the LED should light up, as shown in Figure 8-11.The LED should not light up until you press the button on your circuit. If the light comes on before you press the button or does not light when you press the button, go back and check your wiring using the diagrams.

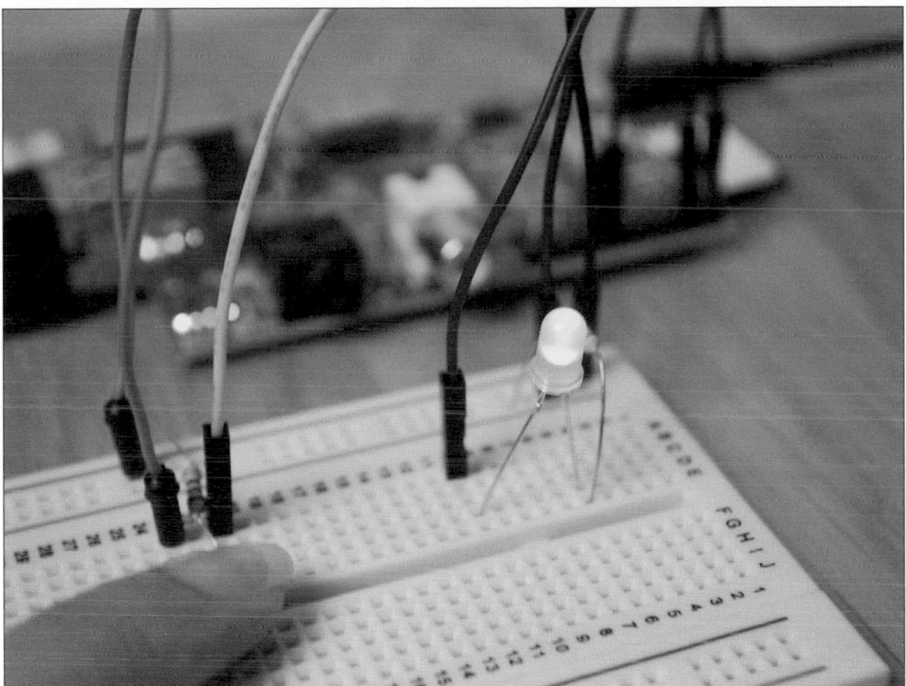

FIGURE 8-11 Pressing the button makes the LED light up!

CHALLENGE

Why not improve your code so that when you press the button once it turns on the LED, and when you press the button again it turns off the LED?

The Marshmallow Challenge

Using the Raspberry Pi GPIO pins for electronic projects can be a great way to learn. However, you can have some fun too. In this project, you will use your new GPIO pin Python programming knowledge to use a marshmallow as an input button, map it to a keyboard letter and use it to control a game that you have created in Scratch! Figure 8-12 shows the game in action.

You will need these items:

- Two female-to-female jumper cables
- Some marshmallows (yes, real ones!)
- Two metal pins or metal paper clips
- Your Raspberry Leaf to help you identify the GPIO pins that you need to use

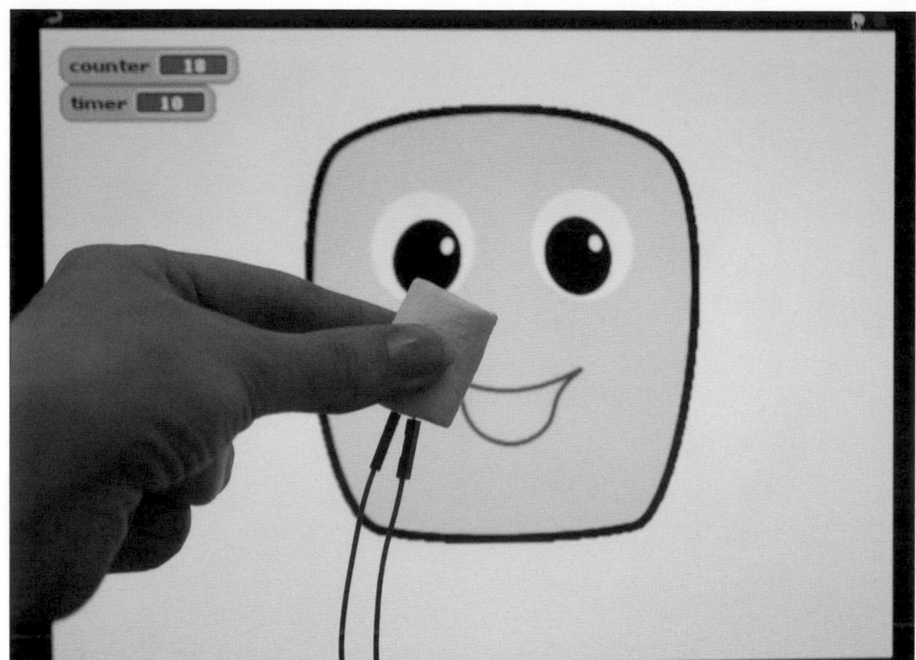

FIGURE 8-12 The Marshmallow Game

Creating the Marshmallow Button

The next step is to write the code to create a marshmallow button.

1. Open an LXTerminal window and type the following lines:

   ```
   cd Documents
   nano marshmallow.py
   ```

   This code opens a new text editor window for you to type your Python code into without having to open a Python IDLE shell and a text editor, and will name the file `marshmallow.py`.

2. Next type the following code:

   ```
   import RPi.GPIO as GPIO
   import time

   GPIO.setmode(GPIO.BCM)
   GPIO.setup(2, GPIO.IN)

   while True:
     if GPIO.input(2) == False:
   print("marshmallow makes a good input")
     time.sleep(0.5)
   ```

Press CTRL+X, followed by y (for yes) and Enter to save the file.

3. Take a jumper cable and carefully push a pin into the end. (You could even use a paper clip that has been straightened out.) Take the other end of the jumper cable and push it into GPIO pin 2 on your Raspberry Pi.

   Do the same again with the second jumper cable, only this time plug it into a ground pin on the Raspberry Pi.

   Poke the other ends of both jumper cables (the metal pin ends) into a marshmallow, as shown in Figure 8-13.

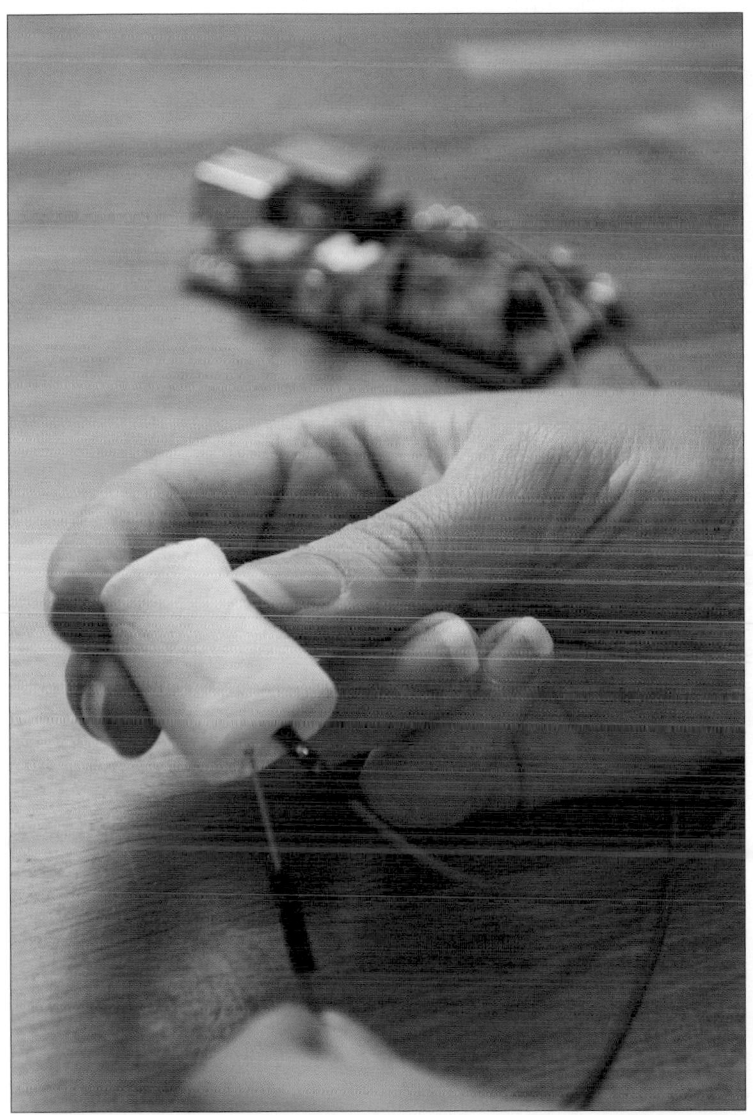

FIGURE 8-13 Connecting jumper cables to GPIO pins and a marshmallow

4. Go back to the LXTerminal window and type the following command:

```
sudo python marshmallow.py
```

Now gently squeeze the marshmallow and your marshmallow message will be printed to the LXTerminal window. If nothing happens, check that you have pushed the pins into the marshmallow and cables as far as they will go.

Now that you have tested to see that your marshmallow button works, you need to map it to a keyboard key so that when the marshmallow is pressed, the game will think that the letter *a* on the keyboard is being pressed. This will become important when you make or download a Scratch Marshmallow Game.

Mapping Marshmallow Input to a Keyboard Key

Follow these steps to map your marshmallow button to a key on the keyboard:

1. In the LXTerminal window type:

```
cd Documents
wget https://launchpad.net/python-uinput/↩
  trunk/0.10.0/+download/python-uinput-0.10.0.tar.gz
```

This will download `uinput`, an application and library that you need to be able to map your keyboard keys in your Python code. Once the `.tar.gz` file is downloaded, type the following command to extract the files into your home directory (`/home/pi`):

```
tar -zxvf python-uinput-0.10.0.tar.gz
```

Figure 8-14 shows the code for this step.

2. After the files have been extracted, type:

```
cd python-uinput-0.10.0
python setup.py build
sudo python setup.py install
sudo modprobe uinput
```

If you reboot your Raspberry Pi, you will need to run the command `sudo modprobe uinput` again in a terminal window, as the `uinput` driver will not install by default.

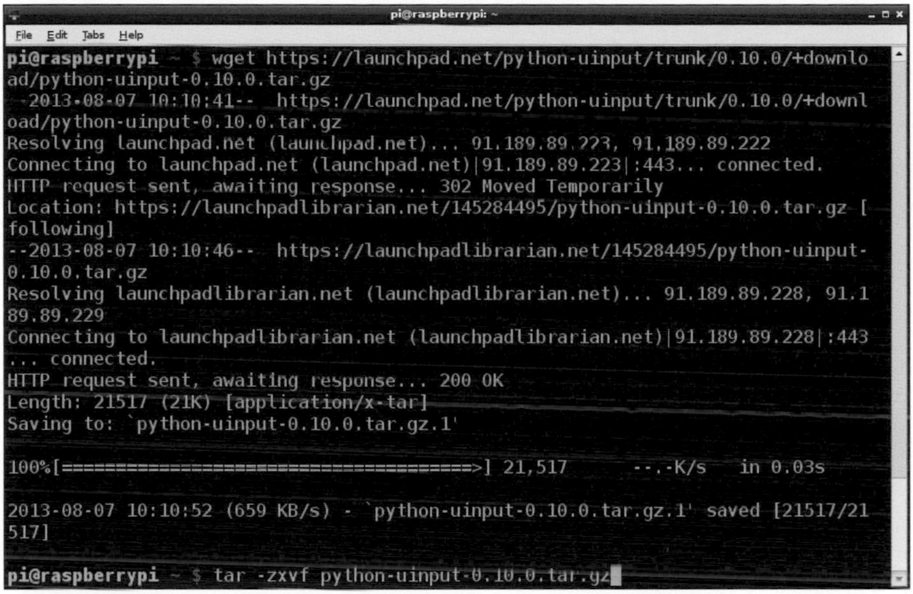

```
pi@raspberrypi ~ $ wget https://launchpad.net/python-uinput/trunk/0.10.0/+downlo
ad/python-uinput-0.10.0.tar.gz
--2013-08-07 10:10:41--  https://launchpad.net/python-uinput/trunk/0.10.0/+downl
oad/python-uinput-0.10.0.tar.gz
Resolving launchpad.net (launchpad.net)... 91.189.89.223, 91.189.89.222
Connecting to launchpad.net (launchpad.net)|91.189.89.223|:443... connected.
HTTP request sent, awaiting response... 302 Moved Temporarily
Location: https://launchpadlibrarian.net/145284495/python-uinput-0.10.0.tar.gz [
following]
--2013-08-07 10:10:46--  https://launchpadlibrarian.net/145284495/python-uinput-
0.10.0.tar.gz
Resolving launchpadlibrarian.net (launchpadlibrarian.net)... 91.189.89.228, 91.1
89.89.229
Connecting to launchpadlibrarian.net (launchpadlibrarian.net)|91.189.89.228|:443
... connected.
HTTP request sent, awaiting response... 200 OK
Length: 21517 (21K) [application/x-tar]
Saving to: `python-uinput-0.10.0.tar.gz.1'

100%[======================================>] 21,517      --.-K/s   in 0.03s

2013-08-07 10:10:52 (659 KB/s) - `python-uinput-0.10.0.tar.gz.1' saved [21517/21
517]

pi@raspberrypi ~ $ tar -zxvf python-uinput-0.10.0.tar.gz
```

FIGURE 8-14 Downloading and extracting `python-uinput`

3. Next, edit the `marshmallow` script to use the `uinput` Python library to map the input of the marshmallow to a key on the keyboard. You can open `marshmallow.py` in IDLE3 or type the following command in the LXTerminal window to open the file:

```
cd Documents
nano marshmallow.py
```

Amend the Python code to include the new lines (shown in bold):

```
import RPi.GPIO as GPIO
import time
import uinput

GPIO.setmode(GPIO.BCM)
GPIO.setup(2, GPIO.IN)
device = uinput.Device([uinput.KEY_A])

while True:
        if GPIO.input(2) == False:
device.emit_click(uinput.KEY_A)
print("marshmallow makes a good input")
        time.sleep(0.5)
```

Here the keyboard key *a* has been used for the marshmallow button. You could use any letter of the alphabet.

DIGGING INTO THE CODE

uinput is a special hardware driver that allows other programs to inject key-presses into the system as if you had pressed a real key on the keyboard. It is a special kernel driver that has to be installed inside the Linux kernel in order to do its work. **modprobe** is an administration command that installs that kernel driver for you.

4. Save and exit nano using CTRL + X, followed by y and Enter. Test that your program works by running `marshmallow.py` with the following command and then squeezing the marshmallow.

   ```
   sudo python3 marshmallow.py
   ```

   You should also test the program by pressing the *a* key on the keyboard. The message `marshmallow makes a good input` will be displayed.

The marshmallow button may not work if you do not have a keyboard plugged in.

Scratch Marshmallow Game

Now that your marshmallow is mapped to the *a* key, you can create a Scratch game with a counter to count each time you squeeze the marshmallow. The completed Scratch Marshmallow Game can be downloaded from the Adventures in Raspberry Pi website at `www.wiley.com/go/adventuresinrp`. The object of the game is to see how many marshmallow presses you can record in 10 seconds, using the marshmallow input button that you have created. Refer to Figure 8-15, the completed game in Scratch, as you work through the following steps.

1. To open Scratch double-click the icon or open the main menu on the bottom left of the screen, and navigate to Education➜Scratch. Select File➜Save As and name the file `Marshmallow Game` before clicking Save.
2. Delete the Cat Scratch sprite by right-clicking on the sprite and selecting Delete from the drop-down menu that appears.

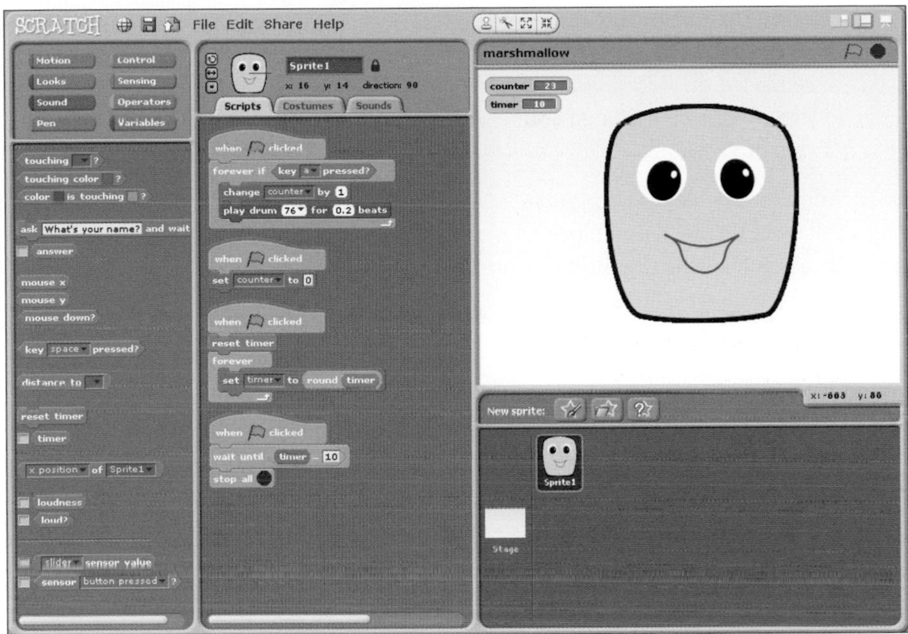

FIGURE 8-15 Scratch Marshmallow Game

3. Click on the Paint New Sprite icon above the Sprites palette (the icon with the paintbrush and star) and draw a marshmallow character using the paint editor. You can use the rectangle or circle shape tools to create your marshmallow, or if you feel confident try using the paintbrush tool to draw freehand. Once you are happy with your design, click OK to exit the Paint Editor window.

   Alternatively, if your Raspberry Pi is connected to the Internet, you can down load the marshmallow sprite used in this project (`marshmallow.png`) from the Adventures in Raspberry Pi website at `www.wiley.com/go/adventuresinrp`.

4. You need to create two variables for this game. Click Variables in the Blocks palette and then click Make a Variable. The New Variable window opens and asks you to type a name for your variable. Name the first variable `counter` and ensure that *For all sprites* is checked before clicking OK. This variable will count the number of times the marshmallow button has been pressed.

   Follow the same steps to create a second variable and name it `timer`. This variable will set the time limit for the marshmallow challenge.

5. Now that all the blocks you need to create the scripts for the marshmallow game are available, click Control on the Blocks palette and drag the control block `When` `clicked` onto the Scripts tab for the marshmallow sprite. Add a `forever if` control block underneath and connect them.

6. Click on the Sensing blocks palette and select the `key space pressed` block. Place it into the hexagonal space on the `forever if` control block. Once you have placed this block you will need to change `space` to `a` or the letter of the key to which you assigned your marshmallow button-press in the previous part of this project.

7. Add the variable block `change counter by 1` inside the `forever if` block, followed by the sound block `play drum 48 for 0.2 beats`. Change the drum to 76 using the drop-down menu.

8. When the game begins, the counter will need to be reset to 0 to record the player's score. Add another `when` 🏁 `clicked` control block to the Scripts tab and connect a `set counter to 0` variable block to it.

9. Remember to save the work you have done so far by clicking File→Save. Then test that your game script written so far works, by clicking the 🏁 icon and using your marshmallow button to check if the counter records how many times it is pressed. Don't forget that the Python script you created for the button needs to be running too!

10. To give the player a time limit, you will need to add two more scripts. Add another `when` 🏁 `clicked` control block to the Scripts tab and connect the sensing block `reset timer` to it. Underneath, connect a `forever` looping control block, and a `set timer to 0` variable block inside it. (You may need to select Timer from the Variable block drop-down menu.)

    Next click on the Operators blocks palette and select the `round` block. Place it inside the `set timer` variable block where the value `0` is. Then add the sensing block `timer` inside the empty space of the `round` operator block you just placed.

    This completed variable block should now read: `set timer to round timer`. This script will reset the timer at the start of the game to 0, and then count upwards every second.

11. The final script will set the time limit for the game. Add a `when` 🏁 `clicked` control block to the Scripts tab, and connect a `wait until` control block to it, followed by a stop all control block.

    Drag the operators block `_ = _` (equal to) and place it inside the `wait until` hexagon space. In the left-hand space before the `=` sign, add the variable block `timer` and on the right-hand side type the value `10`.

    This script will wait until the timer reaches 10 seconds before stopping the game.

12. Finally, save your game by clicking File→Save. Then test that your scripts work by clicking the 🏁 icon and using your marshmallow button to check whether the counter records how many times it is pressed, and the timer counts up to 10 before stopping the game.

CHALLENGE

What other functionality could you add to this game? Here are some ideas:

- Costumes for the marshmallow sprite so that when the button is pressed it becomes animated.
- A Stage background with a Game Over screen. This would also require scripts to broadcast a message, like the one for the Adventurer Game in Adventure 3.
- A scoreboard for the highest number of presses.

You could also make a similar game using Python.

Further Adventures with GPIO Pins

As you can see, programming the GPIO pins on the Raspberry Pi opens a Pandora's box of opportunity. With a little electronics know-how and some imagination you can control lots of things in the real world. The Raspberry Pi website (`www.raspberrypi.org`) is full of great examples of how people are controlling their environments with their Pis.

Now that you have learned how to combine some basic electronics powered and commanded by the Raspberry Pi you may want to continue learning more. Here are some resources to take you further:

- Alex Eames' website RasPi.TV has an RPi.GPIO basics set of tutorials: `http://raspi.tv/category/raspberry-pi`
- If you want to learn how to control the Raspberry Pi GPIO pins using Scratch, Simple Si's blog has some great ideas: `http://cymplecy.wordpress.com/2013/04/22/scratch-gpio-version-2-introduction-for-beginners`
- To learn more about electronic projects and using the Raspberry Pi GPIO pins, the Adafruit Learning System is a great platform to start with: `http://learn.adafruit.com/adafruits-raspberry-pi-lesson-4-gpio-setup`

GPIO Pins Command Quick Reference Table	
Command	**Description**
`import RPi.GPIO as GPIO` `GPIO.RPI_REVISION`	Checks the revision number of the Raspberry Pi board you are using.
`import RPi.GPIO as GPIO`	Imports the Raspberry Pi GPIO module.
`GPIO.setmode(GPIO.`*`mode`*`)`	Sets the numbering mode of the GPIO pins, either `BCM` or `BOARD`.
`GPIO.setup(`*`GPIO number`*`, GPIO.OUT)`	Sets a GPIO pin as either input or output.

Achievement Unlocked: Conquering electronics with a Raspberry Pi!

In the Next Adventure

The final adventure in this book is a humongous Raspberry Pi project. It draws on all the computational skills you have learned on your Pi journey so far, to enable you to make a Pi Jukebox with LCD display, Play, Stop and Skip buttons—and a box! It will also involve acquiring extra parts for your Raspberry Pi, like an LCD screen. The project may seem intimidating at first, but as with all challenging endeavors, you will feel triumphant when it is completed.

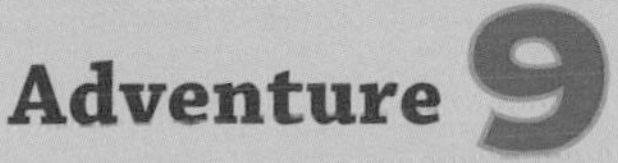

Adventure 9

The Big Adventure: Building a Raspberry Pi Jukebox

ONE OF THE Raspberry Pi's special qualities is the fact that you can transform it into a dedicated device of its own. In this adventure, you will transform your Raspberry Pi into a jukebox, complete with buttons to select and play tracks, and an LCD screen to display the song names. Figure 9-1 shows my version of the completed project.

I hope this adventure will whet your appetite for more big Raspberry Pi projects. If you want to continue your Raspberry Pi journey, I've included a few resources at the end of the adventure to give you some ideas. The more you work with the Raspberry Pi and learn about what it can do, the more you'll come up with your own big project ideas!

FIGURE 9-1 The completed *Adventures in Raspberry Pi* Big Jukebox Project!

An Overview of the Jukebox Project

This final adventure is slightly more complicated than the other projects in this book. A big project like this is great for drawing together many of the skills you have learned in previous adventures. Because this project is complex, I've broken the instructions into four parts. But before you dive in to the details, here's a short road map of what you'll be doing.

- In Part One, you use Python to create the LCD screen for the jukebox.
- In Part Two, you add the software to download and play MP3 files.
- In Part Three, you use the GPIO pins to connect buttons to your circuit and write a program so that you can use the buttons to play, pause and skip tracks.
- In Part Four, you write the code to make the LCD screen information about the MP3 files that are being played.

Finally, you may want to finish up your project by designing a box for your Pi jukebox, to conceal the wiring and circuitry, make it more user-friendly and enhance the way it looks.

All the completed code files for this project are available for download from the companion website at `www.wiley.com/go/adventuresinrp`. As I've said in other adventures, you will learn far more by following the instructions in this book, typing in the code yourself and figuring out how to fix any problems. However, if you have difficulty getting something to work, you might want to compare your code to the download files to check whether you've missed something.

For a video that walks you through the entire jukebox project, visit the companion website at `www.wiley.com/go/adventuresinrp`. Click the Videos tab and select the JukeboxProject file.

What You Will Need

To complete this big project, you will need your Raspberry Pi and a number of extra components. You can purchase all the components from online electronic retailers, and none of them require soldering. Here's what you'll need:

- Your Raspberry Pi and peripherals including an SD card with a Raspbian image installed (see Adventure 1)
- A small speaker that uses the headphone/speaker port on your Pi (like the speaker in Figure 9-1)
- A full-sized breadboard
- A 16 x 2 character 3.3v parallel **liquid crystal display** (**LCD**)
- A 10K **potentiometer**
- Four buttons, like the one used in Adventure 8 to turn on and off an LED
- Four 10k ohm resistors
- Solderless headers
- Female-to-male jumper cables and male-to-male jumper cables
- A printed Raspberry Leaf diagram to help connect components with GPIO
- A cardboard box
- Some decorations or paint to make your jukebox look cool

A full list of products used in this adventure and where they can be purchased can be found on the *Adventures in Raspberry Pi* website at www.wiley.com/go/adventuresinrp.

An **LCD (liquid crystal display)** is an electronic display, usually quite thin and flat, that is typically used in digital calculators and digital watches to display information like the time. In this project, your LCD screen will show the names of the songs playing on the jukebox—you don't need a monitor for the Pi jukebox.

A **potentiometer** is a variable resistor. In this project, it will enable you to adjust the contrast on the display to make it easier to read what is on the LCD screen by turning an adjuster wheel.

Many big electronic projects require you to solder parts together. If you have spent money on expensive components this can be a daunting task, even for proficient tinkerers. It can also be very painful should you accidentally burn yourself with a soldering iron. Luckily, items like breadboards, jumper cables and solderless headers make it possible to make cool electronic projects without the need to solder. If there is an adult in your household or at school who is nifty with soldering tools and has some experience, however, it may be a good idea to ask them to help you solder headers onto any expensive components to save you from fiddling around with solderless headers in this tutorial.

Part One: Creating the LCD Screen

In the first part of this project, you need to assemble the electronic components for your jukebox. This project involves many more cables and components than previous adventures, so you should be extra careful about checking your work against the figures and wiring diagrams. Then, after you have set up the electronics, you will download some files that you'll use later to be able to display text on the LCD screen.

Preparing the LCD Screen by Adding Headers

When you buy or receive your LCD screen, you may find that the header pins that you need in order to connect the LCD screen onto a breadboard are not included with it. In this case, you may need to ask an adult to solder the headers on for you; or, alternatively, you can use solderless headers, which need to be pushed all the way into the holes to make a good connection. Although it may seem easier to use solderless headers, they can be quite difficult to push into place and you might need a lot of patience to do it. I find that wiggling the headers in small groups of five or six at a time, while applying pressure, is the best way to add them to the LCD screen.

Mounting the LCD Screen and Wiring Up the Breadboard

Follow these steps to set up the LCD screen. Refer to Figure 9-2 for additional guidance as you work.

1. Lay your full breadboard out lengthways in front of you so that the longest side runs parallel to the edge of the table directly in front of you. Push your prepared LCD screen's header pins into the holes, starting from C5 and going all the way to C21.
2. Next, add the potentiometer into pins F1 to F3 above the left end of the LCD screen. You will be using the potentiometer to adjust the contrast of the LCD screen.
3. Place your unplugged Raspberry Pi next to the breadboard (see Figure 9-2) and add the Raspberry Leaf (`www.doctormonk.com/2013/02/raspberry-pi-and-breadboard-raspberry.html`) for your Raspberry Pi board revision over the top of the GPIO pins (you'll remember the Raspberry Leaf from Adventure 8). You will be connecting quite a lot of jumper cables from the LCD screen to your Raspberry Pi, and you'll find it easier with the Raspberry Leaf in place as a guide.
4. In order to send data to the LCD screen, it needs to be wired as follows. Start with pin 1 (the far left) of the LCD screen and attach the cable to the correct destination (use the diagram in Figure 9-2 to help you):
   - Pin 1 of the LCD goes to the ground or negative blue strip of the breadboard (black male-to-male cable on diagram).
   - Pin 2 of the LCD goes to the 3.3v or positive red strip of the breadboard (red male-to-male cable on diagram).
   - Pin 3 (Vo) connects to the middle of the potentiometer (orange male-to-male on diagram). Note that the potentiometer has three pins; the orange wire should be placed in a breadboard slot above the potentiometer in the middle.
   - Pin 4 (RS) connects to the Raspberry Pi GPIO 25 (yellow male-to-female cable).
   - Pin 5 (RW) goes to the ground or negative of the breadboard (black male-to-male cable).

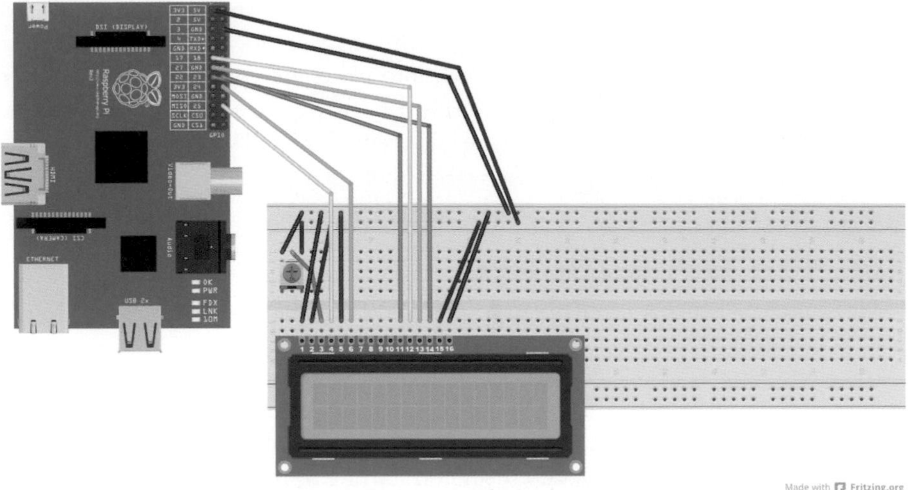

FIGURE 9-2 Circuit diagram for wiring the LCD screen and potentiometer

- Pin 6 (EN) connects to the Raspberry Pi GPIO 24 (green male-to-female cable).
- Skip LCD Pins 7, 8, 9 and 10.
- Pin 11 (D4) connects to the Raspberry Pi GPIO 23 (blue male-to-female cable).
- Pin 12 (D5) connects to the Raspberry Pi GPIO 17 (yellow male-to-female cable).
- Pin 13 (D6) connects to the Raspberry Pi GPIO 27 (green male-to-female cable).
- Pin 14 (D7) connects to the Raspberry Pi GPIO 22 (blue male-to-female cable).
- Pin 15 (LED +) goes to the Raspberry Pi 3.3V (red male-to-female cable).
- Pin 16 (LED -) goes to the Raspberry Pi ground or GND (black male-to-female cable).
- On the potentiometer, connect the left pin to the ground or negative blue strip of the breadboard (black male-to-male cable), and the right pin to the 3.3v or positive red strip of the breadboard (red male-to-male cable).

5. Double-check the diagram (Figure 9-2) and picture (Figure 9-3) to check that you have wired up your LCD and potentiometer correctly. When you are happy that your wiring is correct, plug your Raspberry Pi, complete with SD card, into a monitor, keyboard, mouse, network (Ethernet) cable, and finally, power supply.

FIGURE 9-3 Mounted LCD screen and potentiometer

Remember, if you connect GPIO pins incorrectly you could damage your Raspberry Pi. Always double-check your wiring before you connect it to a power supply.

6. The LCD screen should light up. If it does not, return to the wiring diagram and instructions and check your work. Twist the potentiometer until you see the first line of the LCD fill with boxes.

Adding Scripts to Drive the LCD Screen

Next, you need to download the Python code required to display information on the LCD screen. Make sure that your Pi is connected to the Internet either by an Ethernet cable or by WiFi, so that you can download the files you need.

1. After logging into your Pi and running `startx`, open an LXTerminal window, type the following line and press Enter:

   ```
   sudo apt-get update
   ```

   After you have checked that all your application packages are up to date, type the following line and press Enter:

   ```
   sudo apt-get install git
   ```

   This command checks that the git application that allows you to make a copy of this open source code is already installed on your Raspberry Pi. It should already be installed as part of the Raspbian operating system but, if it is not, this command will download and install it. Once the git application is installed, you can make a copy of the Adafruit Raspberry Pi Python files that I've modified, by typing:

   ```
   git clone https://github.com/MissPhilbin/Adventure_9.git
   ```

2. After the code is copied, navigate to the directory or folder containing the Python code for a 16x2 LCD screen by typing the following into the command line of the LXTerminal and pressing Enter:

   ```
   cd Adventure_9
   ```

3. Now run the Python code by typing the following command and then pressing Enter (Figure 9-4):

   ```
   sudo python3 Adafruit_CharLCD.py
   ```

   You should see the following appear on your LCD screen:

   ```
   This is a test!
   ```

4. As you twist the potentiometer back and forth, the letters will fade and become more vibrant.

5. Next, copy the files into your `Documents` directory where you will be saving your jukebox Python program by typing:

   ```
   cp Adafruit_CharLCD.py /home/pi/Documents/
   ```

Later in this project you will use these files to help you write a program that displays MP3 track information onto the LCD screen of your jukebox.

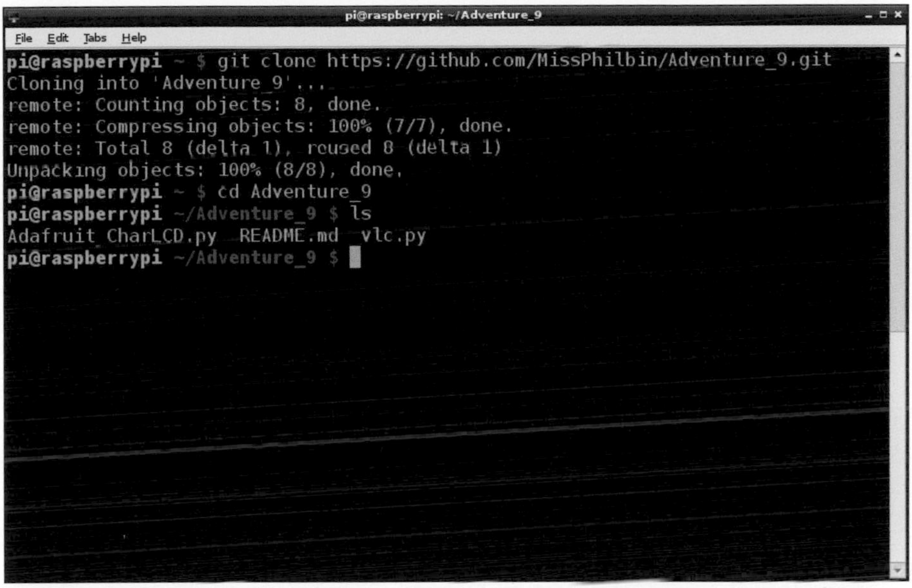
pi@raspberrypi: ~/Adventure_9
File Edit Tabs Help
pi@raspberrypi ~ $ git clone https://github.com/MissPhilbin/Adventure_9.git
Cloning into 'Adventure_9'...
remote: Counting objects: 8, done.
remote: Compressing objects: 100% (7/7), done.
remote: Total 8 (delta 1), reused 8 (delta 1)
Unpacking objects: 100% (8/8), done.
pi@raspberrypi ~ $ cd Adventure_9
pi@raspberrypi ~/Adventure_9 $ ls
Adafruit_CharLCD.py README.md vlc.py
pi@raspberrypi ~/Adventure_9 $

FIGURE 9-1 Downloading the modified `Adafruit_CharLCD.py`

Part Two: Downloading and Playing MP3s

Now that the LCD screen is set up, it's time to download and play some music files on your Raspberry Pi. To play music files on your Raspberry Pi, you will need to download and install a media player and test that it works. Once you have the player installed and some music to listen to, you'll write a program that will let you create a playlist and shuffle or skip tracks.

Installing a Media Player and Getting Music Files

To download and install a media player, type this command in an LXTerminal window:

```
sudo apt-get install vlc
```

The `vlc` application is a media player. It enables you to play different types of media, such as videos and music, from the command line. This is helpful for your jukebox project as the plan is to control the player from the LCD screen using input buttons that you will add later in this project.

Next, you need some music files to play. You may have some MP3s on a desktop, laptop or computer that you can transfer to your Pi using a portable storage device like a USB memory stick. Alternatively, you could download an album from the Free Music Archive using a web browser on the Raspberry Pi. To do this, your Raspberry Pi will need to be connected to the Internet, either through an Ethernet cable or through a WiFi dongle like the WiPi.

1. Open the Midori web browser by double-clicking on the desktop icon or by clicking on the main menu and selecting Internet➜Midori. In the URL address bar of the web browser, type the following URL and press Enter (Figure 9-5):

   ```
   freemusicarchive.org
   ```

FIGURE 9-5 Using the Midori web browser to download legal MP3 audio files

The Free Music Archive is home to high-quality audio files that you are free to download and listen to. The content is cleared for certain types of use by the artists and is not prohibited from download by copyright laws.

2. Find some music that you like by browsing the website. When you have located a song that you like and want to download, click on the download arrow next to the name of the song. A dialogue box will appear, prompting you to open or download the file. Click Save and the MP3 file will start to download. You can check its progress by looking at the progress bar at the bottom of the web browser window. When the bar is full, the download is complete. This file will download to your `/home/pi` directory.

3. Once the download is complete, test to see if `vlc` can play the MP3 music file. In an LXTerminal window, type `cvlc` followed by the path or folder structure and then the MP3 file name. For example:

```
cvlc /home/pi/CAP_01_Adventures_In_Pi.mp3
```

The `vlc` application outputs a lot of things to the console screen, many of them claiming to be "errors", but you don't need to worry about them.

`vlc` will play your downloaded MP3 file. Make sure that you have headphones or a speaker plugged into your Pi so that you can hear the file.

To stop the file from playing, press CTRL + C on the keyboard.

4. The `vlc.py` file that you downloaded earlier is in the `Adventure_9` directory. You need to copy this file into your `Documents` folder so that you can use it in your Python jukebox program. To copy the file, type:

```
cp /home/pi/Adventure_9/vlc.py /home/pi/Documents
```

You can download an entire album from the Free Music Archive using the Download Album link. Extract the MP3 files from the compressed zip folder by clicking on the completed progress bar at the bottom of the web browser page and following onscreen extraction instructions. Alternatively, type the following into an LXTerminal window to unzip the files, after using `cd` to change to the destination directory or folder:

```
unzip filename.zip
```

You may also want to create a folder to store all your MP3 files. You could use the File Manager application to do this, but why not practice the commands you learned in Adventure 2 for use in an LXTerminal window or at the command line?

To create a directory or folder, use the `mkdir` command, as follows:

```
mkdir music
```

This command creates a folder named `music`.

To move a file from one directory or folder to another, you use the `mv` command; for example:

```
mv CAP_01_Adventures_In_Pi.mp3 music/
```

This line moves the MP3 file from the current directory into the `music` directory.

To play all the MP3 files inside a directory or folder, type `cvlc` followed by the name of the folder, followed by an asterisk (*); for example:

```
cvlc music/*.mp3
```

Figure 9-6 shows the output.

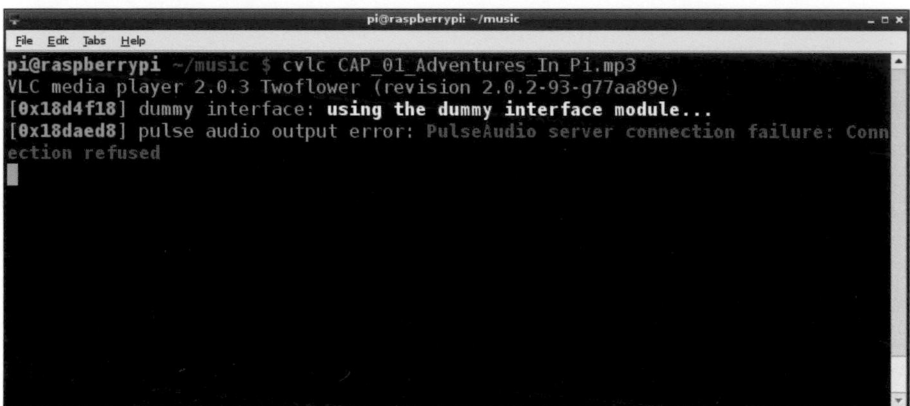

FIGURE 9-6 Playing audio MP3 files using vlc in LXTerminal. The MP3 file plays, despite the error message.

So easy, right?

Writing a Jukebox Python Program

Playing one MP3 at a time is fine, but any real music lover wants to play an entire directory or playlist, and perhaps shuffle the songs, or even skip tracks. This is the part of any big project where you can decide the functionality you wish to add, as you are going to write a program in Python to interact with the `vlc` application using its library.

As in previous adventures, you will use Python 3 to create the jukebox controls.

1. Open IDLE 3 by double-clicking the desktop icon or by selecting the application from the main menu. Click File➜New Window to open a new text file. Alternatively, you could use a command line text editor like nano.

2. In the first line, as in previous projects using Python, you import the modules and libraries that you need. For example, the `glob` module is used for getting a list of MP3 files in a directory, the `random` module is used to shuffle the MP3 files inside the list, `sys` is used for `sys.exit` and getting command line arguments, and `vlc` is the Python interface to the `vlc` library `libvlc`. Type:

   ```
   import glob, random, sys, vlc
   ```

3. Leave a one-line gap underneath and then type:

   ```
   if len(sys.argv) <= 1:
     print("Please specify a folder with mp3 files")
     sys.exit(1)
   ```

   `sys.argv` is a list that contains the arguments passed to the program on the command line. You may remember in earlier adventures we accessed programs from the command line. For instance, if you typed `sudo python3 jukebox.py /home/pi/music` into the command line, then the list would contain `jukebox.py` at position 0 and `/home/pi/music` at position 1 (the zero position always contains the name of the program that was run). So the first argument is at position 1.

4. The next part of the program will load a list of MP3s:

   ```
   folder = sys.argv[1]
   files = glob.glob(folder+"/*.mp3")
   if len(files) == 0:
     print("No mp3 files in directory", folder, "..exiting")
     sys.exit(1)
   ```

   As described before, position 1 in `sys.argv` is the first command line argument. The `glob` function allows you to get a list of files matching a pattern. The pattern `"*.mp3"` expands to any file which ends in `.mp3`, so `files = glob.glob(folder+"/*.mp3")` will produce a list of all files ending in `.mp3` inside the folder given on the command line. If the directory contains no MP3s there won't be anything for the jukebox to play, so you exit early using `sys.exit`.

5. Now you are able to use the `random` module to shuffle the list of MP3 files to put them in a random order. Underneath the previous code, type:

   ```
   random.shuffle(files)
   ```

6. Leave a blank line and then type the following lines:

```
player = vlc.MediaPlayer()
medialist = vlc.MediaList(files)
mlplayer = vlc.MediaListPlayer()
mlplayer.set_media_player(player)
mlplayer.set_media_list(medialist)
```

   This part of the code sets up how you will be using the `vlc` library. The details aren't important, but you set up a `MediaListPlayer`, which is a `Player` that plays a `MediaList` (rather than just having one track queued at a time).

7. Later in the project, you are going to add buttons to play, pause and skip between tracks, so here you need to add a `while` loop to read the input of buttons, and use keyboard buttons 1, 2, 3, 4 to test that it works. Begin your `while` loop with this code:

```
while True:
  button = input("Hit a button ")
  if button == "1":
    print("Pressed play button")
    if mlplayer.is_playing():
      mlplayer.pause()
    else:
      mlplayer.play()
  elif button == "2":
    print("Pressed stop button")
    mlplayer.stop()
```

   The 1 key on your keyboard will act as the play/pause button, while the 2 key will act as the stop button. Inside the `while` loop, you have used some conditionals. Be careful with your indentation here!

   The first level of the condition depends on which button is pressed: `if` 1 is pressed or else if (`elif`) 2 is pressed. Inside each button press is a second condition. If button 1 is pressed when a track is playing, the media player will pause. If nothing is playing, the media player will play a random track. If button 2 is pressed, the media player stops the track after printing `Pressed stop button` to the screen.

8. When the stop button is pushed, you want to make it so that when you hit play again the tracks have been reshuffled. To do that, you sort the list of files again using `random`, and then replace the `MediaList` using that reshuffled list of files. Directly underneath the last line of the previous code, and at the same level of indentation, type these lines:

```
    random.shuffle(files)
    medialist = vlc.MediaList(files)
    mlplayer.set_media_list(medialist)
```

9. Now add two more buttons to this loop to skip back and forward. Be careful of the indentation of your code, as you are continuing the first conditional (see Figure 9-7). Directly underneath the last line type the following:

```
elif button == "3":
  print("Pressed back button")
  mlplayer.previous()
elif button == "4":
  print("Pessed forward button")
  mlplayer.next()
else:
  print("Unrecognised input")
```

10. Save your file as `jukebox1.py` inside your `Documents` directory, by clicking File➜Save As and navigating to `Documents` inside `/home/pi`.

11. Finally, test to see if your code works by clicking Run➜Run Module, or from the LXTerminal by changing to the `Documents` directory and typing `python3 jukebox1.py`

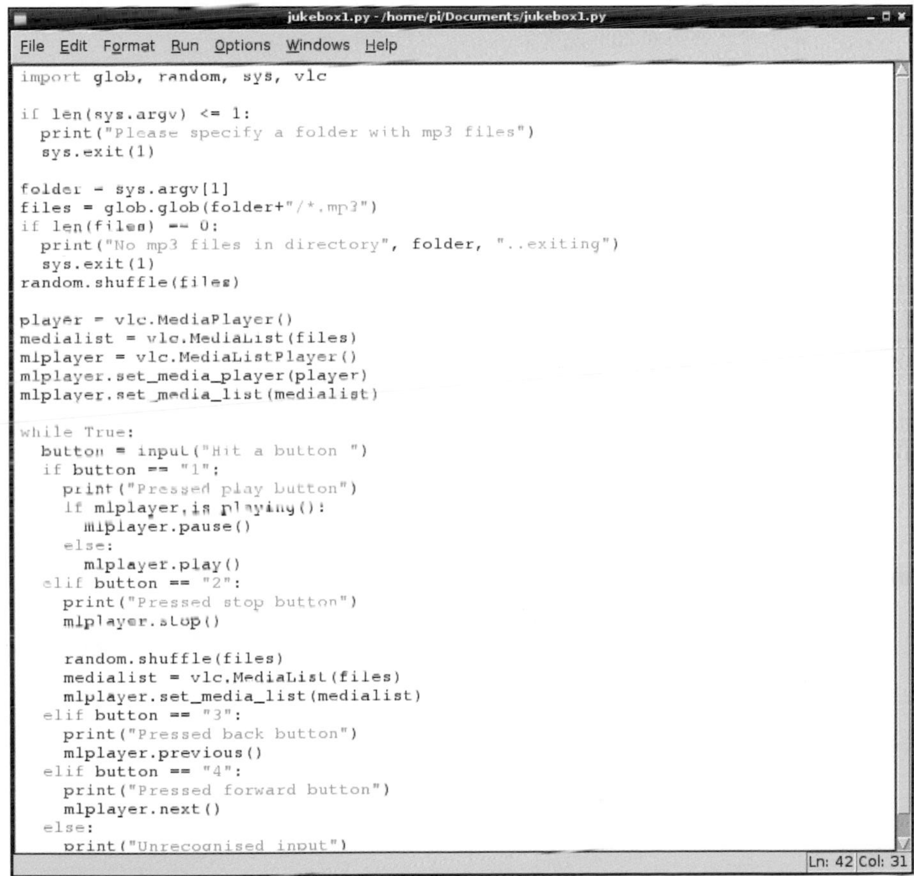

FIGURE 9-7 Writing a jukebox program in Python IDLE 3

Part Three: Controlling the Jukebox with Buttons

You jukebox will use buttons to control the playback of music on your Raspberry Pi. In this part of the project, you connect your buttons to your circuit and modify your program so that you can use the buttons to play, pause and skip tracks. You will require four buttons: one to play, one to pause, one to skip tracks backwards and one to skip tracks forwards. You'll add these buttons to the breadboard next to the LCD screen.

Connecting the Buttons

In the following steps, you add the four buttons to the breadboard and connect them with wires to the Raspberry Pi GPIO. Refer to the wiring diagram in Figure 9-8 as you work.

You **must** turn off the power supply before doing Step 5, so I advise you to go ahead and do that now.

1. Push the buttons into the breadboard so that the legs bridge the gap along the center of the board (in the same way as the LED button project in Adventure 8).
2. Take a 10K ohm resistor and push one end into a hole, one down from the left button leg on the side of the breadboard where the LCD screen is mounted (the south side). Place the other end of the resistor into a hole in the blue (negative) power column of the breadboard, again on the south side.
3. Next take a male-to-male jumper cable and place one end into a hole on the north side of the breadboard, on the same row as the other leg of the button (a white cable in Figure 9-8), and place the other end into the red (positive) power column on the north side of the breadboard.
4. Repeat Steps 2 and 3 for the three remaining buttons, using three more resistors and male-to-male jumper cables.
5. Now you need to connect the buttons to the Raspberry Pi GPIO pins. **Make sure your Raspberry Pi is powered off before you start.** You have already used many of the pins for the LCD screen—but don't worry, you only need four, one for each button. Take a male-to-female jumper cable, and push the male pin into the hole that you left between the button leg and the resistor. Push the female end into GPIO 11 (a green cable in Figure 9-8). This first button is the play button.

6. Repeat this step for the stop button, only this time connect the female end of the jumper cable to GPIO 7 (a red cable in the Figure 9-8).
7. Repeat Step 5 again for the skip tracks backwards button, connecting to GPIO 4; and the skip tracks forwards button, connecting to GPIO 10 (blue cables in Figure 9-8).

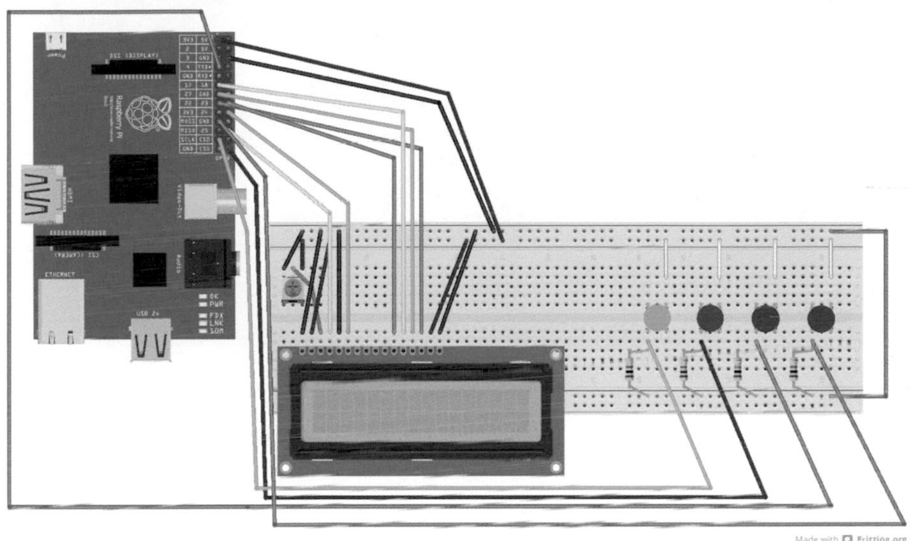

FIGURE 9-8 Wiring diagram for the four jukebox buttons

If you are using a full-sized breadboard, the power and ground rails should run all the way down the strip, which means that your LCD screen and buttons will be powered. However, if you are using a full-sized breadboard that has two halves, like the one used in Figure 9-9, you will need to bridge the channels so that power and ground extend all the way along the strip. To do this, take two male-to-male jumper cables and bridge the gap by pushing one end of the cable into the red (positive) power column hole on one side of the breadboard and the other end into a hole on the other side of the breadboard in the same red (positive) power column. Repeat this step for the blue (negative) ground column. See Figure 9-9.

The circuit being used here has pull-down resistors, which are as valid as pull-up resistors and will not damage your Pi.

FIGURE 9-9 Completed wiring of Pi jukebox with buttons

Adapting Your Jukebox Program to Include GPIO Buttons

With the physical buttons connected to the breadboard and Raspberry Pi GPIO pins, you need to adapt the jukebox program code for them to work.

1. Open `jukebox1.py` using Python IDLE 3 and edit the code to include the parts highlighted in the following code:

```
import glob, random, sys, vlc, time
import RPi.GPIO as GPIO
```

   As well as the modules you imported earlier, you will need to import the `time` module so that you can use the `sleep` function in your code, and you need to import `RPi.GPIO` so that you can set up the buttons for input in the code.

2. The next part of the code remains the same:

```
if len(sys.argv) <= 1:
  print("Please specify a folder with mp3 files")
  sys.exit(1)
folder = sys.argv[1]
files = glob.glob(folder+"/*.mp3")
if len(files) == 0:
  print("No mp3 files in directory", folder, "..exiting")
  sys.exit(1)
```

```
random.shuffle(files)

player = vlc.MediaPlayer()
medialist = vlc.MediaList(files)
mlplayer = vlc.MediaListPlayer()
mlplayer.set_media_player(player)
mlplayer.set_media_list(medialist)
```

3. Next, add the code to set up the GPIO to use the physical buttons you added to your breadboard and connected to your Raspberry Pi:

```
GPIO.setmode(GPIO.BCM)

PLAY_BUTTON=11
STOP_BUTTON=7
BACK_BUTTON=4
FORWARD_BUTTON=10

GPIO.setup(PLAY_BUTTON, GPIO.IN)
GPIO.setup(STOP_BUTTON, GPIO.IN)
GPIO.setup(BACK_BUTTON, GPIO.IN)
GPIO.setup(FORWARD_BUTTON, GPIO.IN)
```

In this code, you assign each GPIO that you are using to appropriately named variables. Putting these in all uppercase is a convention often used in Python when you don't intend to reassign or change those variables. The advantage of this method is that you can refer to a pin (for example, `PLAY_BUTTON`) multiple times in your code. This has two advantages: it's easy to see what the name refers to; and if you change the GPIO pin for some reason the name only needs to be updated in one place.

4. Next, amend the `while` loop code that reads and reacts to the input. The new code uses methods from `RPi.GPIO` to detect when a physical button is pressed. The changes are highlighted in bold in the following code (be sure to add the hash marks, also in bold, to comment out the lines as shown):

```
while True:
  # button = input("Hit a button ")
  if GPIO.input(PLAY_BUTTON):
    print("Pressed play button")
    if mlplayer.is_playing():
      mlplayer.pause()
    else:
      mlplayer.play()
  elif GPIO.input(STOP_BUTTON):
    print("Pressed stop button")
    mlplayer.stop()
    random.shuffle(files)
```

```
    medialist = vlc.MediaList(files)
    mlplayer.set_media_list(medialist)
  elif GPIO.input(BACK_BUTTON):
    print("Pressed back button")
    mlplayer.previous()
  elif GPIO.input(FORWARD_BUTTON):
    print("Pressed forward button")
    mlplayer.next()
  # else:
    #  print("Unrecognised input")
  time.sleep(0.3)
```

Detecting GPIO input here uses the same methods as you used in Adventure 8; you just check each of the GPIO's to see if it is connected to 3.3V (a logic high) or connected to ground (a logic low). You want to add a `sleep` for a short time (0.3 seconds) at the end, otherwise the same press might register multiple times. When a mechanical switch is pressed, it "bounces" between logical high and low which would be read as multiple presses. Here you are "debouncing" it by ignoring changes that happen just after pressing the button.

5. Save this file as `jukebox2.py` inside your `Documents` directory.
6. It is now time to test to see if your code works with your buttons. However, you need to run this program as the super user by using `sudo`, exactly as you did in Adventure 8 when you programmed the Raspberry Pi GPIO. To run your adapted jukebox program, open LXTerminal, and navigate to your `Documents` folder using the command:

   ```
   cd Documents
   ```

   Then type the following command:

   ```
   sudo python3 jukebox2.py
   ```

Now press your jukebox buttons. Is everything working as you want it to work?

Part Four: Displaying Jukebox Information on the LCD screen

Right at the start of this big project, you connected an LCD screen to a breadboard and wired it to work using some adapted test code from Adafruit. Since then, you've pretty much ignored the display. It's time to use the LCD screen to output information about the MP3 file that is being played—the name of the artist, the name of the track and the name of the album. That information comes from the **metadata** stored within the MP3 file.

Metadata is data that describes some other sort of data. In this case, it is textual data such as the name of the artist and track, which helps to describe the audio data stored in an MP3 file. For MP3s, this can be stored inside the MP3 file alongside the audio data.

The `vlc` library allows you to attach code to certain *events*, such as when the track is changed on an MP3 file. This allows you to have a function that is called any time the selected event happens during playback.

1. Open `jukebox2.py` using Python IDLE 3 and edit the code to add the last line:

```
import glob, random, sys, vlc, time
import RPi.GPIO as GPIO
from Adafruit_CharLCD import *
```

   Here the code has been amended to import the modified `Adafruit_CharLCD` library. You use `from Adafruit_CharLCD` instead of `import` because the class in there is called `Adafruit_CharLCD`. That means that, if you didn't use `import *` as we have done here, you would have to type `Adafruit_CharLCD.AdafruitCharLCD`—which would seem silly!

2. The next part of the code remains the same:

```
if len(sys.argv) <= 1:
  print("Please specify a folder with mp3 files")
  sys.exit(1)
folder = sys.argv[1]
files = glob.glob(folder+"/*.mp3")
if len(files) == 0:
  print("No mp3 files in directory", folder, "..exiting")
  sys.exit(1)
random.shuffle(files)

player = vlc.MediaPlayer()
medialist = vlc.MediaList(files)
mlplayer = vlc.MediaListPlayer()
mlplayer.set_media_player(player)
mlplayer.set_media_list(medialist)
GPIO.setmode(GPIO.BCM)

PLAY_BUTTON=11
STOP_BUTTON=7
BACK_BUTTON=4
FORWARD_BUTTON=10

GPIO.setup(PLAY_BUTTON, GPIO.IN)
```

```
GPIO.setup(STOP_BUTTON, GPIO.IN)
GPIO.setup(BACK_BUTTON, GPIO.IN)
GPIO.setup(FORWARD_BUTTON, GPIO.IN)
```

3. After setting up `vlc` and GPIO, you can set up the LCD screen by typing the following lines:

```
lcd = Adafruit_CharLCD()
lcd.clear()
lcd.message("Hit play!")
```

4. Next, leave a blank line to update the LCD screen when the track changes and then type the following code:

```
def handle_changed_track(event, player):
  media = player.get_media()
  media.parse()
  artist = media.get_meta(vlc.Meta.Artist) or "Unknown artist"
  title = media.get_meta(vlc.Meta.Title) or "Unknown song ;
    title"
  album = media.get_meta(vlc.Meta.Album) or "Unknown album"
  lcd.clear()
  lcd.message(title+"\n"+artist+" - "+album)

playerem = player.event_manager()
playerem.event_attach(vlc.EventType.MediaPlayerMediaChanged,;
  handle_changed_track, player)
```

Let's walk through some of this code. The two lines at the end make it so that the `handle_changed_track` function is called any time the file being played changes. This function is called if you start playback or press one of the skip buttons, but also when a track finishes and the next one starts.

Looking inside the `handle_changed_track` function, `media.parse()` causes the program to read the metadata stored in that MP3 file (the artist, track name, and so on).

`artist = media.get_meta(vlc.Meta.Artist)` gets the Artist metadata. The line `artist = media.get_meta(vlc.Meta.Artist) or "Unknown artist"` is, roughly speaking, a handy short way of writing the following:

```
if media.get_meta(vlc.Meta.Artist):
  artist = media.get_meta(vlc.Meta.Artist)
else
  artist = "Unknown artist"
```

You include this code to handle the case where the MP3 didn't have any embedded metadata.

For the `lcd.message` there are two important things to note. First, anything after the newline (`\n`) is displayed on the second line of your LCD screen. Second, you use the `+` character to join strings together into one longer string.

5. Next, add one last line of code beneath the `while` loop:

```
while True:
  # button = input("Hit a button ")
  if GPIO.input(PLAY_BUTTON):
    print("Pressed play button")
    if mlplayer.is_playing():
      mlplayer.pause()
    else:
      mlplayer.play()
  elif GPIO.input(STOP_BUTTON):
    print("Pressed stop button")
    mlplayer.stop()
    random.shuffle(files)
    medialist = vlc.MediaList(files)
    mlplayer.set_media_list(medialist)
  elif GPIO.input(BACK_BUTTON):
    print("Pressed back button")
    mlplayer.previous()
  elif GPIO.input(FORWARD_BUTTON):
    print("Pressed forward button")
    mlplayer.next()
  # else:
  #   print("Unrecognised input")
  time.sleep(0.3)
  lcd.scrollDisplayLeft()
```

The `while` loop is repeated roughly every 0.3 seconds, so the LCD screen scrolls that often. This means that you can read artist and track names that are longer than the LCD screen and it scrolls at a pleasantly readable speed using `lcd.scrollDisplayLeft()`.

6. Save this file as `jukebox3.py` inside your `Documents` directory, by clicking on File→Save As and navigating to `Documents` inside `/home/pi`.

To run your final jukebox program, open LXTerminal and navigate to your `Documents` folder using the command:

```
cd Documents
```

Then type the following command:

```
sudo python3 jukebox3.py
```

Press your jukebox buttons and check to see if the MP3 metadata is now being displayed on the LCD screen and whether it changes when you move between tracks using the buttons (Figure 9-10). You may see some warnings but you can ignore them.

FIGURE 9-10 Jukebox LCD in action displaying MP3 metadata

USING THE JUKEBOX WITHOUT A MONITOR

If you want the Jukebox program to run whenever your Raspberry Pi is turned on, without needing it to be plugged into a keyboard, mouse or monitor, you will need to modify the `/etc/rc.local` file. The `/etc/rc.local` script runs when your Raspberry Pi is starting up, at the end of the boot process. Adding the command to run the `jukebox` Python program to this script means the program will run whenever the Raspberry Pi starts up, so that you do not have to give the command to run it.

To set up the jukebox to run after booting, type the following line into the LXTerminal:

```
sudo nano /etc/rc.local
```

Next, scroll down through the code and add the following line before `exit 0` (see Figure 9-11):

```
python3 /home/pi/Documents/jukebox3.py /home/pi/music &
```

Save and exit the nano txt editor using Ctrl + X, accept the changes to the file by pressing Y, and press Enter.

Restart your Raspberry Pi to make sure that the program automatically runs, using the command:

```
sudo shutdown -r now
```

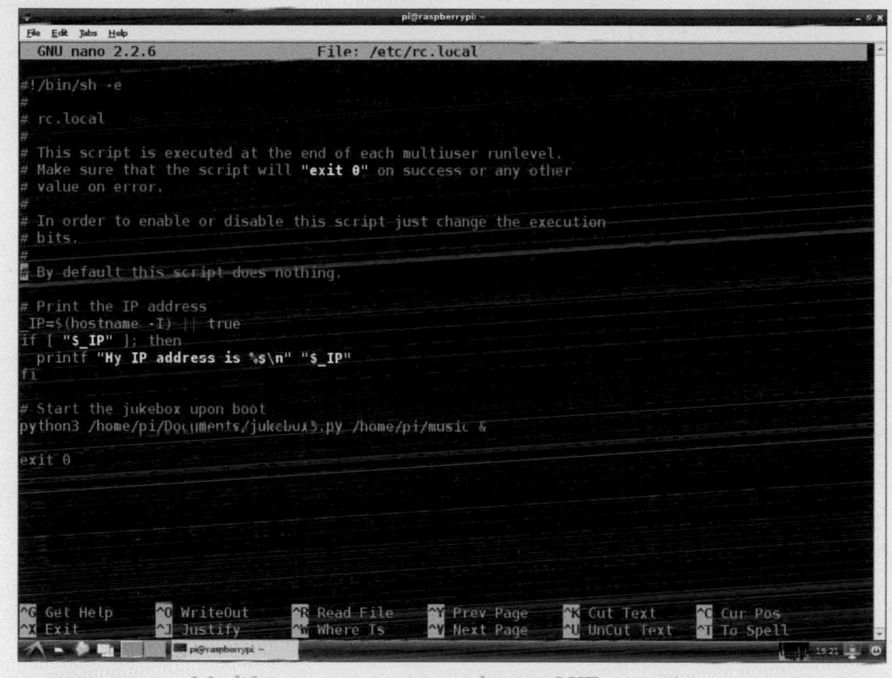

FIGURE 9-11 Modifying `/etc/rc.local` using LXTerminal

Finishing Up

Once you have tested everything and are happy that it all works, you can transfer your Raspberry Pi, wiring, components and breadboard into a cardboard box that you have prepared by measuring and cutting holes for the LCD screen, buttons, speaker and power supply. You could also wrap the box in copies of album covers, paste on a couple of old vinyl records, or add your own designs with pens or stickers to suit your taste.

Achievement Unlocked: Your big Raspberry Pi project!

Further Adventures: Continuing Your Journey with the Raspberry Pi

Its ability to enable you to create big standalone projects like the jukebox, which let you practice your computer programming and electronics skills and use some ingenuity and creativity all of your own, is what makes the Raspberry Pi such a special little device. It allows you to be the creator of technology around you—and should you get tired of your latest project, you can reincarnate your Pi in a new project!

Here are a couple of resources to help you on your way:

- *Raspberry Pi Projects* (`http://eu.wiley.com/WileyCDA/WileyTitle/productCd-1118555430.html`) by Dr Andrew Robinson and Mike Cook (Wiley, 2014) contains 16 super projects using the Raspberry Pi. They include a chicken that reads out your tweets, lights that respond to music and a computer-controlled slot car racing project.
- The official Raspberry Pi website (`www.raspberrypi.org`) adds a new post every day featuring Raspberry Pi projects from around the world, often with links to tutorials on how to make your own.

Appendix
Where to Go from Here

NOW THAT YOU have completed the adventures in this book, it's likely that you will want to embark on your own exciting expeditions with Raspberry Pi. Hopefully you have learned some skills that will help you begin your own projects and you may wish to learn more.

There are an abundance of resources that can take you further:

- Websites
- Clubs
- Inspiring projects/tutorials
- Videos
- Books and magazines

Websites

A great way to further your adventures with Raspberry Pi is to use some of the fantastic websites that are springing up all over the Internet. There is a great culture flourishing there and plenty of opportunities for you to show off your Raspberry Pi projects and explain how you created them so that others can have a go too. Some of the most notable and popular websites are listed here.

- **The official Raspberry Pi Foundation website** (www.raspberrypi.org) This is the official website of the Raspberry Pi Foundation. It's more than simply a resource to download the latest software for your Pi; the front page features a new article every day on new developments, project ideas and inspirational stories, and the entire Raspberry Pi community uses the website's forum to discuss ideas, projects, and future developments. It is designed mainly for adults, which means it can be a little daunting at first, but if you are stuck on a project you can post a question and someone will know the answer and be able to help you out.
- **Rastrack** (www.rastrack.co.uk) You may recognise this website from the very start of your Raspberry Pi adventure, when you installed the New Out Of the Box Software from Raspberry Pi. During installation you were given the option in the `raspi-config` to add your Pi to Rastrack. This website allows you to register your Raspberry Pi and your location. You can then see where other owners of Pis live, using an interactive map. The website was created by Ryan Walmsley when he was 16 years old and has been a huge success.
- **Adafruit Learning System** (http://learn.adafruit.com/category/learn-raspberry-pi) The Adafruit learning system website features detailed lessons on electronics. You may recall that for the jukebox project in Adventure 9 you used some code from Adafruit to get the LCD display up and running. Not only does Adafruit provide open source code for electronics projects on its site but it also has a dedicated section with lessons on Raspberry Pi GPIO that you can follow at your own pace, as well as project ideas and tutorials featuring both Pi and electronics.
- **<Stuff about="code" />** (www.stuffaboutcode.com) In Adventure 6 you had a taste of what it is like to be a games developer of sorts by using Python code to make something happen in the world of Minecraft. If you enjoyed that project and would like more tutorials on Minecraft Pi, head over to Martin O'Hanlon's website, *Stuff about="code"*, where you'll find one of the largest collections of Minecraft Pi tutorials on the Internet. Projects range from having live Twitter feeds appear in Minecraft Pi blocks to firing cannons. There are plenty of fun ideas just waiting for you to try.
- **The official Python website** (www.python.org/doc) The Python Software Foundation has placed all the documents relating to the Python programming language online. The website includes tutorials as well as reference material for all the commands you are likely to use. It's a great site if you get stuck with writing code, especially if your program is generating syntax errors! The site can be quite confusing to navigate at first, but you will find it a valuable reference point when coding.

Clubs

It is always fun to share your computing ideas and projects with other people of your own age. There are many clubs for young people and their Raspberry Pis. Some of these are run at weekends by adults who work as professional coders. They can give you inspiration for new projects, teach you new skills and help you if you are stuck. Here is a list of some popular clubs and groups.

- **Code Club** (`www.codeclub.org.uk`) Code Club is a nationwide network of free after-school coding clubs for children aged 9-11. They are usually located in schools—you can use the Code Club website to find the nearest one to where you live.
- **Coder Dojo** (`www.coderdojo.com`) At Coder Dojo you can learn how to code, as well as develop websites, apps, programs, games and more. Dojos are set up, run by and taught at by volunteers, many of them professional programmers. Some Dojos organise tours of technology companies, bring in guest speakers to talk about their careers and what they do, and organise events. In addition to learning to code, you get to meet like-minded people, and show off what you've been working on. You can find out if there is a Coder Dojo near you by using the CoderDojo search on the website.
- **Raspberry Jam** (`www.raspberryjam.org.uk`) Raspberry Jam is a rapidly growing global network of user groups that meet regularly to support hobbyists, developers, teachers, students, children and families—in fact, anybody who would like to put their Raspberry Pi to good use. You can find out what Raspberry Jams are happening in your area on the website. Some events are held especially for young people and take place in computer-based offices.
- **Young Rewired State** (`https://youngrewiredstate.org`) Young Rewired State, called YRS for short, is a network of computer programmers and designers aged 18 and under. YRS holds large collaborative coding events across the UK, as well as in New York, San Francisco, Berlin and Johannesburg. Events typically last for a week, during which teams of young programmers work together to create a new website or app using public data. They are assisted by professional programmers who volunteer their time to help. At the end of the week all the teams come together to present their work to a panel of judges, with prizes to be won! Not only is it a great way to learn how to code, but it's also a great way to meet other young people across the world and develop a network of friends—and a lot of fun!

- **School clubs** Check to see if there is a Raspberry Pi or coding club at your school. If not, why not approach your ICT or computing teacher and ask about helping to start one? To start your own school club you will need:
    - A teacher or adult willing to help supervise and run the club. This could be a teaching assistant, technician or a parent.
    - A venue, such as a classroom, with tables, chairs and access to power sockets and possibly the Internet, although that is not essential.
    - A suitable time to hold the club, perhaps after school one night every week. Your teacher will be able to help you with this.
    - Some posters to advertise your club.
    - Some enthusiastic club members who own their own Raspberry Pi to bring along.

Inspiring Projects and Tutorials

Once you have had an idea for a Raspberry Pi project and you have spent the time making it happen, you may wish to share your success with others. Many people do this through attending Raspberry Jams. Others write posts in a blog, or they add their projects to a Raspberry Pi ideas website so that others can have a go too!

- **MAKE:** (`http://makezine.com/category/electronics/raspberry-pi/`) The popular magazine MAKE: features a Raspberry Pi section full of Pi projects on its website. Projects include step-by-step tutorials with pictures and videos that are easy to follow.
- **Raspberry IO** (`http://raspberry.io`) This website was created by the Python Software Foundation, and features lots of Raspberry Pi projects in tutorial form using the Python programming language. If you enjoyed the Python exercises in this book, especially those from Adventures 4, 5 and 9, you could find this website very helpful.

Videos

There are some great video resources on the Internet on how to use your Raspberry Pi, some of which include tutorials on how to create a particular project.

- ***Adventures In Raspberry Pi* companion website** (`www.wiley.com/go/adventuresinrp`) You'll find video tutorials to complement this book on the *Adventures in Raspberry Pi* companion website.

- **Raspberry Pi 4 Beginners** (www.pibeginners.com) On this website you will find lots of short video explanations, tutorials and projects to teach you material specific to Raspberry Pi. For example, if you want to learn how to add your Pi to a wireless network or how to view your Pi's file system information, this is the place for you. The videos are created by Matthew Manning and the website is curated by a team of Pi enthusiasts willing to help people learn about Linux.
- **RasPi.TV** (http://raspi.tv) If you are interested in learning more about the GPIO pins on the Raspberry Pi, or how to control real-world objects like lights, for example, you'll find this website and the video tutorials created by Alex Eames really helpful. Programming electronics adds an extra element of fun but it can also be quite difficult to understand what is happening in a circuit. Alex's videos contain simple explanations to help you learn. RasPi.TV has some detailed projects for enthusiastic learners, using extra hardware that interfaces with the Raspberry Pi, like the Gertboard.
- **Geek Gurl Diaries** (www.geekgurldiaries.co.uk) The Geek Gurl Diaries are a collection of video logs, interviews and tutorials designed for young girls. There are a number of Raspberry Pi-based tutorials, including the famous Little Box of Geek project that demonstrates how to turn your Raspberry Pi into a fortune printing box.

Books and Magazines

If you have enjoyed learning from this book, you may like to progress onto other books. There are a number of publications that will take you further after *Adventures in Raspberry Pi*. Here are some recommendations:

- ***Raspberry Pi User Guide***, by Eben Upton and Gareth Hardacree (Wiley, 2012)
- ***Raspberry Pi For Dummies***, by Sean McManus and Mike Cook (Wiley, 2013)
- ***Raspberry Pi Projects***, by Dr Andrew Robinson and Mike Cook (Wiley, 2014)
- ***The MagPi Magazine*** (www.themagpi.com) This monthly magazine for Raspberry Pi users contains articles that cover coding, robotics and electronics. Each issue is free to view online. All you need to do is navigate to the website, click on an issue, and follow the download links. You can buy hard copies of the magazine from Pi Supply (www.pi-supply.com/product-category/books-and-magazines/the-magpi-magazine).

Glossary

algorithm A set of rules to be followed to calculate or solve a problem. Common algorithms are those used for sorting information or data.

argument A piece of information given to a function, which the function then uses to perform its task. The argument goes inside the brackets that follow the function name. In the function `time.sleep(2)`, for example, you use the argument `(2)`, which is the number of seconds you want the program to wait before executing the next line.

boot The first thing a computer does when you turn it on is to start up, or *boot*, the operating system.

breadboard A reusable device that allows you to create circuits without needing to solder all the components. Breadboards have a number of holes into which you push wires or jumper cables and components to create circuits. The two columns of holes on either side of the breadboard are for power. The column next to the red line is for positive connections and the column next to the blue line is for negative connections.

broadcast A message used to coordinate the actions of different sprites and the stage in Scratch. The broadcast message keeps all the scripts running for each sprite and keeps the stage synchronized.

capacitor Electronic component used to store an electric charge. The capacity of this component is measured in farads (F). A farad is a very large quantity, so most of the capacitors you see will be measured in microfarads.

circuit diagram A diagram showing which electronic components, represented by symbols, are connected to complete a circuit and in what order they should be placed.

CLI (command-line interface) The CLI screen allows you to communicate with a computer by typing in text commands.

comments Notes within your code that explain what a line or section of code in intended to do. Each comment line begins with the # symbol, which tells the computer running the program to ignore that line.

conditional A conditional statement is a piece of code that instructs the program to take an action only if a certain condition is true. The most commonly used conditionals are `if` and `if…else` statements.

current The rate at which electrical energy flows past a point in a circuit. It is the electrical equivalent of the flow rate of water in pipes. Current is measured in amperes (A). Smaller currents are measured in milliamperes (mA).

data structure A particular way of storing and organizing related pieces of information. Lists and arrays are types of data structures.

debugging The act of locating the cause of any errors in your computer program code and fixing them.

diode A device that lets current flow in only one direction. A diode has two terminals, called *anode* and *cathode*. Current will flow through the diode only when positive voltage is applied to the anode, and negative voltage to the cathode.

flash memory A type of storage, the same kind you use with a digital camera to store all your photographs.

function A section of code that does a specific task; once the function is created you can use it over and over again. Python, like most programming languages, includes some standard functions that the computer will already understand, like the `print()` function that prints some text to the screen. You can also write your own functions.

GUI (graphical user interface) A way to interact with a computer that uses windows, icons and a mouse pointer.

hardware Refers to the physical elements of the computer that you can see and touch. This includes everything inside the computer case, known as components.

HDMI (High-Definition Multimedia Interface) HDMI devices are used to transfer video and audio data from a source device—such as your Raspberry Pi—to a compatible HDMI device like a digital TV or monitor.

hostname A word that identifies a computing device on a network. The hostname of the Raspberry Pi is `raspberrypi`.

IDE (integrated development environment) A software application used to write computer code in a particular language, for example Python; also referred to as a *programming environment*. The application has the capability to create and edit code, as well as run or execute the code. Many IDEs also provide features to help programmers *debug* or check for errors in their programs.

if/if...else statements Conditional constructs commonly used in computer programming. When you use an *if* statement, you are asking whether a condition is met, and then making something happen if the condition set is true. For example: *If* it is raining, then put up an umbrella. You can add another action for when the condition is false using the *else* command. For example: *If* it is raining, then put up an umbrella; *else,* wear sunglasses.

input The raw data or information entered into a computer system like a Raspberry Pi before it is processed. Input devices include keyboards, push buttons and microphones. The Raspberry Pi has pins that can be connected to these and other devices.

interpreter An application that checks and runs a computer program line by line.

iteration Repeating a sequence.

jumper cables Used to connect the GPIO pins on the Raspberry Pi to a breadboard or other components. They are reusable and do not require soldering. They come in different formats: female-to-male; female-to-female; and male-to-male.

LCD (liquid crystal display) An electronic display, usually quite thin and flat, that is typically used in digital calculators and digital watches to display information such as the time.

library A collection of reusable software functions that allow you do so something useful.

LED (Light Emitting Diode) A diode that lights up when electricity passes through it. LEDs allow current to pass in only one direction. They come in a variety of colours, and have one short leg and one long leg, which helps you to determine which way round they need to be placed in a circuit for current to flow through them.

loop A sequence of code that repeats.

MIDI (Musical Instrument Digital Interface) keyboard A musical instrument that can communicate with a computer. Piano sheet music notes and MIDI keyboard notes are the same, only sheet music notes are represented by letters G, C, A, and so on, whereas MIDI keyboard notes are represented by numbers.

module A collection of reusable Python code that performs a specific function. It may be used alone or combined with other modules. For example, you can use functions from the Python `time` module to add pauses in your programs.

nano A text editor that enables you to write code from the command line.

NOOBS (New Out Of Box Software) A set of software produced by the Raspberry Pi Foundation, to be downloaded onto a computer and copied to an SD card that will be used on a Raspberry Pi.

operating system (OS) A type of software that allows people to create, store and manage files and applications that contain information on a computer. Examples of popular operating systems include Microsoft Windows, Mac OS X and Linux. Raspbian is a popular operating system for the Raspberry Pi.

parameters Options to commands that modify the way that the standard command works (a bit like ticking a tick box in a GUI program). Most Linux commands have lots of parameters that modify the way that they work.

output The data that your computer gives in response, after you have typed in a command. Examples of output devices include speakers and monitor screens.

potentiometer A type of resistor with an adjustable button to vary the resistance of current.

refactoring A way of restructuring code you have already written to make it more efficient and easy to read, and to avoid bugs. If you find yourself copying and pasting large sections of code, this is usually a good indicator that you need to refactor your code!

resistors Electrical components that resist current in a circuit. For example, LEDs can be damaged by too much current, but if you add the correct value resistor in series with the LED in the circuit to limit the amount of current, the LED will be protected. Resistance is measured in *ohms*. You need to pick a resistor with the correct value to limit the current through a circuit; the value of a resistor is shown by coloured bands that are read from left to right.

SD card (Secure Digital memory card) A small memory card that stores data or information. SD cards are most often used in digital cameras, to store images that can then be transferred to a computer using an SD card reader.

SD card reader/writer A device for reading information stored on SD cards and for writing information to SD cards.

software The term given to the programs that run on the computer system. Programs are what make the hardware work, for example by making a calculation or organising your files. There are two main types of software: *systems software*, which runs and manages your computer; and *application software*, which performs a specific task or function.

sprites The characters that can be programmed to do something in Scratch. The sprites wear costumes that can be customised.

stage Refers to the background for the sprites in Scratch. You can add scripts to the stage to allow the sprites to interact with it—for example, you might draw a wall that stops your sprite from moving beyond a certain point.

string Data or information entered as text, i.e., a "string" of characters.

sudo The `sudo` command lets you temporarily act as the *super user* (or *root* user) and gives you permission to do whatever you want on the system.

syntax A set of rules to check whether the code you have typed is valid code. In the same way as the English language has rules about how to properly combine subjects, verbs, objects and so on, each programming language has its own syntax.

syntax error An error that stops a program from running because the computer cannot understand the code.

terminal A screen window that gives you access to the command-line interface. The graphical LXTerminal is an example.

threads A way to run more than one script simultaneously.

turtle An imaginary pen used to create graphic images using a sequence of instructions in the Turtle Graphics program.

uinput A special hardware driver that allows other programs to inject keypresses into the system as if you had pressed a real key on the keyboard. It is a special kernel driver that has to be installed inside the Linux kernel in order to do its work.

USB (Universal Serial Bus) port A type of opening on a computer used to plug in devices such as a webcam, or a portable memory device like a memory stick.

variable A code construct that holds a value that can be changed. The `health` variable in your adventure role-playing game in Adventure 3 is an example of a value that can be changed and used inside different scripts.

voltage The difference in electrical energy between two points in a circuit. It is the electrical equivalent of water pressure in pipes, and it is this pressure that causes a current to flow through a circuit. Voltage is measured in volts (V).

Index

SYMBOLS

A

B

C

D

E

F

G

H

I

J

Q

R

S

T